THE STORY OF THE NEW TESTAMENT TEXT

Society of Biblical Literature

Resources for Biblical Study

Tom Thatcher
Editor (New Testament)

Number 58

THE STORY OF THE NEW TESTAMENT TEXT
Movers, Materials, Motives, Methods, and Models

THE STORY OF THE NEW TESTAMENT TEXT

MOVERS, MATERIALS, MOTIVES, METHODS, AND MODELS

By
Robert F. Hull Jr.

Society of Biblical Literature
Atlanta

THE STORY OF THE NEW TESTAMENT TEXT
Movers, Materials, Motives, Methods, and Models

Copyright © 2010 by the Society of Biblical Literature

All rights reserved. No part of this work may be reproduced or transmitted in any form or by any means, electronic or mechanical, including photocopying and recording, or by means of any information storage or retrieval system, except as may be expressly permitted by the 1976 Copyright Act or in writing from the publisher. Requests for permission should be addressed in writing to the Rights and Permissions Office, Society of Biblical Literature, 825 Houston Mill Road, Atlanta, GA 30329 USA.

Library of Congress Cataloging-in-Publication Data

Hull, Robert F., 1943–
    The story of the New Testament text : movers, materials, motives, methods, and models / Robert F. Hull, Jr.
      p. cm. — (Resources for Biblical study ; no. 58)
    Includes bibliographical references.
    ISBN 978-1-58983-520-7 (paper binding : alk. paper) — ISBN 978-1-58983-521-4 (electronic)
    1. Bible. N.T.—Criticism, Textual. 2. Bible. N.T.—History. I. Title.
    BS2325.H85 2010
    225.4'046—dc22
                                                                    2010034852

18 17 16 15 14 13 12 11 10   5 4 3 2 1
Printed on acid-free, recycled paper conforming to ANSI/NISO Z39.48-1992 (R1997) and ISO 9706:1994 standards for paper permanence.

In grateful memory of
Beauford H. Bryant,
who opened the door,
and
Bruce M. Metzger,
who showed the way.

Contents

Acknowledgments ix
Abbreviations xi
Glossary xiii

Introduction: Getting Hooked on Textual Criticism 1

1. Paul and Luke Become Published Authors.. 7
2. The Precritical Age.. 23
3. The Age of Collecting, Collating, and Classifying................................ 39
4. The Age of Optimism: *The New Testament in the Original Greek* 71
5. The Age of Optimism (Continued): Materials, Methods, Motives, and Models 87
6. The Age of the Papyri: A Harvest of Riches.. 109
7. The Age of Consensus, the Age of Doubt.. 131
8. New Directions: Expanding the Goals of Textual Criticism 151
9. Reassessing the Discipline 169

Bibliography... 193
Index of Biblical Citations... 217
Index of Persons 220
Index of Subjects.. 226

Acknowledgments

This book is largely a chronicle of the work of others. I owe an incalculable debt to the scholars whose work I summarize. In places, my book takes on the character of a review essay, but I do not know any other way to trace the story of the New Testament text. From the frequency of my references to several volumes of collected essays, the reader will be able to identify other scholars whose surveys have been most helpful to me. I single out Eldon Jay Epp, who has done more to trace the development of methodology in New Testament textual criticism than any other scholar in North America. Professor Epp was chair of the New Testament Textual Criticism Section of the Society of Biblical Literature when I read my first paper at a national meeting. I am thankful to him and other members of the section who have continued to stimulate my interest in this discipline through the years.

I am grateful to the students who have given me opportunity to introduce them to the story of the New Testament text during a succession of seminars at Emmanuel School of Religion, especially those who wrote theses on the topic. One of the best of these was Jeffrey D. Miller, now associate professor of New Testament at Milligan College. Jeff read the first draft of this book and gave invaluable criticisms and suggestions. To him I owe much. Many thanks to my editor, Tom Thatcher, whose wise counsel has resulted in a more user-friendly and, I hope, more logically arranged book than this would otherwise have been.

I am enormously grateful to the trustees of Emmanuel School of Religion, whose generous grant of a year's sabbatical leave at full salary made possible the writing of this book.

Finally, to my wife, Loretta, who has, for more than forty years, borne the burdens peculiar to anyone married to an academic, my deepest appreciation.

Abbreviations

AnBib	Analecta biblica
ANRW	*Aufstieg und Niedergang der römischen Welt: Geschichte und Kultur Roms im Spiegel der neueren Forschung*. Part 2, *Principat*. Edited by Hildegard Temporini and Wolfgang Haase. Berlin: de Gruyter, 1972–.
ANTF	Arbeiten zur neutestamentlichen Textforschung
AThR	*Anglican Theological Review*
BASP	*Bulletin of the American Society of Papyrologists*
BASPSup	Bulletin of the American Society of Papyrologists: Supplement
BETL	Bibliotheca ephemeridum theologicarum lovaniensium
Bib	*Biblica*
BTB	*Biblical Theology Bulletin*
BZ	*Biblische Zeitschrift*
BZNW	Beihefte zur Zeitschrift für die neutestamentliche Wissenschaft
CBET	Contributions to Biblical Exegesis and Theology
CBQ	*Catholic Biblical Quarterly*
CRBR	*Critical Review of Books in Religion*
CSCO	Corpus scriptorium christianorum orientalium. Edited by I. B. Chabot et al. Paris, 1903–.
EFN	Estudios de Filología Neotestamentaria. Cordova, Spain, 1988–.
ErJb	*Eranos-Jahrbuch*
HibJ	*Hibbert Journal*
HSCP	Harvard Studies in Classical Philology
HTR	Harvard Theological Review
JBL	*Journal of Biblical Literature*
JECS	*Journal of Early Christian Studies*

JR	*Journal of Religion*
JSNT	*Journal for the Study of the New Testament*
JTS	*Journal of Theological Studies*
NovT	*Novum Testamentum*
NovTSup	Supplements to Novum Testamentum
NTS	*New Testament Studies*
NTTS	New Testament Tools and Studies
NTTSD	New Testament Tools, Studies and Documents
RBL	*Review of Biblical Literature*
ResQ	*Restoration Quarterly*
SD	Studies and Documents
SNTSMS	Society for New Testament Studies Monograph Series
SPap	*Studia Papyrologica*
STDJ	Studies on the Texts of the Desert of Judah
StPat	Studia Patristica
TJ	*Trinity Journal*
TS	Texts and Studies
TU	Texte und Untersuchungen
TUGAL	*Texte und Untersuchungen zur Geschichte der altchristlichen Literatur*
TynBul	*Tyndale Bulletin*
TZ	*Theologische Zeitschrift*
ZPE	*Zeitschrift für Papyrologie und Epigraphik*

Glossary

apparatus (**critical apparatus** or **apparatus criticus**). In a critically reconstructed text, the footnotes in which variant readings and their supporting witnesses are recorded.
archetype. The hypothetical manuscript from which all other manuscripts of the same text-type derive.
catena. A collection or "chain" of quotations from early Christian writers, forming a commentary on a biblical text.
codex (pl. **codices**). A book made by folding sheets of papyrus or parchment (vellum) in half and fastening them together.
codicology. The study of the layout of a handwritten page and the makeup of an ancient book.
collation. A list of the differences between the text of a manuscript and the text of another that is used as a standard.
folio. One side of a leaf; see **recto** and **verso**.
gathering. A stack of sheets of papyrus or parchment folded in the middle and bound together. A gathering of four sheets was a *quaternion*, from which the English word quire derives, now used for a gathering of any number of sheets.
lectionary. A church-service book containing selections of Scripture in the order in which they are used in the church's liturgical calendar.
majuscule. Greek script written in capital letters with each character formed separately; often called **uncial**.
minuscule. Greek script dating from the ninth century, utilizing small letters frequently written in combination by using ligatures; also known as *cursive* script.
palimpsest. A manuscript from which the first text (the "underwriting") has been scraped or washed off and replaced by a new text (the "overwriting"); also called a *rescript*.
quire. See **gathering**.

recension. A revision of an earlier text or the creation of a new standard text from one or more earlier texts.

recto. In a papyrus manuscript, the side of the leaf on which the fibers run horizontally. In a parchment manuscript, the right-hand page.

siglum (plural **sigla**). The "sign" (letter, number, or abbreviation) used to identify a witness to the text.

transcription. A copy of a manuscript conforming to the exact layout of the text, word for word, letter for letter.

uncial. Capital-letter Latin script; often used to refer to Greek **majuscule** script.

verso. In a papyrus manuscript, the side of the leaf on which the fibers run vertically. In a parchment manuscript, the left-hand page.

Introduction
Getting Hooked on Textual Criticism

> I look upon the textual critic as I look upon the man who comes to clean the drains. I should not like to do it myself, but I am very glad that someone likes to do it. (R. P. C. Hanson in Birdsall 2002, 359)

I bought my first Greek New Testament in 1962, when I was a college sophomore, newly enrolled in Elementary New Testament Greek. It was the Nestle-Aland 24th edition (1960). It cost me $1.98 in the college bookstore ("No Disc[ount]," read the penciled note on the inside cover). I still have it, much battered and thumbed, alongside several other editions of the Greek New Testament. Here I was introduced to the wonders and challenges of the Greek text. But, although I completed three years of Greek grammar at Milligan College, the footnotes section on each page (the "apparatus") remained a mystery to me, unknown territory full of cryptic symbols, numbers, and letters, with snatches of Greek and Latin here and there. In my senior year I began to explore that territory just a little, in the exegesis courses of Beauford H. Bryant. When I transitioned into seminary at Emmanuel School of Religion, Dr. Bryant, who had become one of the founding faculty members of that new seminary, pulled out all the stops and offered a seminar entitled Greek Paleography and New Testament Textual Criticism. He had taken a Princeton Theological Seminary summer course of the same title under Bruce Metzger. I was hooked so strongly that I later did a PhD at Princeton Seminary, where Metzger became my mentor and *Doktorvater*.

What hooked me? Part of it was simply learning to understand the technical terms in the apparatus, to read the map of this strange new world. But more compelling was the story itself, the story of how those variants got into the text and the human-interest accounts of scholars who had searched for ancient manuscripts, recovered text that had been erased and overwritten, or risked their jobs and reputations by challenging certain readings that had become cherished residents in published texts. Fortunately, in the mid-twentieth century, scrolls, scribes, and scholars were big news on seminary campuses and even in the popular press. The discovery (in 1947), sale, and publication of the first of the Dead Sea Scrolls was a story of chance, intrigue, and promise. Here was a copy of the prophet Isaiah a thousand years older than any other manuscript of that writing. The famous Bodmer papyri P^{66} (John) and P^{75} (Luke, John) were published, respectively, in 1956 and 1961. The importance of these ancient copies was only coming to light. My fellow seminarians and I were encouraged to do as much hands-on work as we could. When we learned about Tischendorf's 1844 discovery of Codex Sinaiticus, Dr. Bryant brought to class his personal copy of the full-size facsimile of the New Testament portion (published by Oxford University Press in 1922). We tried our hand at reading fourth-century capital-letter script without word division. He acquired all back issues of the Oxyrhynchus papyri and put our library on standing order for this invaluable series.

Perhaps our budding new seminary was unusual, even for that era, but many of my colleagues educated in other schools around the same time can tell similar stories. Forty years later, the situation is much different. During a sabbatical leave several years ago, I participated in an exegetical seminar for PhD students in a divinity school attached to a major university. On the first day of class, the professor (who was nearing retirement) asked the students to discuss the nature and significance of a textual variant in the passage before us. Out of a class of eight students, seven of them New Testament majors, only one was able to interpret the apparatus.

There are many reasons for the decline of emphasis on basic textual skills in seminary education, perhaps chief among them the multiplication of courses and curricular concerns in a typical student program. The hurry to get on with theology and practical ministries may leave little room for cultivating an interest in what used to be called "lower criticism" (history, language, grammar, textual criticism). And, of course, even professional New Testament scholars cannot be expected to master all the disciplines related to New Testament studies. It is difficult enough to keep up with one's special area of expertise. Besides, the almost universal use of the United Bible Societies *Greek New Testament* (UBS^4) among students, teachers, and Bible translators easily creates the impression that the experts have "delivered the goods" and that we can simply rely on the text they have given us. Even the *Novum Testamentum Graece* (27th rev. ed.), with its more detailed apparatus, has the same text as UBS⁴. For some years its major editor referred to this common text as the new "Standard Text," an expression eerily reminiscent of the old label "Textus Receptus," a publisher's blurb for the 1633 edition of the Greek New Testament (Aland and Aland 1989, 31–36, uses the term "new text" instead of the "Standard Text" of the first edition [1987, 34–35]).

But you would not be reading this introduction unless you had an interest in the text of the New Testament. This book itself is a response to a resurgence of interest in New Testament textual criticism, fueled in part by the burgeoning field of studies in the social world of early Christianity. A new generation is learning that textual variants have stories to tell about the problems the first Christians wrestled with: tensions between Jews and Gentiles; women in family life and church leadership; the divine/human nature of Jesus; the standardization of liturgical texts; social and sexual issues; and others (see ch. 8).

The fact is that textual criticism affects the life of the church at its most basic level, for its results eventually filter down to the ordinary Bible-reading public in the translations in popular use. This has sometimes produced outrage, as it did for John W. Burgon, dean of Chichester, England, when the 1881 revision of the King James Version of 1611 appeared. This Revised Version (RV) abandoned many readings familiar from the late medieval manuscripts used as the base for the KJV in favor of readings that had since come to light from earlier witnesses. Burgon insisted that these earlier manuscripts were corrupt copies exhibiting an untrustworthy text and that the KJV was more reliable (see ch. 4). The publication of the Revised Standard Version of the Bible in 1952 met with an even more incendiary reception in some circles, when readers found missing several familiar passages, including the last twelve verses of the Gospel of Mark, the story of the adulterous woman in John 7:53–8:11, and Luke 22:19b–20 (part of the Lukan account of the Last Supper).[1] A Sunday

---

1. The reaction was quite literally incendiary, including one preacher's public burning of a copy with a blowtorch, the ashes being then sent to Luther Weigle, chairman of the translation committee. Bruce Metzger's comment on this bizarre incident is, "though in previous centuries Bible translators were sometimes burned, today happily it is only a copy of the translation that meets such a fate" (Metzger 1997, 79).

school teacher of mine insisted that the RSV was heavily influenced by communists, which is why it was issued in a red cover. Textual criticism is not just about trivialities. It matters.

To be sure, the professional practice of textual criticism requires a formidable repertoire of skills and a fund of knowledge that relatively few persons can master. So, how can nonspecialists access such a highly specialized field of studies? This book provides one avenue of access. It is not aimed at working text critics. Indeed, it is from them that I gratefully draw so much of the book's contents. It also is not intended to be a "how-to" manual, although the careful reader will learn a great deal about how textual critics do their work. My narrative approach should not be taken to imply that others have not told the story of the New Testament text. Indeed, a recounting of the birth, growth, and fortunes of textual criticism (the "history") is a standard feature of the best manuals on the subject, but it is usually just one section or chapter among others dealing with the sources, the methods, and the practices of textual criticism. In contrast, I have integrated five major components of textual criticism in my telling of the story of the discipline. These five components are Movers, Materials, Motives, Methods, and Models. Since I have chosen these headings in part for their convenience as aids to memory, I should make it clear what I have in mind for each and what you should expect to find as you move along in the story.

Movers are the major players in the story, those who have contributed to the development of New Testament textual criticism in some important way. It would be fair to refer to most of them as textual critics, although in the earliest period the term will not fit all of them. I will give more biographical information about the pioneers (chs. 3 and 4) than about their successors, and I have had to be much more selective in later chapters, especially when referring to my contemporaries.

Under the heading *Materials*, I will highlight the collecting, collating, and evaluating of witnesses to the text: the Greek manuscripts, early versions, and the quotations of the New Testament in the church fathers. Obviously I will have to be quite selective, profiling only witnesses that have been deemed to be especially important and making summary comments about others. Readers more interested in the narrative itself might wish to read over these sections rapidly and refer back to them when particular witnesses are mentioned later in the story. In the first chapter I will also briefly describe the materials and techniques of ancient book production and show why knowledge of these things is important to textual critics.

When I discuss *Motives*, I am asking the question, What are textual critics trying to accomplish as they work with divergent forms of the text of the New Testament? The answer might seem self-evident: they are trying to get back to the original form of the text, but, as we shall see, that is only one motive of the workers in this vineyard. Indeed, some of the first persons to comment on variant readings in the text seem to have had little interest in choosing the earliest form of the text. Some scholars have been more interested in charting the differences than in getting behind them. Today the very question whether it is even useful to talk about an "original" text is debated. The motives of text-critical scholars are not self-evident and must be explored for each era.

The discussion of *Methods* traces such developments as the framing of criteria used to weigh one reading against another and various means of classifying textual witnesses sharing similar distinctive readings into groups and subgroups (chs. 3–5). We will see the difficulty and the necessity of trying to control the burgeoning mass of data by such winnowing and grouping (ch. 7 summarizes an extraordinarily complex set of developments; attempting to read it at one sitting will probably cause the eyes to glaze over). We will also come to appreciate why most working text critics today claim to follow an "eclectic" method in their decisions.

By *Models* I have in mind, in the first place, watershed publications that serve to advance the development of textual criticism. A classic example is the description of the principles Westcott and Hort used to reconstruct what they called *The New Testament in the Original Greek* (1881; ch. 4). A more recent model is Bart Ehrman's influential *The Orthodox Corruption of Scripture* (1993), which argues that scribes frequently altered "better" (i.e., earlier) readings in order to protect and defend the church's developing theological orthodoxy (ch. 8). I also use the term *Models* to refer to examples of how scholars make decisions about specific textual variants. The vast majority of textual variants are mechanical scribal errors of the same kind we ourselves make when hand-copying material; others involve grammatical "improvements" to the text that do not change its essential meaning. But some textual variants materially alter the sense of the text, as noted in the above discussion about the RV and RSV. It is instructive to follow the shifting currents of scholarship on such variants, as they are dealt with in commentaries, articles, and published translations.

Obviously, these are five overlapping categories that cannot be neatly separated. I hope the repetition you will sometimes find between one category and another will be helpful and not tiresome. It has not been possible to organize each chapter formally around these five categories, but I have attempted to see that each gets its due in the narrative.

The past two decades have felt the blowing of new winds that are shaking the house of New Testament textual criticism. No one can predict what the discipline will look like when the dust settles, but I am glad for the energy and enthusiasm of those who will write the next chapter in this continuing story. It is my hope that some of you who read this book will be among them.

1
Paul and Luke Become Published Authors

> I, Tertius, the writer of this letter, greet you in the Lord. (Rom 16:22)
>
> Since many have undertaken to set down an orderly account of the events that have been fulfilled among us ... I too decided, after investigating everything carefully from the very first, to write an orderly account for you, most excellent Theophilus. (Luke 1:1, 3)

The Prehistory of the Text: How Writings Were Produced and Published in the Roman Era

Did you ever wish you could pull back the curtain and watch Paul at work writing one of his letters to an assembly of Jesus followers? The possibility of doing this used to be largely a matter of guesswork, but more than a century of research into ancient letter writing has given us a much clearer picture. In 56 or 57 C.E., while in Corinth as a guest in the home of Gaius (Rom 16:23), Paul wrote a letter to the believers in Rome. In the sketch that follows, we will use this letter as a model to learn how Paul's writings (and perhaps other letters that ended up in the New Testament) were produced and distributed (E. Richards 1991, 2004; Gamble 1995, 1–143; Murphy-O'Connor 1995).

Paul Writes a Letter to the Romans

Our first act of historical imagination must be to think ourselves into a culture where only a small minority of the population, perhaps only about

10 percent, could read and write (W. Harris 1989, 272).[1] Even those who had these skills often dictated their work to a secretary rather than doing their own writing. After all, literacy in writing must be thought of as a continuum, ranging from name literacy (the ability to write one's name on a document), through various levels of skill in spelling and writing, to the competencies required for professional work.

In reconstructing the writing, sending, and publication of Paul's letter to the Romans, much of the process I describe is virtually certain. Other parts are not certain but highly probable, and every practice and piece of equipment is well documented from sources reasonably contemporaneous with Paul.

What eventually became the Letter to the Romans may well have begun weeks, or even months, before Paul actually "wrote" it, for he likely carried with him notebooks for jotting down ideas, useful scriptural texts, quotations, and rough drafts. Writers often used for their notes a set of waxed wooden tablets stacked and joined together with cords or thongs tied through holes at their edges. These tablets could easily be smoothed over and rewritten with the use of a stylus made of wood, metal, ivory, or bone.[2] Such tablets (*tabulae ceratae*) were in widespread use in the Roman world (E. Richards 1991, 55–57). By the time the Letter to the Romans was written, waxed tablets were being supplemented by small parchment notebooks (*membranae*), which were a Roman innovation (Roberts and Skeat 1983, 15–23). These notebooks were widely used for copying out extracts from reading, epigrams, maxims, and the like (see Cribiore 1996, pl. 385, 389, 403, for examples of wooden and parchment notebooks). The writer of 2 Tim 4:13 has Paul asking that his "books [τὰ βιβλία, *ta biblia*, probably scrolls of some of the Old Testament writings] and especially the notebooks [τὰς μεμβράνας, *tas membranas*]" be brought to him.[3] This text

---

1. The heavy use of literature in early Christian communities has occasioned discussion of whether there may have been a higher level of literacy among leaders of these communities than among the wider population (Gamble 1995, 3–10; Epp 1997, 15–37). Millard suggests that the strong emphasis on the importance of education of Jewish males to read the Scriptures in synagogue services likely resulted in greater literacy in Jewish society than in the Hellenistic world in general (Millard 2000, 157–58).

2. For a photograph of a wax tablet used for a school writing exercise, see E. Turner 1971, 33. For a set of five bound into a "codex," see Pestman 1990, 205–6.

3. I disagree with Gamble (1995, 64), who insists that, since *ta biblia* normally

is a valuable reference to the likely practice of Paul, even if, as many scholars hold, 2 Timothy is not written by Paul himself. For a writing as long and carefully constructed as Romans (Paul's longest letter), it is likely that a great deal of preformed material made its way out of his notebooks and into this treatise.

Paul's other writing equipment included a pen, which was simply a section of reed cut to a point (the nib) and slit to help retain ink, the ink itself (made from lampblack or soot mixed with thin gum, usually sold in a dried cake and mixed with water for use), and a sponge (to wash off writing that needed to be replaced). Two famous wall paintings from Pompeii show us what this equipment may have looked like, including the kind of containers in which bookrolls (scrolls) were carried (E. Turner 1971, 34–35). Paul would customarily have used such equipment for writing in his notebooks.

For his letters, however, Paul relied on secretaries to take down dictation. In six of his letters, Paul shows that he has used a secretary; in five of these, Paul intervenes near the end to write a greeting in his own hand (1 Cor 16:21; Gal 6:11; Col 4:18; 2 Thess 3:17; Phlm 19). E. Richards (1991, 172–73) has demonstrated that, when an ancient letter writer adds a postscript in his or her own hand, that is evidence that the rest of the letter has been written by a secretary.[4] In our model letter, Romans, the secretary sends a greeting: "I, Tertius, the one writing the letter, greet you in the Lord" (Rom 16:22). From this brief subscription we know that Tertius was himself a believer, and we can infer that he was personally acquainted with some of the Roman believers (Tertius was a Latin name). We should not necessarily conclude that all of Paul's letters were dictated to fellow Christ followers. It is not likely that his circle of acquaintances would always have included a trained scribe, and we should not imagine that just any literate friend would have been capable of taking dictation, which entailed a set of skills well beyond the ability to read and write. Since Paul's letters were

---

designates proper books, i.e., scrolls, the phrase "especially the parchments" must refer to what we might call published books in leaf form, not rough notebooks; Murphy-O'Connor (1995, 36–37) cites Martial's epigram entitled "Pugillares Membranei" (Fist-Sized Notebooks): "Imagine these tablets are waxen, although they are called parchment. You will rub out as often as you wish to write afresh" (*Epigrams* 14.7).

4. Even if, as many scholars hold, 2 Thessalonians and Colossians are not by Paul, there is no doubt about the other examples above. Cumulatively, there is a "favorable presumption" that Paul customarily used a secretary (Murphy-O'Connor 1995, 7).

vastly longer than the private letters that have survived from antiquity, he may well have required a secretary versed in shorthand, at least for the two longest letters, Romans and 1 Corinthians. Not every secretary will have been so skilled. E. Richards (1991, 26–43), demonstrates the use of shorthand systems in both Latin and Greek for the time of Paul, although he does not believe Paul would have had access to such highly trained scribes for all of his letters.

A plausible surmise is that Tertius was a slave of one of the few upper-class members (Gaius?) of the church in Corinth, since many of the known secretaries of Roman times were either slaves or freedmen (Haines-Eitzen 2000, 21–40, 53–64). In any case, Tertius was not hired at random from the marketplace, although Paul may on other occasions have needed to hire from the market.

For the production of the Letter to the Romans, Tertius could have done his writing almost anywhere, for he would have sat cross-legged on a small stool, or even on the ground, the skirt of his tunic stretched tightly across his knees to form a flat surface on which he laid a papyrus roll held in place by his left hand. (Surprisingly, scribes did not begin to use tables or desks for writing until the early Middle Ages [Skeat 1956, 179–208].) Laid within easy reach were the tools of his trade: a penknife, sponge, inkpot, brick of dried ink, and pumice for smoothing the writing surface. Paul could well have dictated the letter over a period of several days, working only a few hours at a time—even handing the secretary his notebooks for inserting scriptural quotations and other preformed material. Based on what we know of the average number of syllables per line generated by trained copyists and the estimated average number of lines a secretary could write per hour, Richards suggests that two to three working days would have been needed for a single draft of Romans (E. Richards 1991, 164–65). This allows about five hours of actual writing each day, with additional time needed for the preparation of the papyrus, mixing of ink, periodic sharpening of the pen nib, conferring with the author, and resting. If the rough draft was written on wax tablets, the work may have gone faster.

The expected practice would be for Paul then to go over the rough draft and enter (or dictate) revisions. A fair copy would then be made, perhaps on better-quality papyrus, to be sent out to the addressees. Finally, the secretary would make a copy in Paul's notebook for his own records. Although it is impossible to estimate the time spent in actual dictation, revising, and copying, the production of the letter to the Romans may well have occupied two weeks or more, not counting the hours Paul may have spent thinking and jotting down notes before the secretary even began to work.

THE LETTER TO THE ROMANS IS SENT

Writers of private correspondence had to find their own letter carriers. Paul's usual practice was to send one of his co-workers, for example, Timothy (1 Cor 4:17; 16:10), Titus (2 Cor 7:15–16), Epaphroditus (Phil 2:25–30), Tychicus (Eph 6:21; Col 4:7; Titus 3:12), Epaphras, and Onesimus (Col 1:7; 4:7–9) to carry his letters. The letter to the Romans was evidently entrusted to a colleague of Paul's, otherwise unknown to us, named Phoebe (Rom 16:1–2). The care with which he introduces and commends her confirms what we see from the references to Paul's other colleagues who were entrusted with his letters, namely, that letter carriers often did more than simply deliver the mail. We have abundant evidence in private letters from Egypt that other letter carriers in Hellenistic and Roman times were expected to bring personal news of the writers whose mail they carried (Epp 1991, 46–48): Timothy will "remind you of my ways in Christ" (1 Cor 4:17); "Tychicus will tell you all about my affairs. … I have sent him to you for this very purpose, that you may know how we are" (Col 4:7–8). It is clear from these and other references that Paul's known letter carriers communicated news of Paul's circumstances.

Paul held these letter carriers in high esteem. Timothy is his "beloved and faithful child in the Lord" (1 Cor 4:17); the Corinthians are asked to "put him at ease among you" (1 Cor 16:10). Epaphroditus has brought to Paul financial support from the Philippians (Phil 4:14–18) and is being sent back to the Philippians as Paul's "brother and co-worker and fellow-soldier, and your messenger and minister to my need" (Phil 2:25). Phoebe is introduced as "deacon [or perhaps 'minister' (διάκονος, *diakonos*)] of the assembly that is in Cenchrea" (Rom 16:1). The Romans are asked to "assist her in whatever she may have need, because she has been a patron [προστάτις, *prostatis*] of many and of me" (v. 2). Although it is impossible to know how the congregations might be called upon to assist her, we can construct a very likely scenario of what Paul may have expected of Phoebe as his representative. Not only could she have brought more personal information about Paul, especially to those he greets by name in 16:3–15, but she may well have been asked by Paul to read the letter aloud to the several house-church groups in Rome (see Rom 16:5, 10, 11, 14, 15).

Public reading of a letter required careful attention to what we now call "oral interpretation," that is, use of the voice and even gestures to convey the author's intentions clearly (E. Richards 1991, 202). It is likely that Paul would have coached Phoebe on how the letter was to be read.

The Letter to the Romans Is "Published" and Dispersed

Odd as it may seem to moderns, publication of a piece of literature in the ancient world was simply the public reading of the composition and its release in the form of a copy available to the broader community (Turner 1968, 112–13). We cannot know whether Phoebe would have carried the one letter around to each of the Roman house-churches or would have left a copy for each of these groups (Gamble 1995, 97). E. Richards (2004, 157) points out that Paul expected his original letter to the Galatians to be circulated to all of the churches in that province, because his calling attention to his large signature at the end of the letter (6:11) would have been meaningless to anyone reading a copy of the original. A single reading of one of Paul's letters would not have exhausted its usefulness to its addressees; indeed, all of these writings would have required much time for reflection and discussion within the community. Paul felt so strongly that his letters should be read before the whole congregation that he wrote to the Thessalonians (1 Thess 5:27), "Put yourselves under an oath to the Lord that you will read this letter to all the brothers [and sisters]." In any case, when the letter had been read aloud to its intended public and a copy had been made available for further use, the letter to the Romans had been "published."

Luke Writes a Gospel[5]

The textual mechanics of writing and publishing a Gospel would likely not have differed from those involved in the production of Paul's letters (or, indeed, of the other writings in the New Testament). Nevertheless, the process of gathering materials and fashioning them into a narrative about the life, death, and resurrection of Jesus was different from the process of writing a pastoral letter to a congregation. Moreover, the existence

---

5. I use the name Luke on the basis of tradition and without prejudice to the question of the actual author of this Gospel.

of multiple sources of traditions about Jesus and the eventual publication of multiple Gospels influenced the subsequent copying of these works in ways that set them apart from the New Testament letters.

I use Luke as the example for the production of a Gospel because, of all the Gospel writers, only he includes a preface with information about his working methods (Luke 1:1–4). Luke writes with the awareness that "many" persons had already written up their own accounts "of the events that have been fulfilled among us" (Luke 1:1). This is not the place for a discussion on the origins and interrelationships of the canonical Gospels, which any good critical introduction to the New Testament can supply. For the purposes of what follows, I accept these hypotheses: (1) that Mark was the first of the canonical Gospels to be written; (2) that the Gospel of Mark was the primary source document used by Luke; (3) that Luke's major secondary source was a collection of non-Markan traditions about Jesus (labeled Q by scholars) that was also used by Matthew; (4) and that, in addition to these sources, Luke had access to additional material, both written and oral, that contributed to his project.

The question of the nature and origin of the source material in all of the Gospels is still much debated. The earliest Christian tradition, attributed by Papias, bishop of Hierapolis (ca. 120 C.E.), to "the Elder," reports that Mark (presumably the John Mark who is associated in the Acts of the Apostles with Peter, Paul, and Barnabas) was "the interpreter (or translator) of Peter" and that he wrote down, but "not in order," what Peter recalled of the sayings or deeds of Jesus. Near the end of the second century, Clement of Alexandria (d. before 215), citing a tradition of "the elders," claims that Mark put down in writing the preaching of Peter in Rome (*Hypotyposes* 6; quoted by Eusebius, *Hist. eccl.* 6.14.5–7). The historical worth of this tradition is debated, but for our purposes the major point is that oral reminiscences or sermons about Jesus were reduced to writing and that these "notes" formed the basis for a more formal written composition that came to be called a Gospel (on the origin and significance of the term Gospel, see Hengel 2000, 34–115). We must assume that all of the Gospel writers drew from a wealth of Jesus tradition, both written and unwritten.

In comparing the work of Paul in writing his letters and Luke in writing his Gospel, it is certain that both used preformed written tradition. Paul quotes snatches of confessions of faith and hymnic material that were part of the churches' developing liturgy; he also seems to have drawn upon "virtue and vice" lists as well as other catechetical material.

Luke clearly knows other written narratives about Jesus. Both Paul and Luke may well have made use of "testimony collections" of Old Testament scriptures useful to their projects.[6] We are in the dark about how they accessed and adapted these materials or even the physical form in which these source materials were available. Testimony collections may have been available on papyrus scrolls; wax tablets and parchment notebooks were possible vehicles for source material. It is likely, but not certain, that Luke had the Gospel of Mark available in roll form, but we do not know whether he handled it physically or had assistants who read out from the text the portions Luke wished to use. That Paul customarily used secretaries is certain; that Luke did so as well is almost certain, for this was the common practice for persons writing treatises of any length. Besides, the Theophilus to whom Luke's work is dedicated (Luke 1:3) was likely a well-to-do patron who bore the expense of the project.

As for the target audiences of Paul and Luke, Paul's letters were clearly directed to particular congregations and individuals. The Gospel of Luke was directed to the instruction of Theophilus, who may well have published the letter by reading it to his circle of friends. Whether Luke's Gospel was shaped to meet the needs and interests of a wider church community in a particular geographic region is a much-debated issue.[7]

In any case, once the original work (Romans, Luke) was made available for copying, not only was it copied for use by its first recipients, but there soon developed a lively exchange of writings, the church in one city sending copies of Christian writings it possessed to the church(es) in another city. Colossians 4:16 directs its readers to make sure there is an exchange of letters between the church at Colossae and the church at Laodicea. Although Gamble believes Colossians is not an authentic letter of Paul, he rightly concludes that "the notice does show that the author either knew that letters of Paul were circulating among Pauline churches or wanted to encourage their circulation by offering a Pauline warrant" (Gamble 1995, 97). We have evidence that copies of Romans circulated without the words "in Rome" in 1:7, 15, thus allowing readers to receive

---

6. A testimony collection is a list of Old Testament texts useful for supporting themes or claims relating to Christ and his ministry, death, resurrection, and redemptive work (see Rom 15:9–12).

7. The question whether each of the Gospels was written for a particular community or region or all were intended for wider use has recently been reopened (Bauckham 1998).

the letter as generally applicable to all churches. We have similar evidence for 1 Corinthians and possibly Ephesians (Gamble 1995, 97–99).

Just as the church itself was expanding rapidly during the first two centuries C.E., we are right to surmise a quite-rapid expansion in the number of copies not only of Paul's letters but of the Gospels and other early Christian literature as well. Older studies used to suppose that it would have taken a period of several years, even decades, for the dissemination of a writing from its place of origin to a distant city in the Mediterranean world, but a study of the speed with which dated private letters and documents traveled to and from distant cities has made it clear that the writings of the New Testament "could easily, in a matter of a few weeks, have moved anywhere in the Mediterranean area" (Epp 1991, 56).

But who made these copies of the originals? Did the churches have ready access to professional scribes, and could they afford their services? Probably not. The great number and variety of textual variants that are found in the earliest manuscripts of New Testament writings suggest that, from the beginning, the churches relied on the relatively few literate persons among them to make the copies they needed (Royse 2008, 28–31; Cribiore 1996, 5, 10). Although only the elite made it to the top of the educational ladder, even those on the lower rungs learned writing by means of copying: first the alphabet, then words and phrases, and, finally, longer models. We have no direct evidence of Christian copying practices from the first century, but the second-century Shepherd of Hermas depicts its author as having been given the book in a vision; he then copies the text "letter by letter" (πρὸς γράμμα, *pros gramma*), a procedure suggesting that the slave Hermas (whether a real or fictional character) was not a professional scribe (Haines-Eitzen 2000, 36). What we can demonstrate is that very few of the earliest New Testament papyri known to us (late second century) exhibit the practiced hand and careful eye of professional scribes. Furthermore, a professionally produced copy of a single Gospel, even of second-quality scribal work, might well have cost the equivalent of $1,000 today (Bagnall 2009, 50–69).

But would a person not have needed permission from the author before making a copy for private use? The answer is no. There was no concept of copyright or intellectual property in the ancient world. To be sure, there was a commercial book trade in Rome during the time of the early empire, but it was vastly different from a modern publishing enterprise. From references in Martial, Quintilian, and Pliny, Harry Gamble infers that these authors delivered copies of their new works to booksellers for a

> **THE WRITINGS OF THE NEW TESTAMENT ARE PUBLISHED**
>
> ▶ Authors compile notes, outlines, traditions on wax tablets or parchment notebooks.
> ▶ Authors dictate their material to secretaries (scribes).
> ▶ Scribes write first drafts on wax tablets.
> ▶ Authors correct first drafts.
> ▶ Scribes write final drafts on papyrus rolls.
> ▶ Scribes make copies of final drafts for authors to archive.
> ▶ Each writing is sent to its designated audience.
> ▶ Writings are read aloud in congregational gatherings.
> ▶ Each writing is "published" when a copy is made available for others to copy.

flat fee. The dealer then paid to have multiple copies made, thus generating profits for himself (Gamble 1995, 86–87). There is no reason to believe Christian scriptures would have been available in a commercial book stall. It remains the case that any work could be copied by anyone who had access to it and was literate enough to make a copy.

The very form of book production that Christians adopted sometime in the first century may also have implications for the somewhat casual way in which early copies seem to have been made, for Christian copyists and writers moved quickly from using the roll (scroll) form of book to adopting the codex, or leaf-form book, as a proper medium for copying their religious literature (Roberts and Skeat 1983). The rationale for this move is under debate, and I will discuss it in chapter 9. Meanwhile, this much can be said: in general, the papyrus (or parchment) roll continued to be the preferred medium for copies of classical literature until the late third or early fourth centuries C.E. (the parchment or leather roll for Jewish Scriptures even longer). In addition to Christians, the early adopters of the codex seem to have been writers of professional handbooks and manuals—practical writings. As a working hypothesis, Gamble's comment is worth noting: "Christian texts came to be inscribed in codices not because they enjoyed a special status as aesthetic or cult objects, but because they were practical books for everyday use: the handbooks, as it were, of the Christian community" (Gamble 1995, 66).

Thus, both the form of the early Christian book and the rapid accumulation of copying errors and other alterations to the text indicate that

1. PAUL AND LUKE BECOME PUBLISHED AUTHORS   17

the earliest copies were "working texts" for the immediate use of the individuals and communities who saw to it that copies were made. As early as the late second century, however, Christian writers (and some of their opponents) were beginning to notice and compare variant readings in the text, thus practicing a rudimentary form of textual criticism.

The Need for Textual Criticism

What exactly is textual criticism? The classical scholar A. E. Housman put it this way: "[Textual criticism] is the science of discovering error in texts and the art of removing it" (Housman 1961, 131). As we will see, removing error is not the only motivation for the critical study of texts, but variant readings in texts do invite critical attention. In his study of Origen and textual criticism, Bruce Metzger quotes Origen's famous comment about variant readings in the Gospels, part of which will be used as the caption to the next chapter: "The differences among the manuscripts have become great, either through the negligence of some copyists or through the perverse audacity of others; they either neglect to check over what they have transcribed, or in the process of checking, they make additions or deletions as they please" (Metzger 1963b, 78). Origen (185–232 C.E.) was probably the greatest scholar of the pre-Nicene church and one of the first Christian intellectuals to devote attention to the transmission of the biblical text. His comment is a convenient point of departure for us to consider the causes of scribal errors and alterations in the manuscripts Origen and his near contemporaries saw and used.

Scribal Errors in the New Testament Text

Every reader of this book has committed many of the same errors as ancient scribes, just as thoughtful readers develop a certain expertise in sorting out the copying or printing errors we encounter, as David C. Parker cleverly reminds us:

> Everybody who reads the newspaper is an expert in textual criticism, in coping with those distctive errors of omssion and displaced lines, and jumbling of letrset. This sophisticated process of recognizing nonsense and picking up the sense is so natural to us the classical scholars of ancient Alexandria or the Benedictines of that we perform it without thinking, unaware of our kinship with

St Maur. Textual criticism is not an arcane science. It belongs to all human communication. (Parker 1997, 1)

Scholars frequently distinguish between unintentional and intentional changes in the text. I prefer, with Parker, to speak of unconscious and conscious alterations (Parker 1997, 37). Even when scribes consciously altered the text they were copying, they often assumed they were *correcting* a mistake in the exemplar, thus bringing the text back to its original wording, rather than creating a new variant reading.

Unconscious alterations are those that occur during one of the four stages in the ancient copying process: reading (a line or phrase), remembering (as one's eye turns from the exemplar to the blank page), repeating (aloud, as most reading was done in antiquity), and writing the line or phrase in the new copy (so Dain 1975, 41–46). The three most common categories of unconscious alterations are scribal leaps, confusion of letters, and confusion of sounds.

Scribal leaps occur when the scribe copies a word, phrase, or line, then looks back and copies the same thing again (dittography) or looks ahead and leaves out material (haplography). For example, the scribe of our earliest manuscript of Paul's letters (known in the standard list as P[46]) has duplicated the phrase "with thanksgiving" (μετὰ εὐχαριστίας, *meta eucharistias*) at Phil 4:6, producing nonsense: "with thanksgiving with thanksgiving let your requests be known." The same scribe has omitted the words "zeal, the one doing acts of mercy with" (σπουδῇ ὁ ἐλεῶν ἐν, *spoudē ho eleōn en*) at Rom 12:8 because his eye skipped from the "with" in the previous phrase ("with zeal") to the "with" in the following phrase ("with cheerfulness"). In this second example, the text still makes sense, but it is short one of the spiritual gifts of Rom 12.

Confusion of letters sometimes occurred when the exemplar (the text in front of the copyist) was poorly written or faded or the copyist did not see well. Most manuscripts prior to the ninth century were copied in capital letters, in which the Greek letters *sigma* (C), *epsilon* (Ꮛ), *theta* (Θ), and *omicron* (O) could be confused. The double *lambda*, ΛΛ, could also be read as a *mu*, M, which apparently happened at Rom 6:5, where the word ΑΛΛΑ "but" has been misread as ΑΜΑ "together" by some copyists (Metzger and Ehrman 2005, 251).

Confusion of sounds sometimes resulted in certain vowels and diphthongs being interchanged because they were pronounced alike (Caragounis 2006, 339–96, with pronunciation chart on 352). This could have occurred when the letter was first dictated (and not corrected by the author) or even when a copyist, pronouncing aloud the words before writing them, unconsciously wrote a same-sounding vowel or diphthong. Thus, the Greek vowels *iota*, *ēta*, and *upsilon* (ι, η, υ) were pronounced the same, and the diphthongs ει, οι, and υι were pronounced the same as the vowels above. The diphthong αι was sounded the same as ε. *Omicron* (ο) and *omega* (ω) were pronounced identically. Additional orthographic confusion resulted because of certain vowel/consonant combinations. The New Testament is replete with variations between the first- and second-person pronouns (ἡμεῖς, ὑμεῖς, *hēmeis, humeis*) because these sounded alike. Since both readings often make good sense, it is frequently difficult to decide between them. To be sure, Phoebe was "our" (ἡμῶν, *hēmōn*) sister from the standpoint of the Corinthian Christians, but when Paul commends her to the Roman church (Rom 16:1), is it possible he describes her as "your" (ὑμῶν, *humōn*) sister, as read by many witnesses to the text? It has been conceded that the variation between the subjunctive form ἔχωμεν, *echōmen*, and the indicative form ἔχομεν, *echomen*, at Rom 5:1 ("let us have peace with God"/"we have peace with God") may go back to the autograph (the original). Paul may have dictated one form; Tertius may have written the other; and Paul may then have let the copied form stand. In any case, the variation undoubtedly arose because of the identical pronunciation; both forms have had their champions in antiquity, as they do today.

Conscious alterations are the results of someone's attempts to improve on a text he or she judged to be faulty in some way. Metzger notes Jerome's observation that many copyists, trying to correct the errors of others, simply "expose their own" (Metzger and Ehrman 2005, 260). Although such changes are routinely said to be the fault of scribes or copyists, it is more probable, as we will see in chapter 9, that the scribe was simply copying into the text marginal or interlinear changes already suggested by a previous reader or owner of the exemplar.

Improvements to grammar, spelling, and sense intrude into the text in various ways. Common intrusions include the addition of prepositions, articles, pronouns, conjunctions, and adverbs. At 1 Cor 15:49 we find dropped into the text of P[46] the little particle δή, *dē*, before the verb φορέσωμεν, *phoresōmen* (φορέσομεν, *phoresomen* in most witnesses), so that the text reads "just as we bore the image of the earthly, well then [δή, *dē*] let us bear the image of the heavenly," thus changing a statement ("we shall bear") into an exhortation ("let us bear").

Corrections to historical and geographical references may be a way of protecting the reader from difficulties. All three of the Synoptic Gospels have the variant readings "Gadarenes," "Gerasenes," and "Gergesenes" in their accounts of Jesus' healing of the demoniac(s) (Matt 8:28; Mark 5:1; Luke 8:26), apparently because of the difficulty of settling on one location that satisfied all the conditions implied in the story (near the Sea of Galilee, with tombs and a steep bank nearby). At Mark 1:2, where there is a composite quotation (from Exodus, Malachi, and Isaiah) introduced by the words "Just as it stands written in Isaiah the prophet," the text has been corrected in several witnesses to read "just as it is written in the prophets."

Conflations occur frequently throughout the Gospels, as those who handled manuscripts found it difficult to resist the temptation to fill out a story by adding details from its parallel version(s). The piercing of Jesus' side by a spear (John 19:34) was so important in early Christian tradition that it was added to the account in Matt 27:49 in a number of manuscripts. Some editors or copyists thought that a reference to "scribes" ought always to be completed by "and Pharisees." In short, every one of the Gospels, especially the Synoptics, contains textual variants with additional material drawn from parallel accounts.

Alterations to the text to protect theological points of view eventually entered the stream of textual tradition, although we cannot know how early. During the doctrinal debates of the second and third centuries, Irenaeus, Clement of Alexandria, Origen, and others frequently accused their opponents of falsifying Scripture. In fact, it was not only the heretics who altered the text to buttress their dogmas, but also the orthodox (Ehrman 1993b). Consider an example from Mark 1:41: Was Jesus "compassionate" (σπλαγχνισθείς, *splanchnistheis*) or "angry" (ὀργισθείς, *orgistheis*) when he stretched out his hand and touched the leprous man? An early reader might well have had second thoughts about a representation of Jesus acting in anger to heal someone and thus have edited the text in the direction of a friendlier Jesus.

With the rapid expansion of the church all over the Roman world, it is certain that copies of the writings that later became the New Testament were multiplied freely for the use of local congregations. Although relatively few individuals will have been able to afford their own copies, it is clear that by the last quarter of the second century C.E. some of the church's bishops and intellectual leaders possessed, or at least had access to, multiple copies of some Christian texts. Troubled by variant readings, they began to compare these readings and comment upon them. Thus was ushered in the dawn of New Testament textual criticism.

2
The Precritical Age

> The differences among the manuscripts have become great, either through the negligence of some copyists or through the perverse audacity of others. (Origen of Alexandria, *Comm. Matt.* 15:14)

Origen's comment above demonstrates that variant readings in the text of the New Testament did not go unnoticed by learned readers. Although it would be many centuries before a formal, critical discipline of textual criticism would be employed on the New Testament texts, we can trace the outlines of a developing process already as early as Irenaeus, who was bishop of Lyons around 170 C.E. Beginning in this chapter and continuing through the chapters ahead, we will trace the development of New Testament textual criticism by asking these questions:

1. Who were the *movers*, the major players in the development of the discipline of textual criticism of the New Testament?
2. What were the *materials*, what scholars today call the witnesses to the text, available to the early fathers and their successors?
3. What were their *motivations* for engaging in the comparison of these witnesses: to get to the original text? to get to the earliest form known from the copies? just to collect all the variants? to refute the deliberate "falsifications" of others?
4. What were the *methods* of study they used: scientific? intuitional? Did they make lists or charts? What kinds of controls did they develop for making decisions?
5. What *models* have they left as guides or challenges for those

who came after them? How did they deal with particular variant readings? What did they publish to advance the discipline of studies? What questions did they raise for their successors?

Not every chapter will lend itself to a clear-cut development around these five markers, but they will remain guiding concerns throughout the book. In the present chapter, before textual criticism has become a recognized discipline in the modern sense, we will omit the formal category of movers, although we will meet a good number of persons who laid the foundations upon which modern textual criticism has been built.

Materials

Origen's comments demonstrate that it was possible for a scholar in the second century to have access to the text of the New Testament in multiple copies. We can trace over the centuries between Origen and Erasmus remarkable developments in the ways in which the text may have been encountered by ordinary Christians who heard it read and preached, as well as by scholars who gave themselves to its study. Since my main interest is in tracing the development of textual *criticism*, that is, the critical *study* of the text, I will do only a rapid survey of the growth in materials that became available from the second through the sixteenth centuries (see Parker 1997, 19–29). I will not discuss in detail any particular manuscripts or other material, because such details become important largely during the *rediscovery* or careful restudy of these resources during the centuries following the publication of the first printed New Testament in 1516.

Greek Manuscripts

Just over 5,500 Greek New Testament manuscripts have been catalogued (see Epp 2007, 77–106, for statistics). The official list is kept by the Institut für neutestamentliche Textforschung/Institute for New Testament Textual Research in Münster, Germany, with updates on the Institut's website (http://www.uni-muenster.de/NTTextforschung/). Many of these manuscripts are highly fragmentary—some containing only a few verses or even portions of a few verses. In fact, only fifty-three manuscripts contain the complete New Testament, and only one of these is dated as early as the fourth century. Scholars today divide the Greek manuscripts into four categories: papyri, majuscules (or uncials), minuscules, and lectionaries. As we saw above, the earliest extant Christian manuscripts are papyrus codices. Majuscules are written entirely in capital letters and usually in large script (the biblical papyri are also written in capitals, but are distinguished from the majuscules by the medium used, namely, papyrus rather than parchment). Minuscules, written in a small, running hand, began to displace majuscules in the ninth century, to enable more-rapid production of books. Lectionaries may be in either capitals or in minuscule script; they are distinguished from the other categories in that they contain selections of Scripture, rather than being running texts, as we will see below. In the next chapter, I will explain how textual critics developed ways of cataloging these four categories of manuscripts. We have no way of estimating how many copies of the New Testament in Greek, in whole or part, were known to any one person during this first period of our study.

We now know that by the late second century, papyrus codices were being used to copy multiple books, not only single ones. That is, we have papyrus codices dating from around 175–250 C.E. that contain two or more Gospels (P^{75}), all four Gospels and Acts (P^{45}), and as many as ten letters attributed to Paul, plus Hebrews (P^{46}), to mention only three. I do not deal here with the question of the collection of Paul's letters into a corpus and the first publication of the four Gospels. By the third century, such multiple-text codices, especially for the Gospels, were proliferating.

Up to the fourth century, we still find few indications of professional scribal activity; all the textual variants mentioned above, conscious and unconscious, abound in our manuscripts, most notably the tendency to harmonize and conflate passages. Since we know that oral tradition about Jesus was circulating alongside the written Gospels, it is likely that some of this material also found its way into some Gospel manuscripts. This is, for example, the likeliest explanation for how the story of the adulterous woman entered the manuscript tradition at various places, most notably John 7:53–8:11. We can also see the beginnings of regional texts, that is, patterns of distinctive readings emerging in various regional centers, as copyists repeat the alterations to the text they find in the local models available to them. I will expand on this point in the next chapter.

At the same time, there are indications of a broader network of Christian scribal contacts from a very early period. One of these markers, mentioned above, is the almost exclusive use of the codex format for Christian texts. Another, running parallel to it, is the development of a system for abbreviating a number of words of an especially sacred character, so-called sacred names (*nomina sacra*), a designation bestowed upon them by Ludwig Traube (Traube 1907). Beginning with the words for Jesus, God, Christ, and Lord (Ιησους, θεος, χριστος, κυριος, *Iesous, theos, christos, kyrios*), the system was gradually expanded until, by the fifth century, fifteen to eighteen words were marked out for special treatment in Christian manuscripts of all kinds, usually by abbreviating the forms and drawing a line over the compendium.[1] Since no mention is made of this practice until the tenth century, we can only speculate about its origins and significance, but it cannot have developed randomly and still have made its way into all known Christian copies of Scripture. Because major scholarly attention to this feature did not develop until the twentieth century, I will reserve treatment of it until the last chapter.

Between the years 303 and 313, the emperor Diocletian enforced an edict ordering the destruction of books the Christians considered holy. Massive numbers of manuscripts were lost. With the peace of Constantine (313), the church flourished and began to replace its lost texts (Aland and Aland 1989, 64–67). The emperor ordered that fifty copies of the sacred Scriptures be made on fine parchment by skilled scribes (Eusebius, *Vit. Const.* 4.36). Now, perhaps for the first time, manuscripts of the complete Bible (Old and New Testament) were being produced, not on papyrus but on high-quality parchment and not by amateurs but by skilled scribes writing in a beautiful hand. From this point on, professionally prepared New Testament manuscripts—copies also continued to be made on papyrus by nonprofessionals—begin to contain a number of "helps for readers," including chapter divisions and headings, the Eusebian canon tables (which alerted readers to parallel passages in the Gospels), prologues, titles, and other aids (Metzger 1981, 33–48).

The growing influence of church officials in major centers (Rome, Alexandria, Antioch, Constantinople) resulted in more controlled copying and in the perpetuation of somewhat standardized forms of the text (Parker 1997, 26). By the fifth century, Latin had replaced Greek as the preferred language in the Western part of the empire, affecting the church's liturgical usage and resulting in the displacement of the Greek Bible in the West

---

1. The additional terms are the Greek words for "son" (when referring to the Son of God), "spirit" (when referring to the Holy Spirit), "savior," "cross," "father" (when used of God as Father), "mother" (in reference to the mother of Jesus), "man" (as in Son of Man), "heaven," "David," "Israel," and "Jerusalem," in addition to a few other terms that did not catch on in more than one or two manuscripts (Roberts 1979, 26–48).

by Latin translations. The copying and dispersion of the Greek text was largely confined to the East and was increasingly standardized to conform to the text of the capital city, Constantinople. For the next thousand years, there were relatively few changes in the *textual* character of the New Testament in Greek, although helps for readers continued to be added, including accents, punctuation, and ornamentation (Parker 1997, 27–28). By the end of our period, it was largely this "standard" form of the text (now referred to as Byzantine or *koinē*) that was available to Erasmus and his contemporaries. From the eighth century on, a worshiper was likely to hear the New Testament read not from a running text but from a lectionary, that is, a service book containing selections of Scripture in the order in which they were used in the church's liturgical calendar (Osburn 1995, 61–74).

Vernacular Translations

Beginning sometime in the second century, the Bible began to be available in languages other than Greek, although the origins of these translations are debated and we have no certain evidence for any of them before the third century. They probably had their beginnings as oral translations, produced on the spot as the Greek text was read out in the church's worship, similar to the practice of providing an Aramaic *targum* in synagogue worship for those who did not speak Hebrew (Metzger 1977, 286; Parker 1997, 25). These translations are important in our efforts to trace the transmission of the New Testament because they presumably represent the form of the Greek text prominent in the respective location where each was translated.

The New Testament in Syriac is known in its earliest form only for the Gospels, in one fourth-century and one fifth-century manuscript, both of which may preserve a text going back to the third century (Metzger and Ehrman 2005, 96–100). The Old Syriac version of other portions of the New Testament is known only from quotations made from it by church fathers writing in that language. The text of the complete New Testament was standardized and published in the fifth century and is known as the Peshitta, that is, the "common" version (the Orthodox Syriac canon does not include 2 Peter, 2–3 John, Jude, and Revelation). By the time of Erasmus, several other translations into Syriac had been published.

The New Testament in Latin would have been needed by the early third century, when the Latin language was gradually displacing Greek in the churches of the West, although our earliest Latin manuscripts date from the fourth century. Translations (or perhaps revisions of a single ancient translation) can be traced to North Africa, Italy, Gaul, and Spain, resulting in a welter of different renderings in these Old Latin versions. Jerome observed that there were "almost as many forms of text as there are manuscripts," and Augustine complained that "every man who happened to gain possession of a Greek manuscript [of the New Testament] and who imagined he had any facility in both languages, however slight that might have been, dared to make a translation" (Metzger 1977, 334, 290). Pope Damasus therefore commissioned Jerome (346?–420?) to revise these texts and produce a translation conformed to the Greek text. We know this revision as the Vulgate, that is, the "common" text. Far from displacing the Old Latin versions, however, most copies of the Vulgate show evidence of corruption from these older versions, just as many manuscripts of the Old Latin have been affected by readings from the Vulgate. The English monk Alcuin attempted a revision in the eighth century, about the same time the Spaniard Theodulf did the same. Another revision was undertaken by Stephen Harding in the twelfth century. It was Harding who divided the text into numbered verses, a system still in use in Bible translations in many languages.

Although more than 10,000 manuscripts of the Latin Vulgate, in whole or in part, are known today, we cannot be certain how many of these were available, at any one time, to the many scholars and revisers of the medieval era. Before the time of Erasmus, however, Johannes Gutenberg had printed the Latin Bible (1456) using whatever manuscripts of the Vulgate were available to him.

The New Testament in Coptic must have been largely available by the early fourth century to serve the Copts, that is, Egyptian Christians (Metzger 1977, 105–6). Christianity had been brought to Egypt in the first century and was well established by the end of the second century (Roberts 1979, 49–73). Although educated Egyptians spoke Greek, the largely rural, uneducated inhabitants spoke one of several local dialects that had developed along the lengthy Nile Valley. A complex writing system known as demotic had mostly replaced the old hieroglyphic forms, but Christians developed a simpler system, adopting twenty-four letters from the Greek alphabet (written in uncial form) and adding seven letters from demotic script (for sounds that spoken Greek did not use). Thus was the Coptic alphabet formed.

Portions of the New Testament are available in manuscripts representing a half-dozen Coptic dialects, the earliest of which is the Sahidic, from Southern Egypt, and the most influential of which is the Bohairic, from the Delta region in the north. The Bohairic dialect became dominant in the sixth century and was edited into the standard Coptic version in the seventh century. It is this version that is used today in the liturgy of the Coptic church. Since critical study of the Coptic versions with an eye to their text-critical value does not begin until the seventeenth century, I will revisit them later.

Other early versions, notably the Armenian, the Ethiopic, the Georgian, and the Gothic, are also important in the history of the transmission of the New Testament text but are all judged to be later than the three above. They are of varying usefulness for the purpose of reconstructing the underlying Greek text and are somewhat marginal for my purposes.

QUOTATIONS IN THE CHURCH FATHERS

As soon as there was a New Testament to quote, the church fathers began quoting it. Textual critics turn to these quotations to learn about the characteristics of the text available to each of the fathers in the location(s) where they lived and wrote. In fact, patristic quotations, more than any other factor, confirm that distinctive patterns of readings emerged in particular church centers. If the quotations of a church father agree consistently with one Greek or Latin manuscript, or with a type of text preserved by only one group of manuscripts, we can infer that an ancestor of that manuscript or type of text was once available in the place where that father lived.

But isolating these quotations is notoriously difficult. The fathers are not equally careful in the ways they cite Scripture nor equally reliable when they cite from memory, as opposed to looking at a text. If they are writing a commentary or refuting an argument, they may be more likely to give an exact quotation than if they are just giving a moral example or a sermon illustration. Then, too, a father may have had more than one copy of the text available to him and have quoted now from one, now from another or, as is true of several of them, have lived in different regions where different forms of the text were available (Fee 1995).

Before the quotations of a church father are deemed useful for textual criticism, a truly critical text of that father has to be established, based on everything that can be known about his citing habits and purposes as well as his geographical movements. Unfortunately, since we do not have any of the original writings of the fathers, we have to reconstruct their texts from later copies, and scribes or those who employed them were prone to adjust the quotations of a father to conform to the text the copyist knew. Later fathers also sometimes copied the quotations of an earlier father word for word. In the chapters ahead we will trace the efforts of scholars to develop careful methods for isolating the texts of the fathers. The 27th edition of the Nestle-Aland text includes references to more than seventy patristic writers up through the eighth century. Metzger and Ehrman (2005, 131) give a list of the thirty they regard as "the more important" ones, including Justin Martyr (d. ca. 165), Irenaeus (d. 202), Clement of Alexandria (d. ca. 212), Hippolytus of Rome (d. 235), Origen (d. 253/254), Eusebius (d. 339/340), and Jerome (d. 419/420), to mention only a few.

But what use was made of manuscripts, versions, and patristic quotations here at the dawn of New Testament textual criticism?[2] Not surprisingly, the fathers do not enumerate the copies each has available to him, but, as Metzger notes, "the disquieting possibility remains that the evidence available to us today may, in certain cases, be totally unrepresentative of the distribution of readings in the early church" (1979, 208). A reading supported by "most of the ancient copies" known to a church father may be extant in only a very few manuscripts today. In any case, the persecution under Diocletian no doubt radically reduced the number of copies available during much of the fourth century.

As noted above, during the Byzantine period the number of manuscripts increased dramatically, especially after the monastic scriptoria developed, in which multiple copies could be made from dictation. The advent of minuscule script in the ninth century further supported the rapid copying of the Bible. By this time the text had been standardized such that there were relatively few conscious alterations to copies of the New Testament made during the Byzantine era and later. Presumably, manuscripts with texts diverging from the standard text were relegated to the personal libraries of scholars or the monastic collections. A noteworthy exception is minuscule manuscript 1739, a tenth-century manuscript that is a *copy* of a fourth-century text (Metzger and Ehrman 2005, 91).

In addition to purely Greek manuscripts, from the fifth century (or possibly earlier) there is an interest in producing bilingual versions of the New Testament. These are in facing columns, usually Greek and Latin but

---

2. I do not include lectionaries here because we have no fragments earlier than the sixth century and no complete manuscripts before the eighth century.

also with examples in Greek and Coptic and a small number with Greek and another vernacular language (Metzger 1984, 327–34; Parker 1992, 50–69).

Jerome had both Greek and Latin manuscripts at his disposal and readily commented on the differences between them. For more than a thousand years after Jerome, however, there is very little evidence that the scholars of the church, in the East or West, compared Greek and Latin copies, let alone other versions, of the New Testament texts with an interest in getting back to the earliest form. In the West, the Bible *was* the Latin Bible to an extent scarcely imaginable to modern students (Smalley 1952). There were revisions of the Vulgate by Alcuin (eighth century), Theodulf (ninth century), and Stephen Harding (twelfth century), who perhaps used some Greek evidence, but text-critical interests seem not to have been a priority in these efforts. In the thirteenth century, some efforts were made to collect variant readings in Greek and Latin manuscripts as well as patristic sources and to enter these as corrections to the Latin Vulgate, but these in no way sought to replace the Vulgate, only to amend it. As Metzger points out, the Greek New Testament was not published until fifty years after the advent of Johannes Gutenberg's printing press, even though some one hundred editions of the Latin Bible were published during that time (Metzger and Ehrman 2005, 137). As for the other materials available to support textual criticism, the later fathers had the texts of the earlier fathers, although these were used not to illustrate the form of the New Testament text in a particular time and place but to support the exegesis, commentary, and spiritual reading of the Bible that formed the curriculum of the medieval cathedral schools and universities. Roughly the same is true of Erasmus; even though he gives the names of several church fathers on the title page of his Greek New Testament, he uses them not as witnesses to the early Greek text but as support for his exegetical comments, which are attached to his volume.

What, then, were the motives of the fathers, the medieval scholars, and the first editors of the Greek New Testament for publication?

Motives

The practice of textual criticism began among the Greeks, and its flowering is connected especially with the great library, the Museum, founded at Alexandria around 295 B.C.E. The librarians there sought to compensate for the copying discrepancies in the thousands of books they were collecting by issuing standard texts, especially of Homer, and by developing a number of aids for the reader, including punctuation, a rudimentary system of accents, critical signs calling attention to omissions, interpolations, transposition of word order, and other noteworthy features (Reynolds and Wilson 1974, 5–15). A "standard text," to use the term of Reynolds and Wilson, may not have been, by modern standards, a "critical text," however, but only a model for other copyists (see the cautions of Holmes 1996, 143–47).

It might logically be expected that Christians in Egypt would have applied these methods to their own texts, but, as indicated above, virtually all the early Christian papyri appear to have been copied not by scholars, nor even by professional copyists, but by those who made immediate use of the texts. Nevertheless, the rudiments of textual criticism may be detected in the late second century, as we begin to encounter comments in the church fathers about variant readings in manuscripts available to them. Although we cannot even estimate how many copies of a given text any one of the fathers may have had, we find in various of the fathers such terms as "few," "many," "most," "other," "certain," "some," "almost all," "true," "good," and "ancient" copies. Bruce Metzger was able to compile a list of forty-six patristic authors who mention, collectively, variant readings in more than a hundred passages (Metzger 1975, 208–10). Irenaeus, for example, who wrote less than a hundred years after the Revelation to John, already knows that some Greek manuscripts have the "number of the beast" in 13:18 as 616, while "all the good and ancient copies" read 666 (Metzger 1980, 190).[3]

But what were their motivations for referring to textual variants? This is not always possible to discover. Presumably, Irenaeus judged these "good and ancient copies" to reflect the earliest text of Revelation, in contrast to later, corrupt manuscripts. Even Origen, perhaps the father most likely to have absorbed the methods of Alexandrian textual scholarship, usually simply notes the variant readings without choosing between or among them. This seems to be consistent with what Origen does in the Hexapla: he gives in successive columns the Hebrew text of the Old Testament (with its transliteration into Greek characters), then four (or five)

---

3. Ancient copies reading 616 were virtually lost to view until 1998, when a third- or fourth-century papyrus, P[115] (P.Oxy. 4499), was published. Prior to that, only one Greek manuscript, the fifth-century Codex C, was known to contain it.

Greek versions, *without choosing among them* (Wright 1988, 48-92). Metzger lists twenty-two New Testament texts about which Origen makes explicit reference to textual variants. In perhaps a quarter of these, he signals a preference for one of the variants, and when he does so, "his criteria were not derived from a study of the manuscripts themselves, but from various more or less inconsequential and irrelevant considerations" (Metzger 1963b, 94). Presumably, when he states a preference for one reading over against another, he assumes the preferred reading is the original, but since he so frequently is content to let variants coexist peacefully, his interests go beyond identifying the original reading to include supporting dogmatic convictions and harmonizing Gospel accounts. As we will see below, he does not follow a clear and consistent method for choosing between or among readings.

In another study, Metzger lists twenty-seven passages that draw comment from Jerome about textual variants (Metzger 1979). Confirming previous studies, Metzger concludes that Jerome was, by modern standards, more critical than Origen in his treatment of variant readings. As the pope's designated reviser of the Latin version, Jerome saw his task as producing a translation that would conform to the Greek original, so it is not surprising that when the Latin copies he knows differ from the Greek copies before him, he often supports the Greek. He distinguishes between "certain copies" and "true copies." He is aware of the common scribal errors, such as confusion of similar letters, scribal leaps resulting in dittography or haplography, transposition of letters, and the like (Hulley 1944). He is willing to make judgments on the grounds of which reading makes most sense to him.

Of the forty-six patristic authors Metzger lists as referring to variant readings, more than half of them mention only one variant reading and few of them defend one of the readings against the other(s). When we look through the works of the late medieval church scholars, there is even less interest in variant readings in the Greek text. It is fair to conclude that, during the long period from Irenaeus, the earliest of the fathers to refer to a textual variant, to Erasmus, the first scholar to publish a Greek New Testament, three motives can be identified for dealing with textual variants: (1) to recover the earliest or original text; (2) to reconcile passages in the Gospels that are at variance with one another; and (3) to exploit the interpretive possibilities presented by two or more variant forms of a passage. The so-called long ending of Mark (Mark 16:9-20) is a curious case in point. There is patristic evidence for this passage as early as Justin Martyr (ca. 155). Many fathers quote or clearly allude to the passage; those who know both the short and the long ending may express a critical judgment about which is more accurate (so Eusebius, Jerome, Hesychius of Jerusalem, Victor of Antioch), but they usually also go on to reconcile Mark's account with that of Matthew (Metzger 1975, 343–45; Kelhoffer 2000, 169–77).

When these early practitioners of textual criticism compared the witnesses to the text at their disposal, what were the methods they used for distinguishing better readings from rejected ones, or, when they did not choose, how did they decide, methodologically, to let variant readings stand side by side?

Methods

Even though Irenaeus makes explicit reference to only one textual variant, the number of the beast in Rev 13:18 as 666 or 616, Metzger finds it instructive that, in arguing for the reading 666, Irenaeus invokes what today we would call standard text-critical criteria: he prefers "good and ancient" copies to others; he relies on "internal evidence," suggesting that John would more likely have written 666, using the letters of the Greek alphabet to yield six hundreds, six tens, and six ones, than the less-balanced number; and, finally, he seeks to account for the rejected reading as owing to a scribal confusion of letters (Metzger 1975, 341). Nevertheless, we do not know how Irenaeus judged the copies that read 666 as "good and ancient copies." In the place where he refers to the variant reading (*Haer.* 5.30.1), he is making an allegorical application of the text, adding the years of Noah's life to the dimensions of the image Nebuchadnezzar erects, to arrive at the total of 666, thus showing that the beast and his number were predicted in the Old Testament. It is possible that Irenaeus first chose his preferred reading and then set out to support it.

Origen invokes various rationales for his textual decisions. The best-known case, cited by many scholars, is the Barabbas/Jesus Barabbas textual variant at Matt 27:16–17. At this text, which recounts the trial of Jesus, most witnesses mention a noteworthy prisoner named Barabbas. A few witnesses, however, read "Jesus Barabbas." Origen prefers the reading "Barabbas," explaining that no evil person would have been named Jesus, apparently oblivious to the ubiquity of the name Yeshua among Palestinian Jews. Although Origen is not, by modern standards, a critical judge of the best/better reading, he does use many of the techniques of scholarship developed at Alexandria for the study of classical texts, including attention to geographical terms, etymology, grammar, and logic. In the end, Origen could let variant readings stand side by side because his interpretive methods privileged multiple senses in the text over the literal sense.

Those who have studied his citations generally conclude that Jerome was a more discriminating textual critic than most of the fathers. Not only does he usually prefer the Old Greek copies to the Latin; he values copies held by great scholars over other copies. He frequently tries to account for the origin of a reading he rejects as resulting from the errors of copyists. He appeals to internal evidence, as in his rejection of the reading "without a cause" in Jesus' statement in Matt 5:22, "if anyone is angry with his brother," holding that "in the true copies the meaning is plain and anger is totally abrogated" (Metzger 1979, 180). This is all but an enunciation of the principle that a scribe is more likely to make a text easier to read than harder. Sometimes, however, Jerome declines to make a choice and sometimes he makes a clearly wrong choice. For example, he holds that Gal 2:5 makes better sense if we follow a Latin copy that omits the words οἷς οὐδὲ, *hois oude*. This results in Paul's saying that he "yielded for a time" to the "false brothers who slipped in," rather than saying "to whom I did not yield even for a time" (Metzger 1979, 185).

We should not expect, and do not find, anything like a consistent and rational set of goals and operations for dealing with textual variants during the fourteen centuries we have briefly surveyed. But some of the church fathers were asking the right questions; their decisions and the processes by which they arrived at them are sometimes surprisingly agreeable with modern critical practice. During the late medieval period, few scholars in Western Europe even had access to the Bible in any form except Jerome's Vulgate. Although the Old Latin versions continued in circulation for centuries, we can detect very little interest in solving the problem of divergent readings, especially since exegetical methods welcomed multiple senses of the text. Nevertheless, at the end of our period, we have two models for settling on a form of the Greek New Testament suitable for publication.

Models

The first Greek New Testament to come off the press was printed in 1514 as volume 5 of the famous six-volume Complutensian Polyglot. Its editor, Cardinal Archbishop Francis Ximenes de Cisneros, printed the New Testament in two columns, Greek and Latin. Although Ximenes is reported to have spent an enormous amount of money to purchase manuscripts, it is not possible to identify a single Greek manuscript used for this edition. Its text generally conforms to that found in medieval manuscripts from the tenth century and later. The project did not receive the imprimatur of the pope until 1520 and was not actually published, that is, distributed for purchase, until 1522, by which time it had been "scooped" by the edition of Erasmus (for details on the Complutensian, see Scrivener 1894, 2:176–81; Metzger and Ehrman 2005, 138–42, with plate at fig. 22).

It was precisely to beat the Spaniards to the punch that the publisher John Froben of Basel contacted Desiderius Erasmus in 1515, while Erasmus was in England, and asked him to edit a Greek New Testament for publication. Erasmus had long been working on annotations for a projected revision of the Latin version. He hurried back to Basel, rounded up what manuscripts he could and, within ten months, "rushed out" his *Novum Instrumentum* to the publisher. ("Hurried out rather than edited" [*praecipitatum verius quam editum*] were his own words [Rabil 1972, 92]). He used the most complete manuscripts available to him as copy, marking them up with corrections and sending them directly to the publisher. The bulk of his Gospels text was taken from a single manuscript and his Acts and Epistles text from another manuscript, both of these from the twelfth century. From his friend John Reuchlin he borrowed a manuscript of the Apocalypse (again, twelfth century) lacking the last six verses. These he back-translated from the Latin, thus producing for this section a form of the Greek text not known in any other Greek manuscript whatsoever. He also interpolated a few other bits from the Vulgate, most notably Paul's question in Acts 9:6, "Lord, what will you have me do?" and Acts 8:37, which Erasmus supposed to have been incorrectly omitted in his manuscripts but which is now judged to be a late addition to the text. (One can find information on the manuscripts Erasmus used in Tarelli 1943, 155–62; Reicke 1966, 254–56; Krans 2006, 335–36.)

Perhaps it was Froben's promise to match any other offer Erasmus might receive (from another publisher) that inspired Erasmus to work in such haste. In a letter to William Bude he frankly admitted, "Some things I purposely passed over, and shut my eyes to many points upon which soon after publication I held a different opinion" (Nichols 1962, 2:282). Indeed, his second and third editions contain numerous corrections to the

Gospels, Acts, and Epistles, although these do not result in a substantially better text. In fact, he inserted into the third edition (1522) the famous Johannine Comma, 1 John 5:7–8, which states, after the words "there are three who bear witness in heaven," the following (in the language of the KJV): "the Father, the Word, and the Holy Ghost, and these three are one. And there are three that bear witness on earth." This addition to the text had already appeared in the Complutensian Polyglot (taken, apparently, from the Vulgate), and one of its editors, Stunica, challenged Erasmus to add it to the text of his *Novum Instrumentum*. It has been famously reported (although without hard evidence) that Erasmus agreed to add the passage to his next edition if it could be found in a single Greek manuscript, whereupon such a copy was in due time presented to him—apparently having been made just for the purpose! Metzger traces the history of this addition to the text back to a fourth-century Latin work known as *Liber apologeticus*, where it may have been an exegetical comment that was later written into the margin of a Latin manuscript of 1 John. It was added to manuscripts of the Vulgate around the ninth century and then made its way as a marginal textual variant in some Greek manuscripts beginning in the fourteenth century (Metzger and Ehrman 2005, 145–48).

Erasmus's fourth edition (1527) benefited substantially from his examination of the Complutensian and his decision to follow that text in numerous places, especially in the Apocalypse. He issued his final edition in 1535, giving up the Vulgate text for his revised Latin but altering the Greek side very little.

Today the general conclusion is that the Complutensian Polyglot was a more careful piece of work than what Erasmus produced, but his had the advantage of being first off the press, and so it stood for nearly four hundred years as the standard against which all New Testament textual criticism must be judged. Its effect upon the readers of the English Bible is beyond all calculation, because it was essentially the text upon which the translators working for King James I of England based their translation issued in 1611, which is still read by millions today. Of course, the work of Erasmus has to be judged on the basis of what was possible at the time. Had he been given more time and expended more effort to gather manuscripts, he could have produced a better text (by today's standards) than what he did produce—but only marginally so, for the science of textual criticism was not far enough advanced to prepare him to make the judgments needed, even if he had been able to acquire many more ancient manuscripts.[4] As we will see in the next chapter, as "debased" as Erasmus's text was (Metzger's term; Metzger and Ehrman 2005, 149), it served as a catalyst for an immense effort to collect, collate, and classify the witnesses to the text of the Greek New Testament. To this effort we now turn.

---

4. It is in his annotations, not his text, that Erasmus often demonstrates remarkable judgment about readings. Not only was he familiar with the usual causes of unconscious scribal errors, he also anticipated some of the text-critical criteria that were yet to be articulated, such as "the harder reading is to be preferred" (Krans 2006, 9–191). Modern readers also need to take into account that the Latin Bible was still the standard for church usage and that Erasmus's text-critical comments were made to justify the differences between his Latin translation and the Vulgate, not to contribute to a better Greek text than he found in the manuscripts before him.

3
THE AGE OF COLLECTING, COLLATING, AND CLASSIFYING

> It would be highly desirable to publish an edition of the New Testament in which the text itself should in every instance clearly exhibit the genuine reading, and leave not a single passage in dispute. The present age, however, cannot accomplish this. (J. A. Bengel)

To our thinking, nothing would have been more natural than for scholars and publishers to want to put out a Greek New Testament as soon as printing from moveable type became possible (around 1450). However, not only did many editions of the Latin Bible precede the first printed Greek New Testament, so did the first printed Hebrew Bible (1488) as well as Bibles in a number of European languages, including Czech, French, German, and Italian (Metzger and Ehrman 2005, 137). But once the edition of Erasmus "hit the streets," the publishing floodgates opened and new editions were offered nearly every year. The problem was that very little was done to improve the quality of the printed text itself in these successive editions; except for minor changes, everyone printed the text of Erasmus. In the world of publishing, there is no substitute for being first. Even so, the act of publication of the Greek New Testament stimulated a desire among scholars to collect manuscripts and compare their readings, efforts which laid the groundwork for truly critical study of the text. In this chapter we will meet the best-known contributors to this enterprise, those who moved the discipline along.

Movers

Robert Stephanus (1503–1559) came from a famous Parisian family of printers (the family surname Estienne is usually latinized as Stephanus, English Stephen). Stephanus edited four editions of the Greek New Testament, the most famous of which is the third, issued in 1550 (called the Royal Edition because of its dedication to the French king, Henry II, from whose press the volume was printed). The text of this beautiful folio edition differs very little from the last two editions of Erasmus, but Stephanus inserted in the margin a selection of variant readings from fifteen manuscripts collated by his son, also named Henry II, and others, as well as from the Complutensian. The 1550 Stephanus was the first Greek New Testament with a printed apparatus. The preface enumerates these witnesses by using lowercase letters of the Greek alphabet with the accent mark to show they are numbers, not letters: $\acute{α}$, $β'$, $γ'$, and so on (J. Elliott 2009, 390–95, lists the manuscripts Stephanus is known to have used). Although many of these manuscripts have not been identified, the most famous of them is now known as Codex Bezae (D),[1] a fifth-century Greek-Latin bilingual containing the Gospels and Acts. This edition became enormously popular in England and was republished as late as 1877. It was the 1550 Stephanus that was used as the basis for the 1560 Geneva Bible, the English translation that accompanied the Pilgrims to the New World. The Geneva Bible included twenty-one variant readings in its margins, ten of which are supported by Codex Bezae in Acts (Metzger 1961–1962, 72–77). Stephanus's 1551 edition introduced another innovation by providing the verse numbers that are still followed in printed Greek New Testaments.

Theodore Beza (1519–1605), classical and biblical scholar and Calvin's successor at Geneva, published four separate editions of the Greek New Testament (1565, 1582, 1588, and 1589) and five reprints, each accompanied by his own Latin translation. In 1562, Beza came into possession of the remarkable manuscript mentioned above in connection with the 1550 Stephanus, known henceforth as Codex Bezae. A description of the manuscript and its significance follows later in this chapter, in connection with the detailed study made of it in the eighteenth century.

---

1. D represents one system later developed to classify manuscripts by assigning them letters from the roman alphabet.

Beza also owned a number of other manuscripts, including what is now known as Codex Claromontanus, containing the Pauline Epistles. Beza's chief importance for us is that he included among the many annotations in his several editions references to a number of textual variants. For example, Beza cited ancient witnesses that did not include John 7:53–8:11 (the pericope of the adulterous woman) and frankly stated that he regarded this text as suspect. These annotations show that he was the first to use the Syriac and Arabic versions of the New Testament (the latter available only for Acts and 1–2 Corinthians) to add support for textual variations already known in the Greek (Krans 2006, 208, 243). But he did not use any of these textual resources to make substantive changes to the printed text; he remained under the spell of Stephanus and his predecessors. Metzger suggests that Beza did not use Bezae and Claromontanus in any critical fashion precisely because they differed so much from the accepted text (Metzger and Ehrman 2005, 151). The popularity of Beza's editions only added to the status of the Erasmian-type text as the default standard Greek New Testament. The translators of the Authorized Version (KJV) of 1611 relied primarily on the 1589 edition of Beza and secondarily on the 1550 and 1551 editions of Stephanus (Schaff 1883, 238–39, 348–49).[2]

Bonaventure (1583–1652) and **Abraham** (1592–1652) **Elzevir** are mentioned here not because their endeavors did anything to aid scholars in moving toward a more ancient and reliable form of the Greek text but because they (actually, one of their editors) did precisely the opposite. The Elzevirs issued three editions of the Greek New Testament in Leiden in 1624, 1633, and 1641. The text was essentially Beza's smaller 1565 edition. The preface to the second edition contains what Metzger describes as a publisher's "blurb": "You have the text [*textum*] now received [*receptum*] by all, in which we give nothing changed or corrupted."[3] This brash claim led to the Elzevir text's being referred to as the "Textus Receptus" (TR), which soon came to mean the standard, the orthodox, the only reliable and true text of the Greek New Testament. It thus commanded on the

---

2. Schaff also has photographic facsimiles of the title page and one other page of each of the major editions of the Greek New Testament from Erasmus (1516) to Westcott and Hort (1881).

3. "Textum ergo habes, nunc ab omnibus receptum: in quo nihil immutatum aut corruptum damus." We now know that this comment was the product of the editor, the philologian and University Librarian at Leiden, Daniel Heinsius (de Jonge 1971).

European continent the same allegiance as the third edition of Stephanus did in England. For all practical purposes, the text of Erasmus, cobbled together from a few late medieval manuscripts, had now been canonized and would have a stranglehold on biblical scholars and translators for the next 250 years.[4] If "nothing succeeds like success," nothing promotes success quite as well as a good advertising slogan.

The only road to a better text was the systematic collection and comparison of all the witnesses to the text that could be found in libraries, museums, and monasteries. For a long time, there was no common system of reference to distinguish one manuscript from another, so we enter a period of experimentation on how best to record variant readings in manuscripts, versions, and fathers. Although Stephanus had used Greek letters as numerals to refer to manuscripts available to him, Beza backed away from this practice, referring instead to "some manuscript," "two manuscripts," "my old manuscript," and similar designations. Both Stephanus and Beza could refer to the Vulgate as simply "the Latin" or "the old Latin." The fathers were sometimes cited by name, at other times left unidentified. Although it would be almost a hundred years before anyone had the temerity to desert the Textus Receptus in favor of more critically selected readings, the foundation for a critical text was about to be laid. The heroes of this chapter, many of them unknown and unsung, are those who did the patient and meticulous work of deciphering and collating the texts of varying ages and types of handwriting.

Brian Walton (1600–1661) published in London in 1657 a multilingual Bible (now known as the London Polyglot) in six large folio volumes.[5] Volume 5 contains the New Testament in Greek (the 1550 edition of Stephanus) with the interlinear Latin translation of Arius Montanus, the Vulgate, and the Syriac, Ethiopic, Arabic, and Persian (only in the Gospels) versions, each with its own translation into Latin. At the bottom of each page were entered the variant readings of a manuscript that had

---

4. "So superstitious has been the reverence accorded the Textus Receptus that in some cases attempts to criticize or emend it have been regarded as akin to sacrilege" (Metzger and Ehrman 2005, 152). Indeed, as we will see in ch. 8, a form of the text very much like that of the Textus Receptus is still championed by a small but influential cadre of scholars and preachers.

5. Few readers will have access to the early printed Bibles mentioned here, but Walton's Polyglot was reprinted in a full-size photographic facsimile by Akademische Druck in Graz, Austria, 1963.

> **What Is a Manuscript Collation?**
>
> In textual criticism, collation is the recording of all the differences between one textual witness and a "base text." The base text could be a single manuscript or any standard agreed upon for the purposes of comparison. Since scholars of the seventeenth to the nineteenth centuries were mostly interested in how a newly discovered manuscript differed from the Textus Receptus, the TR became the collating base and remains so for some projects even today. In recent years, the Nestle-Aland/UBS text has often been used as the collating base.
>
> At Acts 1:14, where the disciples of Jesus are gathered in Jerusalem in an upper room, all available witnesses to the text read "with [their] wives" (συν γυναιξιν, *syn gynaixin*) except for Codex D, which adds "and children" (και τεκνοις, *kai teknois*). The variant reading might be represented in a collation this way, where D is being collated against Nestle-Aland[27]: Acts 1:14 συν γυναιξιν] + και τεκνοις. If a collation is carefully done, the complete text of the new manuscript can be known to scholars without their having access to the manuscript itself.*
>
> *A simplified model for recording a collation is found in Greenlee 1995, 132–39. For a more technical introduction, see Parker 2008, 95–100. For the definition and presentation of textual variants, see Epp 1976b, 153–73; Fee 1993, 62–79.

been presented in 1627 to King Charles I by Cyril Lucar, patriarch of Constantinople. Walton was the first to use the capital letter A to refer to this manuscript, which is today known as Codex Alexandrinus because Lucar had been patriarch of Alexandria prior to his move to Constantinople. The manuscript will be described later in this chapter.

In volume 6, Walton included a large number of variant readings, taken from the annotations of several scholars, from Stephanus's 1550 edition and from sixteen manuscripts, thirteen of which had been collated specifically for Walton's project. He identified these manuscripts either by the name of their owner or by reference to the college or library where they were held (e.g., Magd. 1, Magd. 2 referred to manuscripts held at Magdalen College, Oxford; Em. was the sign for a manuscript held at Emmanuel College, Cambridge). Why was Codex Alexandrinus given such special attention as to be the only manuscript whose variants are included in volume 5, where the Greek text was printed? Probably because it was more ancient than any of the others, it was a nearly complete manuscript of both the Old Testament and the New Testament, and it was a prized possession of the king.

John Fell (1625–1686), dean of Christ Church, Oxford, took a small step forward by issuing (anonymously, perhaps for fear of reprisal) in 1675 the first Greek New Testament to be published at Oxford. The text was largely the 1633 Elzevir edition, but the apparatus contained variant readings from some one hundred manuscripts, although about twenty of these were cited in groups, so that we cannot always be certain which manuscripts in a certain group support a particular reading.[6] Fell was the first to offer evidence from the Bohairic version of Coptic and from the Gothic. His greatest contribution was to further and support the work of our next mover.

John Mill (1645–1707),[7] another Oxford scholar, casts a very large shadow among these pioneers of textual criticism. Mill spent almost thirty years preparing his edition of the Greek New Testament, which came out only two weeks before his death. Some scholars describe Mill as the founder of New Testament textual criticism because he was the first to set the discipline on a scientific foundation. Scrivener famously said of him: "Of the criticism of the New Testament in the hands of Dr. John Mill it may be said, that he found the edifice of wood, and left it marble" (Scrivener 1894, 2:202). He not only collected the variant readings from the editions that had preceded his, he also collated or recollated thirty-three manuscripts and thirteen early printed editions. He described the manuscripts he had used, cited and critically discussed citations from all the important fathers, described thirty-two printed editions of the text, and laid out his understanding of the history of the transmission of the text. So detailed are his discussions that he makes reference to more than 3,000 verses of the New Testament (out of a total of about 8,000) in these prolegomena (Metzger and Ehrman 2005, 154).

Although he printed that old standby, the 1550 text of Stephanus, he made copious references to variant readings, using, like Fell, evi-

---

6. Scrivener (1894, 2:200) and Metzger (Metzger and Ehrman 2005, 154) claim that Codex Vaticanus (B) was among the witnesses of one of Fell's groups. If so, Fell would be the first to cite this manuscript, but it is not clear how Fell's use of Codex B was confirmed.

7. Neé Milne, he changed his name to Mill, sometimes seen as Mills.

dence from more than one hundred manuscripts.[8] In his prolegomena he encouraged his readers to believe they could work out from the evidence in the apparatus (which contained 21,000 notes) what the true reading ought to be at every point of variation. The number of variants in Mill's apparatus was later determined to be some 30,000. With Mill's having vastly increased the size of the apparatus and having made many discerning judgments about better readings, the time seemed ripe for someone to build upon those "Herculean labors" (Mill's own description of his truly monumental work) by editing a better text than the Textus Receptus.

Edward Wells (1667–1727), another Christ Church scholar, ventured out in this direction. His labors are overlooked by many historians of the Greek New Testament, perhaps because he issued the work (accompanied by an English translation) in ten parts, beginning with 1–2 Thessalonians and Galatians (1709) and completing it with Luke, Acts, and John (1719), and because his efforts were somewhat tentative. In the preface, he announced his intention to improve on Mill's work by printing a Greek text "amended according to the Best and most Antient Readings or Copies" (Fox 1954, 96). His zeal for emending the text seems to have waned as he worked, because the number of textual notes declined from nineteen on Galatians to just seven on John. Nevertheless, Wells was a trailblazer, the first scholar to abandon the Textus Receptus and publish his emendations not simply in the notes but in the text itself.

Richard Bentley (1662–1742) thought that by printing a text based on the agreements of Origen and the Vulgate, he would have recovered the form of the New Testament in circulation at the time of the Council of Nicaea (325). Although he failed to issue his planned Greek and Latin edition, he deserves a place among the founders of New Testament textual criticism for the boldness of his proposals and the clarity with which he stated them. The two specimen pages he produced anticipated the results of modern scholars. Günther Zuntz refers to "those lucid two pages which will for ever remain the weightiest contribution to our subject" (Zuntz 1953, 1). His ambitious project resulted in the addition of many more Greek and Latin manuscripts to the collations that had been previously made, including one of the better early collations of the famous Codex Vaticanus (B). But his greatest contribution was his defense of Mill

---

8. Mill was the first to use lectionary manuscripts in his apparatus (Osburn 1995, 64).

and others who had so laboriously recorded the variant readings of the witnesses to the New Testament text against the criticisms of alarmists who claimed that calling attention to these variants would result in the weakening of the authority of Scripture.[9] Bentley pointed out the commonsense fact that Mill did not create any of these variant readings. They had been there for hundreds of years in the witnesses to the text; Mill only exposed them to viewing by a larger readership. If the Christian faith (or "Religion," as Mill called it) was true during all the ages when the variants stood in these witnesses, unseen by most readers, it is still true and safe, even if everybody can now see them. Putting the truth on public display can never "subvert True Religion" (from Bentley's *Remarks upon a Late Discourse of Free-Thinking*, cited by Fox 1954, 113–14).

Daniel Mace (d. 1753) is even less well-known than Edward Wells, perhaps because he published anonymously, he was a Presbyterian and not an Anglican, and he introduced many innovations into the format of both his Greek text and its accompanying English translation.[10] Scrivener dismissively remarks: "The anonymous text and version of William [*sic*] Mace, said to have been a Presbyterian minister … are alike unworthy of serious notice, and have long been forgotten" (Scrivener 1894, 2:210). Mace was raised from obscurity only in the twentieth century (McLachlan 1938–1939, 617–25; Fox 1954, 97–102). In 1729 he published, in two volumes, the Greek New Testament and an English translation in parallel columns, with a title that included the words, "Containing the ORIGINAL TEXT Corrected from the AUTHORITY of the most *Authentic Manuscripts*." Using the text of Mill as his model, he corrected it in numerous places, frequently also preferring readings in other editions to those of the Textus Receptus. He was especially bold in identifying and bracketing interpolations in the text. It may be that Mace's typographical eccentricities, as well as the "many racy and colloquial expressions" (Metzger and Ehrman 2005, 157) in his English translation, were disturbing to his critics. More troubling was his decision to desert the entire manuscript tradition in favor of a conjecture at Gal 4:25, where his translation reads "this Agar answers to the Jerusalem now in being" in place of the conventional "Now Hagar is Mount Sinai in Arabia; she corresponds to the present Jerusalem" (RSV). He thus

---

9. Bentley's controversy with Daniel Whitby and the Free Thinker Anthony Collins is detailed in Fox 1954, 105–15.

10. Nothing is known of Mace's family, date of birth, or education. He died in 1753.

omitted most of a clause in Greek (Ζινᾶ ὄρος ἐστὶν ἐν τῇ Ἀραβίᾳ, *zina oros estin en tē Arabia*). In defense of his reading, Mace "enunciated one original and superbly dangerous canon" (Fox 1954, 99), namely, that "there [is] no manuscript so old as common sense." In fact, Bentley had conjectured that the whole clause ("now this Hagar is Sinai, a mountain in Arabia") was an interpolation, and Mace claimed that Mill would likewise have omitted it, except for the agreement of all the manuscripts. Although this is the only pure conjecture in Mace's edition, he was summarily dismissed by some critics as arbitrarily altering the text according to his subjective notions. Eduard Reuss, however, aptly described Mace as "a true pioneer" (*verum antesignanum*) of textual critics and gave a list of readings in which Mace has been followed by modern editors (Reuss 1872, 175–76).[11]

Johann Albrecht Bengel (1687–1752) is, like Mill, a giant among these pathfinders of textual criticism. As so many of his successors, he was attracted to the study of the transmission of the text because of his commitment to the authority of Scripture. A theology student at the University of Tübingen, Germany, Bengel was a pietist who believed in the plenary inspiration of the Bible. Troubled by the 30,000 textual variants in Mill's Greek New Testament, Bengel determined to give several years to his own study of the text. After satisfying himself that textual variation was not a threat to faith,[12] he published in 1725 an essay announcing his intention to edit a Greek New Testament. In 1734 his edition, which contained a critical apparatus, was issued at Tübingen. The text he printed was still a timid one. It agreed largely with Stephanus, varying from it only when Bengel could find a better reading in some other edition (and in the Apocalypse, where Bengel did more original work and adopted a number of readings without other editorial support). But he freely exercised his critical judgment by an innovative device in the apparatus: he

---

11. Reuss's work is indispensable for anyone chronicling the history of this period. He identified 1,000 passages in the Greek New Testament in which there are significant variant readings and then collated some 600 printed editions at these passages, listing in his book the preferred readings of each edition.

12. He later wrote to one of the pupils he tutored, "Take and eat in simplicity the bread as you have it before you, and be not disturbed if you find in it now and then a grit from the millstone. If the sacred volume, considering the fallibility of its many transcribers, had been preserved from every seeming defect, this preservation would have been so great a miracle, that faith in the Written Word could no longer be faith" (quoted by Steudel 1863, xv).

graded his marginal readings by means of five categories, using the Greek alphabet: *alpha* readings were those he judged to be genuine; *beta* variants were better than those in the text (i.e., of Stephanus or another editor); *gamma* readings were equal to the readings in the text; *delta* readings were inferior; and *epsilon* variants were not approved. The editors of UBS do something similar in assigning to each variant adopted into the text an A, B, C, or D, based on "the relative degree of certainty" of the editors (Preface to the First Edition [1966], x–xi).

More important than Bengel's text are the critical principles that guided him in his evaluation of textual variants.[13] In this regard he made three lasting contributions to New Testament textual criticism. (1) He was the first to group textual witnesses on the basis of their common readings. He reasoned that if certain manuscripts, patristic citations, and early versions exhibit a common pattern of readings not shared by other witnesses, those readings must have a common geographical origin; thus the witnesses to the text could be grouped into "companies, families, tribes, and nations." He judged that the later witnesses were derived from Constantinople and related areas; these constituted the "Asiatic nation." The earlier witnesses, whose readings he generally preferred, were assigned to the "African nation" (with two "tribes," Codex Alexandrinus and the Old Latin). (2) Since the *quality of readings* exhibited by witnesses was more important than the *number* of witnesses, he formulated the principle "manuscripts must be weighed, rather than counted." (3) He enunciated one of the most important principles, or "canons," for deciding between or among variant readings: "The harder reading is to be preferred to the easier" (*proclivi scriptioni praestat ardua*).[14] The easier readings were those modified to make them agree with parallel passages or with lectionary instructions or to make them grammatically or stylistically more pleasing

---

13. Bengel lists twenty-one "admonitions," in which are included his principles for making textual decisions; see the English edition of Bengel's *Gnomon* edited by Steudel 1858, 1:13–19.

14. Bengel articulated this canon in the 1730 *Prodromus*, or "forerunner," where he announced his intention to publish a Greek (and Latin) New Testament. The canon is often expressed today as *difficilior lectio potior*. West (1971, 51) attributes the similar *praestat difficilior lectio*, "prefer the difficult reading," to Clericus in *Ars critica* (Amsterdam, 1696), 2:293. Eldon Jay Epp points out that Mill had anticipated Bengel in the use of this principle, although he did not formally list his canons of criticism (Epp 1976a, 218).

to the reader. Bengel thus invoked what are now called external criteria (the quality of the witnesses to the text) and internal criteria (the quality of each reading in a witness) in his text-critical decisions, although the external evidence was the more decisive.

Johann Jakob Wettstein (1693–1754), like Bengel, became interested in textual variants as a theology student, writing his thesis on this topic for the University of Basel.[15] His first contribution to the discipline was to devise a rational system of reference for manuscripts, assigning capital roman letters to majuscules (uncials)[16] and Arabic numerals to minuscules, including lectionaries. He collated or recollated dozens of manuscripts in Switzerland, France, and England, many of them for Richard Bentley's projected edition of the New Testament. He was the first person to make a full collation of the New Testament portion of the famous Codex Ephraemi (C) in Paris, a fifth-century manuscript that had been erased and later overwritten. Although hampered by a lengthy heresy trial in Basel, he published his *Prolegomena* to an edition of the Greek New Testament in Amsterdam in 1730, critically surveying the entire field of studies, including manuscripts, versions, patristic quotations, and printed editions. He proposed nineteen critical maxims he intended to follow in his projected edition, including these notable ones: (7) a reading in better or clearer Greek is not usually preferable to its contrary reading; (8) a reading with an unusual expression is preferable to one with a more usual expression; (9) a shorter reading is to be preferred over a longer (unless a convincing argument can explain that omissions have been made in order to remove difficulties); (10) a reading found in the exact same words elsewhere should not be preferred over a reading that differs from its parallel; (11) other things being equal, a reading that conforms to the style of the author is preferable; (12) a more orthodox reading is not necessarily preferable; (13) Greek readings that accord with the ancient versions should not easily be set aside; (17) other things being

---

15. For a detailed biography, see Hulbert-Powell 1938.

16. Walton's use of A to designate Codex Alexandrinus was the inspiration for this innovation, but Bentley's two specimen pages, which used the letters A, B, C, etc., and α, β, γ, probably also played a part. Wettstein's system served until the number of known majuscules exceeded the number of letters in the roman alphabet (and the Greek and Hebrew as well). Although a different system based on numbers was later devised by C. R. Gregory, it is customary still to use the alphabetic letters in referring to the majuscules that were at first so designated.

equal, the ancient reading is preferable; (18) other things being equal, the reading of the majority of manuscripts is preferable.[17]

Wettstein initially announced his intention of taking Codex Alexandrinus as his base text (his third critical principle was "the prescription of the Textus Receptus should have no authority"). Unfortunately, during the twenty years between his *Prolegomena* and the date his *Novum Testamentum Graecum* was issued (1751–1752), Wettstein adopted the eccentric notion that the oldest Greek manuscripts had been corrupted by latinization, that is, additions to the text from Latin manuscripts. Consequently, he lost confidence in the more ancient Greek manuscripts, including Alexandrinus. He also lost his nerve when it came to a decision to abandon the Textus Receptus. During his long controversy with the Basel theologians about his orthodoxy, his opponents warned that his new text would undermine true doctrine. For safety's sake, he printed the Elzevir text of 1624, with minor changes. Once again, as in the editions of Mill, Bengel, and others, his preferred readings were consigned to the apparatus in the lower margin, where he cited readings from many manuscripts not previously collated.[18]

Wettstein appended to his new edition a revision and expansion of his 1730 *Prolegomena*. He modified somewhat his list of critical canons, for example, dropping the eighteenth, which preferred the reading of the majority of manuscripts (Epp 1976a, 225). Although he did not always follow his own canons in the marginal readings he approved, many of these principles have stood the test of time. Aside from his contributions to textual criticism, he added to his commentary on the text valuable quotations from scores of Greek and Latin authors, as well as rabbinical literature, a treasure store still drawn upon by scholars.[19]

Johann Salomo Semler (1725–1791) reprinted Wettstein's *Prolegomena* in 1764, adding noteworthy comments. He refined Bengel's

---

17. For all of his canons and Wettstein's explanatory comments on them, see Hulbert-Powell 1938, 114–20. The English printer William Bowyer (1699–1777) printed a Greek New Testament in 1763, into which he inserted Wettstein's approved readings (Metzger 1963a, 155–60).

18. Hulbert-Powell (1938, 252) says Wettstein himself had collated more than a hundred of these witnesses. His edition contains references to twenty-two majuscules (Parker 1995, 263).

19. Like Walton's Polyglot, Wettstein's edition was reprinted in photographic facsimile in Graz, Austria, by Akademische Druck, 1962.

Recap of Major Movers and Their Contributions	
Stephanus	First to publish a Greek New Testament with a critical apparatus
Beza	Greatly increased the number of known textual variants
The Elzevirs	Their third edition (1633) became known as the Textus Receptus
Walton	First to publish the variant readings of Codex Alexandrinus, using the reference letter A
Mill	Included 30,000 variant readings in the apparatus of his edition
Bentley	Defended Mill against his detractors and sponsored the collation of scores of manuscripts
Bengel	First to group textual witnesses on the basis of their shared readings
Semler	Grouped witnessed into three recensions: Alexandrian, Eastern, and Western

classification of witnesses into groups by eventually positing three "recensions": (1) the Alexandrian, which he traced to Origen and saw represented by the Syriac, Bohairic, and Ethiopic versions; (2) the Eastern, embodied in the form of text in the Greek church of Antioch and Constantinople in the late fourth century; (3) the Western, represented by the Latin versions and patristic writers.[20] With modifications (as we shall see), Semler's classification has continued to influence New Testament textual criticism up to the present time.

---

20. By recension, Semler seems to have meant only a form of text characteristic of a region or group. Modern textual scholars use the term to refer to careful editorial work that results in a kind of official edition (so Metzger and Ehrman 2005, 161 n. 58).

Materials

The most impressive accomplishment of the era from Erasmus to Semler was the collection, collation, and cataloguing of hundreds of Greek manuscripts and versional witnesses. Mill and others assembled from these the great store of textual variants that might be described collectively as the apparatus in the successive editions of the Greek New Testament we have surveyed. In the list below, I describe a select few, using the classification system Wettstein himself devised.[21] In order to place the knowledge and study of these witnesses in the eighteenth-century context of Wettstein, I will consign information about later publications on them to the footnotes. Full-color images of many New Testament manuscripts are available from the Center for the Study of New Testament Manuscripts (www.csntm.org/manuscripts.aspx).[22]

Majuscules

The list below references the most noteworthy manuscripts known at the end of our period, using both the sigla of Wettstein and the (Latin) name by which each is known.

A. Codex Alexandrinus, which was presented to Charles I of England in 1627, was moved to the British Museum in 1753, the year after Wettstein's New Testament appeared. Dating to the fifth century, it was the earliest important Greek manuscript available to any of the scholars of the seventeenth and eighteenth centuries. Except for the loss of several leaves, all of the Old Testament is intact. The New Testament is missing all of Matthew up to 25:6, John 6:50–8:52, and 2 Cor 4:13–12:6. The Catholic Epistles follow Acts; Hebrews is found before the Pastorals; all of 1 Clement and a fragment of 2 Clement are included following the Apocalypse.[23]

---

21. For more detailed descriptions, see Metzger and Ehrman 2005, 67–134; Scrivener 1894, 1:97–240.

22. Basic information on most New Testament manuscripts copied before 800 C.E. can be found in the Leuven Database of Ancient Books (LDAB), which can be accessed at www.trismegistos.org/ldab/. The site does not contain any images but does refer the user to publications with images. Each manuscript is indexed according to the inventory number in the collection where the manuscript resides.

23. The table of contents shows that the Psalms of Solomon were also included; these have been lost along with most of 2 Clement.

The manuscript is in two columns on pages about 12.375 inches high and 10.375 inches wide.[24] As indicated earlier, the manuscript was collated for Walton's London Polyglot. Anyone looking at the margins of Walton's edition will quickly notice that Codex A differs from the Textus Receptus far more often in the rest of the New Testament than in the Gospels.

B. Codex Vaticanus was first made known to scholars in 1475, when the Vatican catalogued the holdings in its library, but the guardians of the manuscript frustrated the attempts of all scholars who wished to collate it during this period. Scholars knew of its importance both from the great age (fourth century) and the contents of the manuscript. Originally it contained the complete Old Testament, including all of the apocryphal/deuterocanonical books except for Maccabees and the Prayer of Manasseh; most of Genesis and about thirty psalms have been lost. In the New Testament, Heb 9:15 to the end, 1–2 Timothy, Titus, Philemon, and Revelation are missing. Erasmus knew of the codex and had been furnished a list of 365 of its readings.[25] Bentley succeeded in having a collation made for him in Rome in 1720 and another, more satisfactory, in 1726,[26] but these collations were not published and, hence, were not available to others. Even so, Bengel recognized that if a careful collation of Codex Vaticanus were available, the manuscript "would be almost without an equal" (Steudel 1858, 1:16).

The manuscript is in three columns (except in the poetical books, where there are only two columns), on square pages measuring roughly eleven by eleven inches. The chapter numbers of the letters of Paul run sequentially through the entire corpus, but the order is broken at Ephesians, which begins at chapter 70, although the previous letter, Galatians, ends at chapter 58. Hebrews begins with chapter 59, but follows 2 Thes-

---

24. A photographic facsimile was published in 1879–1883 in London by the British Museum, which produced a reduced facsimile of the New Testament portion in 1909. A facsimile and paleographical description of one page appears in Metzger 1981, 86–87.

25. He cites a reading unique to B (which he refers to as "a Greek codex in the Pontifical Library") in his 1535 *Annotations to the Acts* (Scrivener 1894, 1:109). He knew of the manuscript as early as 1521 (Parker 1995, 26).

26. Many of the editors featured in this chapter had fresh collations of manuscripts made because the earlier collations were often incomplete or slipshod. It took some time before it was understood that every single deviation from the Textus Receptus should be recorded, not only those that affected the meaning of the text.

salonians, not Galatians. The implication is that the scribe of Vaticanus changed the place of Hebrews from the location it occupied in his exemplar (which had Hebrews following Galatians) but did not think to reorder the chapter numbers. Because of its enormous importance in the New Testament textual tradition, four photographic facsimiles have been published.[27]

C. Codex Ephraemi, a fifth-century manuscript, also originally contained the complete Bible, although much of the document is lost, including about three-eighths of the New Testament.[28] The manuscript, which is housed in the National Library in Paris, appears at first to be only a copy of some of the writings of Ephraem of Syria (299–378) in a single column, written in a twelfth-century hand, but it was noticed around 1690 that there was a faint underwriting containing the biblical text, which had been largely erased. The first variant readings from the manuscript were published in a "reconditioned" version of Mill's Greek New Testament edited by Ludolph Küster in 1710 (Fox 1954, 89). Wettstein painstakingly collated it for Bentley in 1716, later recording its variants in his own edition of the New Testament.[29]

D. Codex Bezae (Codex Cantabrigiensis) was introduced above as the first manuscript to have its variations from Erasmus entered into the margins of the text of Stephanus in 1550 (with the siglum β). The manuscript has an interesting history (Parker 1992, 261–78; Callahan 1996, 56–64). As we saw above, it dates to the fifth century (ca. 400, according to Parker 1992, 279–86). On a page of the manuscript, Theodore Beza, for whom the codex is named, wrote that it had been in the monastery

---

27. See *Novum Testamentum e Codice Vaticano Graeco 1209 (Codex B)* (Vatican: Vatican Library, 1968) for a full-color, full-size photographic facsimile. A magnificent limited-edition (450 copies), digitized version with each page sized and shaped like its original (including cuts, rough edges, and other damages) comes with a separate volume of prolegomena, under the title *Bibliorum Sacrorum Graecorum Codex Vaticanus B* (Rome: Instituto Poligrafico e Zecco della stato, 1999). For paleographic description and photograph of a page of the manuscript, see Metzger 1981, 74–75.

28. The exact contents of the New Testament portion of this and other important manuscripts are found in app. 1 of NA[27], 684–720. Codex C is missing parts of every single book in the New Testament (and all of 2 Thessalonians and 2 John).

29. After earlier, unsuccessful attempts to bring out the underwriting by the use of chemical reagents, Constantin Tischendorf succeeded in deciphering most of the text, which he published at Leipzig in 1843. For corrections to Tischendorf, see Lyon 1958–1959, 266–72. For a paleographical description and photographic facsimile of one page, see Hatch 1939, pl. 20.

3. THE AGE OF COLLECTING

of Saint Irenaeus at Lyons until that city was sacked (by the Huguenots) during the civil war of 1562. Subsequent study has disclosed that at Lyons, which had been for centuries a center of scholarly activity, some missing leaves were replaced by newly copied text in the ninth century. We know that the codex was taken by the bishop of Clermont to the Council of Trent in 1546, where the bishop used a reading at John 21:22 known only from this manuscript to support an argument for celibacy. Possibly its use in that council brought it to the attention of some friends of Robert Stephanus, who made a list of its variant readings and sent it to him; this explains how some of these variants made their way into the margins of his 1550 edition. It is likely that one of the scholars, printers, or booksellers who fled during the war brought it to Geneva, where it came into Beza's possession. In 1581, Beza presented it to the University of Cambridge, where it now resides.

The manuscript contains the Gospels (in the order Matthew, John, Luke, Mark)[30] and Acts; since some leaves are missing between Mark and Acts, the manuscript originally contained additional material, presumably from the New Testament. It is a bilingual, with Greek on the left-hand page, Latin on the right. The text is written in cola, that is, each line consists of a clause or phrase, so that the public reader of the text would find it easier to follow the syntax (most manuscripts of this time had no divisions between words, phrases, or sentences).

Few other New Testament manuscripts have incited as much interest as this one, largely because it contains more distinctive readings than any other witness. The relative freedom of its readings in the Gospels and in Acts is a complex issue, with the result, for example, that its text in Acts is roughly one-tenth longer than the printed text in UBS[4]/NA[27]. Its most celebrated unique reading is in Luke 6, where verse 5 is relocated to follow verse 10 and after verse 4 is inserted an otherwise unknown saying of Jesus: "On the same day, seeing someone working on the Sabbath, he said to him, 'Man, if you know what you are doing, you are blessed, but if you do not know, you are cursed and a transgressor of the law.'"

Beza made a few references to readings of the manuscript in his three editions of the New Testament. Walton had a full collation made for his

---

30. The order of the Gospels in D is the Western order, so called because many Old Latin manuscripts contain the Gospels in this order and the Latin version presumably originated in the western part of the Roman world.

London Polyglot. Mill again collated it and gave his opinion that the Greek text had been altered to agree with the Latin column, an opinion shared by Wettstein,[31] who made a full transcription of the manuscript.[32]

D^p. Codex Claromontanus[33] is another Greek-Latin bilingual (sixth century), arranged in the same way as Codex Bezae, with lines in cola, but containing only the Pauline Epistles, including Hebrews. It was known by Beza; Walton had it collated, and Wettstein collated it twice. It is in the National Library in Paris.

L. Codex Regius is an eighth-century four-Gospels manuscript now in the National Library in Paris. Its text is closely related to that of Codex B (Vaticanus), especially in the Synoptics. Although its text is quite valuable, it was copied by an ill-prepared scribe who made copious mistakes (Scrivener 1894, 1:138). This is one of the sixteen witnesses cited by Stephanus in his apparatus (1550). Wettstein collated it, but not carefully. It is the earliest-known witness to contain what is now called the shorter ending of Mark: preceding the traditional long ending (16:9–20), these words occur: "But they reported briefly to those with Peter all the things that had been told. And after these things Jesus himself sent out through them from east to west the sacred and imperishable proclamation of eternal salvation."

Minuscules

Although the early majuscules in general preserve the greatest number of variants from the Textus Receptus, Wettstein and others dutifully and properly collated scores of minuscules, most of which will not have differed significantly from the Textus Receptus, since minuscules are dated no earlier than the ninth century.[34] Nevertheless, some of the minuscule

---

31. This theory has been revived from time to time; Parker (1992, 184–85) appears finally to have laid it to rest.

32. The definitive transcription was made by Scrivener (1864; repr. 1978). A photographic facsimile was published by Cambridge in 1899. For paleographic description and plates, see Metzger 1981, 88–91.

33. Wettstein enumerated manuscripts independently for each of the four parts of the New Testament (Gospels, Acts, Epistles, Rev); today a supralinear "p" is added to distinguish this manuscript from Bezae.

34. In his *Prolegomena* of 1730, Wettstein gives a list of 152 minuscules. Scrivener lists the manuscripts known to have been collated for Walton, Mill, and their

manuscripts collated in this era are important witnesses to the ancient text. Recall that in Wettstein's registration system, minuscules (also called cursives) are identified by Arabic numerals.

1. Codex Basiliensis is a tenth-century manuscript of the complete New Testament except for Revelation. It was known to Erasmus and collated by Wettstein. Codex 1 will later become known as an important member of a closely related family of manuscripts.

33. This ninth-century manuscript contains the complete New Testament except for Revelation. It was used by Mill and was collated by Wettstein. Its text is closer to Codex Vaticanus (B) than that of any other minuscule. Because of the importance of its text, it later came to be called "the queen of the cursives." It is now housed in the National Library in Paris.

69. Codex Leicestrensis is a fifteenth-century manuscript originally containing the complete New Testament in the order Paul, Acts, General Epistles, Revelation, Gospels, but now missing portions of Matthew, Acts, Jude, and Revelation. It was collated in 1671 by Mill and later for Wettstein. In the Gospels it seems to have been influenced by one or more lectionary manuscripts. Although lectionaries were often neglected in the editions mentioned above, Mill used nine, Wettstein twenty-four, and Griesbach fourteen lectionaries (Osburn 1995, 64). Codex 69 will later be identified as an important member of a closely related family of Gospel witnesses.

Versional Manuscripts

Collecting data from the early versions was difficult for the textual scholars of this era. As we have seen, Walton published the New Testament in six languages, but, except for the Vulgate, his evidence was almost as meager as that of Beza, who knew some readings from the Syriac. Mill had to turn to Latin translations of the Syriac, Arabic, and Armenian for the readings in his apparatus. Wettstein had seen some Syriac and Coptic manuscripts and valued these versions, but in his day there was simply

---

successors and indicates which manuscripts were first cited by whom (Scrivener 1894, 2:196–216). Descriptions of the contents and history of several hundred minuscules known through 1894 are found in Scrivener 1894, 1:189–356.

too little known about the Syriac, Coptic, and other non-Latin versions for meaningful progress to be made.

As we saw in the second chapter, the transmission of the New Testament in Latin was already out of control before the time of Jerome; even the copies of his revision (the Vulgate) were soon corrupted by readings from the Old Latin translations. As early as 1504, an edition of the Vulgate was published with a collection of variant readings (Scrivener 1894, 2:62). Bentley had collations made of many Vulgate manuscripts. He was the first to appreciate how important the agreement of readings in the Vulgate and the oldest Greek manuscripts was for recovering a better text. Bengel advanced this theory further, tracing the origins of one part of the African group of witnesses to the Old Latin. Several important manuscripts of the Old Latin were known and collated or edited during the eighteenth century. In the following short list, these are cited by small italic letters of the alphabet, according to the convention established by Karl Lachmann around 1842.[35]

a. Codex Vercellensis, containing the four Gospels in the so-called Western order (Matthew, John, Luke, Mark) was written in silver letters on purple-dyed vellum in the fourth century in Vercelli, in northern Italy, and is the most important of the European Old Latin witnesses. It was collated as early as 1727 and published in 1748.

b. Codex Veronensis is another purple parchment, written in the fifth century with silver (and some gold) ink. Like *a*, it contains the Gospels in the Western order. In the twentieth century, the text of this manuscript would be seen as representative of the type used for the production of the Vulgate (Metzger and Ehrman 2005, 102). It was collated around 1749.

c. Codex Colbertinus is a twelfth-century manuscript of the Gospels and Acts that was later expanded by another hand, which added the text of the rest of the New Testament in the Vulgate. Although deriving from France, the codex contains some readings from the African Old Latin. It was published in Pierre Sabatier's edition of the Old Latin Bible (1743–1749), the first scholarly collection of the remains of the Old Latin versions.

d. The Latin side of Codex Bezae (D) was collated at the same time as the Greek by Archbishop Usher for Walton's Polyglot (1657). Wettstein

---

35. For a descriptive list of all known Old Latin manuscripts, see Metzger 1975, 295–319. Facsimile pages of many of these manuscripts are found in Vogels 1929.

made a transcription in 1716 and a better collation was made in 1732. It was edited by Sabatier before 1743. Although copied in the fifth century, the manuscript has a form of text going back to at least the early third century.

ff². Codex Corbiensis II is a fifth-/sixth-century manuscript of the Gospels in the order Matthew, Luke, John, Mark. It was edited by Sebatier before 1743.

PATRISTIC QUOTATIONS

The quotations of the fathers began to be cited as early as the Complutensian Polyglot, but Mill was the first to make substantial use of them, discussing the importance of patristic citations in the prolegomena of his edition (1707) and listing some eighty fathers whose quotations he included in the apparatus. In his *Prolegomena*, Wettstein reinforced the importance of the fathers for help in ascertaining the text of the New Testament; he was the first to include the quotations of fathers deemed heretical and of secular sources. The problem for all scholars during this era was that no critical editions of the fathers were at hand, nor were the means available to produce such materials. Indeed, only within the past fifty years have we made substantial progress in this area.

MOTIVES

In a sense, a single motive drove the immense labor summarized in this chapter: to print a better text, a text as close to the original as it was possible to recover from the materials available. Even Erasmus, despite the limitations he faced, had this as a goal. Aware of how faulty his first edition was, he set out to improve the second (1519) by giving corrected readings based on a manuscript not used in his first edition.[36] He further improved the fourth edition by readings he took from the Complutensian.

The story of these 250 years shows how this commendable motive was tempered by the need to assure the readers that the editors were not tampering with Holy Writ, thus endangering the faith of those who identified

---

36. He also corrected thousands of misprints; Scrivener's assessment is that Erasmus's first edition had more typographical errors than any other book he knew (Scrivener 1894, 2:184–85).

Scripture with the exact words of God. It is this tension that partly explains how the Textus Receptus continued to dominate the printed editions even while hundreds of manuscripts were being ferreted out and collated, along with the readings of early versions and patristic quotations.

From a strictly scholarly standpoint, there was nothing new about what the early editors of the New Testament were attempting. As we have seen, the critical study of handwritten texts with the aim of producing a single, uncorrupted edition had its beginnings as early as the third century B.C.E., as ancient librarians in Alexandria saw the need to edit, from the numerous discordant manuscripts of Homer and others, a standard text (Reynolds and Wilson 1974, 9; I draw upon this book for much of this section). Successive librarians at the Museum in Alexandria developed marginal signs to mark what they identified as spurious readings and different kinds of variants in the copies known to them. Origen later adapted these Aristarchian signs for use in his famous Hexapla, a sixfold copy of the Hebrew Bible and multiple Greek translations. Although the rationale of these librarians for deciding which readings were best was often inadequate by modern standards, they also made decisions based on such careful criteria as agreement with the author's known usage. The critical signs developed by Greek grammarians to signal textual discrepancies passed eventually to Roman circles and influenced the critical study of Latin authors. We know from Cicero's correspondence that a published author could later make changes in what he had written and request that his friends enter those changes into their copies, but this did not always happen, so that two competing editions sometimes survived (Reynolds and Wilson 1974, 23).[37]

By the fourth century C.E., copies of the classics of literature often contained a subscription with the name of the person who corrected and edited the text. Although serious attention to the classics waxed and waned in the late Roman and Byzantine eras, critical methods for editing texts continued to be refined here and there. Even during the so-called Dark Ages in the Latin West, when study of the classics declined or was discouraged in the monasteries and schools on the continent, other foundations in Ireland and England transmitted the ancient Latin texts and eventually spurred a revival of learning in what soon became the empire

---

37. Ovid (43 B.C.E.–17 C.E.) mentions that his *Metamorphoses* was published before his final revisions; manuscripts of both versions exist (West 1971, 15).

of Charlemagne. The Greek classics fared much worse during this period, but a few Greek-Latin bilingual biblical manuscripts survive from the ninth century.

The Renaissance (ca. 1300–1550) revived interest in the Greek and Latin classics and fostered an ardent search for manuscripts to collate in order to reconstruct the best texts. Hundreds of long-lost literary works were uncovered and made available for wider study. A giant of the period was Lorenzo Valla (1407–1457), who did much to refine the infant science of textual criticism. Using the skills and knowledge he employed on the Latin classics, he emended the text of the Latin Vulgate, based on his study of Greek biblical manuscripts and patristic quotations. It was Erasmus who supervised the printing of Valla's *Annotations on the New Testament* (1505), a publication that troubled many of the clergy. The *Annotations* were problematic precisely because Valla applied the same critical operations to the text of the Bible that he did to secular Latin classics. The response Valla received was an early indication of what Erasmus and his successors were to face. He and most of the scholars profiled in this chapter cut their scholarly teeth on the classics and some of them, notably Bentley, are far better known for their text-critical work on the classics than on the New Testament.

Textual criticism of the New Testament differed (and differs still) in only two important particulars from textual criticism of the Greek and Latin classics: (1) there were far more witnesses to the text of the New Testament (in many cases only one manuscript of a secular author's work might be known, hundreds of years removed from the original); and (2) the text of the Bible, as inspired scripture, was regarded by many as the literal words of God.[38]

To vastly oversimplify the theological issue, the infallible authority in the Catholic Church (both Roman and Orthodox) in matters of church doctrine and practice was the church hierarchy. The Roman Catholic Church decided at the Council of Trent in 1546 that the Vulgate was of equal authority to the original text. For the Protestant Reformers, the infallible authority in matters of church doctrine and practice was the Bible as originally written in Hebrew, Aramaic, and Greek. Although the

---

38. Somewhat strangely, even the Latin translation of the Bible functioned with a similar authority for centuries; Jerome anticipated that he would be called "a forger and profane person for having the audacity to add anything to the ancient books, or to make any changes or corrections in them" (Metzger 2001, 32).

Reformers had various ways of expressing precisely how the Holy Spirit had operated in the writing of the Scriptures, the doctrine of plenary, verbal inspiration became paramount: the Holy Spirit was responsible for the very words of the Bible. The most extreme expression of this view was articulated in the Formula Consensus Helvetica drawn up in 1675 by Swiss theologians, which declared that even the vowel points in the Hebrew Bible were inspired. Faced with evidence of textual variants in some manuscripts, versions, and patristic quotations, theologians often pointed out that the Textus Receptus agreed with the majority of witnesses ("strength in numbers") and that it was on such a text that the great doctrines of the church were based. It was argued, therefore, that except for purely mechanical variant readings, alterations in the text likely sprang from base motives.

As we have seen, Origen attributed some of the discrepancies he found in Greek manuscripts to the carelessness of scribes, others to their "perverse audacity." Eusebius, citing an anonymous source, claimed that the followers of Theodotus of Byzantium willfully corrupted Scripture in the copies they made, that these copies had begotten other copies, and that, furthermore, no one copy agreed with another. But the accusation that one's opponents have corrupted Scripture is widespread in polemical writings.[39] In the case of the Theodotians, Eusebius gives no examples of such corruptions. But we have clear examples where, in an excess of zeal to support their own theological position, some of the fathers supported a "corruption" against the better reading. Metzger cites Ambrose, who charged some of the Arians with removing from the text of John 3:6 ("that which is born of the Spirit is spirit") the words "because the Spirit is God, and is born of God." The additional clause, which is attested only by some Old Latin and Old Syriac texts, is an obvious gloss that had been picked up by one strand of the textual tradition. It is Ambrose who follows the corrupt reading (Metzger 1980, 197).

Erasmus, Stephanus, Beza, Mill, Bengel, Wettstein, indeed, all the "movers" we have looked at, were churchmen, some holding ecclesiastical positions in which they were subjected to the most careful scrutiny by their superiors. When we consider the consequences of challenging church authorities during these tumultuous centuries, it is not surprising

---

39. *Hist. eccl.* 5.28,16–18. The anonymous source is probably the Little Labyrinth and is cited also by Hippolytus (Ehrman 2006, 300–306).

that scholars continued prudently to print the Textus Receptus and allow the better readings to stand in the apparatus. The case of J. J. Wettstein is particularly instructive.[40]

Opposition to the Helvetic Confession (Formula Consensus Helvetica) went back three generations in Wettstein's family, although they were all loyal Calvinists. As a "deacon at large" in Basel, Wettstein had the right to preach, under supervision, wherever he was needed in the town. The publication of his university thesis on variant readings in the text of the New Testament (1713) already raised doubts about his orthodoxy. He came under further suspicion because he was unwilling to defend the Trinitarian position that attributed to the Son and the Holy Spirit the same status as the Father. Accused of being a Socinian,[41] Wettstein was tried by the Basel Town Council and deposed from his ministry in 1730. Among the list of errors set down in the published *Acta* of the Council was the charge that Wettstein intended to publish an edition of the New Testament based on Codex Alexandrinus (A), which "has many readings which can be employed by enemies of religion to weaken orthodoxy" (Hulbert-Powell 1938, 56; this biography contains long extracts of the *Acta* in English translation). One of the passages cited was 1 Tim 3:16, where the Textus Receptus reads "God [$\overline{\Theta\Sigma}$] was manifested in the flesh," against Alexandrinus, which reads "who [$\overline{O\Sigma}$] was manifested in the flesh." Wettstein had collated Codex A in 1715 in London and noticed that the word $\overline{\Theta\Sigma}$ in the manuscript was the result of a corrector, who had added the bar in the *theta* and the stroke above the two letters (all the great majuscules prior to the eighth century have been similarly "corrected").[42]

As we have seen, Wettstein finally decided to print the Textus Receptus after all, recording his disagreements with it in the apparatus. And, to give these pioneers of textual criticism their due, there was simply not

---

40. For the following I rely on Hulbert-Powell 1938.

41. Socinians were anti-Trinitarians, named for Laelius Socinus (Lelio Sozzini) of Zurich, who denied the preexistence of Christ, regarding him not as fully God but as a deified man.

42. Ironically, Macedonius II was removed from his bishopric in Constantinople (495–511) under the charge of being a Nestorian (one who believed that Christ existed in two distinct persons, the human Jesus and the divine son of God). It was reported that he had changed the word $\overline{O\Sigma}$ in 1 Tim 3:16 to $\overline{\Theta\Sigma}$ (to support the opinion that Jesus was not actually God in flesh but only "appeared" as God in flesh). See Stenger 1975.

enough known about the history of the transmission of the New Testament text to attempt a complete reconstruction of it. The time was not right for a wholesale desertion of the Textus Receptus. For that, we must wait until the next chapter.

Methods

The story of this era includes not only the gathering of many more witnesses to the text but the development of sophisticated methods of controlling the data. From haphazard, partial collations, we move to more thorough, careful recording of variants. The practice developed of purchasing several copies of a standard edition of the Greek New Testament and recording the variants of each separate witness in the margins of a different copy of this edition. We begin with vague and inconsistent references to manuscripts ("three manuscripts at Cambridge") and progress to Wettstein's classification system. We begin with an awareness that there are many variants to the Textus Receptus and progress to Mill's apparatus, with its record of 30,000 such variants. Along the way, we perceive a deepening appreciation of versional and patristic evidence. Although the sheer mass of data begins to seem unmanageable, Bengel shrewdly deduces that the witnesses may be divided into "tribes" and "families" based on their shared readings and that readings can be "graded" as to their nearness to the original text.

Methodologically, the most important development was the articulation of principles for sound text-critical work. Traditionally these principles, as we have seen, were called canons, in the sense of standards or measures by which genuine readings can be separated from those that have been corrupted, whether unconsciously or consciously.[43] In 1711, Gerhard von Mastricht (also seen as Maestricht, Maastricht) published a Greek New Testament with extensive prolegomena, in which were included forty-three canons. Although many of these were constructed in such a way as to argue against the variant readings in Mill's edition and to support the Textus Receptus, they drew widespread attention and con-

---

43. The word "canon" derives from an Aramaic term referring to a tall reed that might be used as a rule, standard, straightedge, or yardstick. On the development of text-critical canons, see Epp 1976b, 211–57). Epp (2002a, 24) suggests that "probabilities" or simply "arguments" might be preferable to "canons," since the latter suggest something "fixed and final."

siderable praise. Probably their chief value was to provoke a careful and critical response from Bengel, who addressed them first in the apparatus of his Greek New Testament (1734) and in greater detail in the preface to his *Gnomon Novi Testamenti* (1742). Quoting each of the canons, Bengel showed: (1) that many of them were simply observations, not canons (for example, mechanical copying errors ought to be distinguished from deliberate alterations); (2) that others were simply invalid (for example, the several canons that state or imply that the better reading is the one supported by the greatest number of witnesses); and (3) that Mastricht poorly understood and badly applied even the valid canons he stipulated (for example, copyists sometimes clarify the text by adding explanations or omitting superfluous words).[44]

Bengel preceded his critique of Mastricht with twenty-two "suggestions" (or perhaps "admonitions" [Latin *monita*]) that he employed in treating variant readings in his edition of the New Testament. Among them are these important canons, which he summarized in his succinct style:

> (2) *More* witnesses are to be preferred to fewer; and, which is *more important*, witnesses who *differ* in country, age, and language, are to be preferred to those who are closely connected with each other; and which is *most important of all, ancient* witnesses are to be preferred to modern ones. ... (14) A corrupted text is often betrayed by *alliteration, parallelism*, or the convenience of an *Ecclesiastical* Lection, especially at the beginning or conclusion of it; from the occurrence of the same words, we are led to suspect an omission; from too great facility, *a gloss*. ... (15) There are, therefore, *five* principal *criteria*, by which to determine a disputed text. The *Antiquity* of the witnesses, the *Diversity* of their extraction, and their *Multitude*; in the next place,[45] the apparent *Origin of the corrupt* reading, and the *Native* colour of the *genuine* one. (Steudel 1863, 1:16)

Bengel realized that there is no foolproof set of rules by which to determine the correct reading in every case; sometimes one reading is supported by some criteria, an alternative one by other criteria. In such cases, we simply have to weigh the arguments of critics and decide which

---

44. I am summarizing from Steudel's edition 1863, 1:20–38.
45. I adopt from Epp (1976a, 222) and insert here the phrase "in the next place" (Latin *tum*).

is the more convincing. As we saw above, he assigned "grades" to the readings he evaluated, depending on his relative certainty about them.

As noted earlier, Wettstein obviously had been influenced in the formulation of his canons by Bengel.[46] Both of them sought a balance between external evidence (the age, diversity, and general excellence of the *documents*) and internal evidence (observed habits of the original *author* and of *copyists*); Bengel, however, clearly differentiated the two types of evidence and placed a higher value on external evidence (so Epp 1976a, 222). Put in our own language, we might say that by the middle of the eighteenth century, several criteria had emerged for choosing between or among variant readings. It probably should be understood that each of these canons presupposes the phrase "other things being equal":

1. A reading supported by the most ancient witnesses should be preferred.
2. A reading supported by witnesses from diverse geographical regions should be preferred.
3. A reading that has the support of Greek manuscripts, versions, and fathers should be preferred.
4. A reading that disagrees with its parallels should be preferred.
5. The harder reading (grammatically, stylistically, theologically) should be preferred.
6. A reading that agrees with the author's style should be preferred.
7. The shorter reading should be preferred.

Implied and all but stipulated in the discussions of Bengel and Wettstein is the dictum that the reading should be chosen that best accounts for the origin of the other(s). In addition to these "positive" canons, Bengel and Wettstein agreed with a conclusion widespread in their day, namely, that conjectures ought never to be admitted into the text. They were aware that conjectural emendation was sometimes necessary in recovering the texts of some classical authors whose work was known from only one or two late and/or mutilated manuscripts, but they believed that the New

---

46. This is so even though Wettstein mounted scathing attacks on Bengel both in his *Prodromus* of 1730 and his edition of 1751–1752. Wettstein's actual textual decisions often disagreed with his stipulated criteria.

Testament text was attested by so great a number and variety of witnesses that the true reading in every contested passage could be found in the extant documents. Although these canons would not remain undisturbed in the coming centuries, they provided a clear rationale for making textual decisions without regard to how the Textus Receptus would be affected. Truly modern text-critical methods were being firmly set in place.

Models

In various ways each of the movers stands as a model of how improvements could be made to the text of the New Testament then available, but if we had to single out one publication as the most significant, it would be John Mill's edition of the Greek New Testament. Even though he, like nearly every other editor of this era, printed a form of the Textus Receptus,[47] what sets his work apart is his thorough, careful, and critical survey of scholarship in the field prior to his edition, his collection and evaluation of many more witnesses to the text than had previously been known, and his efforts to frame a history of the transmission of the text. All of these labors were assembled in his massive prolegomena (described in detail in Fox 1954, 67–71). The fruit of these efforts appeared in the critical apparatus to his text, where he displayed a rare judgment in evaluating the evidence for readings. Although he did not offer a list of critical canons for making textual decisions, his discussion of variants and the grounds for his decisions contributed much to the formulation of canons by others, including Bengel and Wettstein. The importance of Mill's edition is shown in both the negative and positive responses to it. On the one hand, Daniel Whitby attacked it in 1710 largely on the grounds that by quadrupling the variations found in the 1550 Stephanus, Mill had made the foundation of faith insecure.[48] On the other hand, every edition of the

---

47. Wells, Mace, Bowyer (1763), and Harwood (1776) are the exceptions, although none of them constructed a completely fresh text. For the latter two, see Metzger and Ehrman 2005, 62–63.

48. Whitby's attack was contained in a Latin appendix to his 1710 reprinting of his *Paraphrase and Commentary on the New Testament*. His critique was used by the religious skeptic Anthony Collins during the so-called Freethinking Controversy as proof that the Scriptures were unreliable, owing to the great number of variant readings in the witnesses; see Fox 1954, 105–9; Metzger and Ehrman 2005, 155 n. 42.

Greek New Testament subsequent to Mill mined his great stock of variants and benefited from his careful judgment about preferred readings.

Relatively few readers of this book will be equipped to work their way through the lengthy discussions of variant readings (almost always in Latin) found in the critical apparatus of the editions we have surveyed. Those who can do so would find the editors recording accumulating evidence against the originality of several passages that had become solidly entrenched in the Textus Receptus and, thus, in vernacular translations. In 1763 William Bowyer published examples of what Wettstein's edition would look like if he had printed a text based on his own critical judgment. Bowyer's Greek New Testament had square brackets around Matt 6:13 (the doxology of the Lord's Prayer), John 7:53–8:11 (the woman caught in adultery), 1 John 5:7–8 (the Johannine Comma), and many other words and phrases (Metzger 1963d, 155–60).

Wettstein's treatment of 1 John 5:7–8 can stand as a good model of how the critical evaluation of this text would finally result in its being relegated to the margins of most editions published by his successors. We saw in the first chapter that Erasmus was induced to add this passage about the three heavenly witnesses to his third edition in 1522. In 1534 Simon de Colinus published an edition based on Erasmus but omitting the disputed passage. For the next 195 years, every edition of the Greek New Testament included the passage, but many of their editors recorded doubts about it (for the following summary see Fox 1954, passim). In 1658 Etienne de Courcelles published a Greek New Testament in which he placed square brackets around the passage, explaining in a long footnote that there was scant support for it in Greek, versional, or patristic sources. Mill devoted nine and one-half pages to this text, finally supporting its retention. Daniel Mace omitted it from his 1729 edition, explaining why in a fifteen-page footnote. Even though Bentley did not follow through on his intention to publish a Greek New Testament, he found it necessary to respond to reports that he was planning to omit the passage.

Why did this text draw so much interest and debate? The answer may be found in the highly charged Trinitarian debates of the seventeenth and eighteenth centuries, which in many ways revived the ante-Nicene controversies on the same subject. If the New Testament plainly said that "the Father, the Word, and the Holy Spirit" were witnesses "in heaven," all agreeing in their testimony that "Jesus is the Son of God" who came "through water and blood," the preexistence and deity of Christ were supported against all varieties of anti-Trinitarian claims, whether unitarian or subordinationist. The theological investment in this text was so huge that even Bengel made an elaborate argument in support of the passage. He claimed that, although ancient evidence is almost confined to Latin translations and some fathers, the documentary support is outweighed by the context in 1 John itself. In fact, his discussion in the *Gnomon* includes the astonishing comment that "the context itself confirms this verse as the centre and sum of the whole Epistle" (Steudel 1863, 5:150).

It was Wettstein who first detailed all the evidence, traced the debate, and offered the most compelling critical arguments against the originality of the three heavenly witnesses (Hulbert-Powell 1938, 247–50). Wettstein had found it necessary to defend his judgment about this reading since 1729, when the Basel Town Council lodged their charge of heresy against him. These theologians noted that Wettstein's planned New Testament would omit 1 John 5:7. In volume 2, he devotes his longest text-critical note, six pages of densely packed type, to this passage. He begins with Erasmus and traces the treatment of the text through subsequent editions, rehearsing the arguments of these editors both for and against the passage. He notes that Martin Luther omitted the words from his first German Bible but that subsequent editors added them after Luther's death. No Greek manuscript prior to the sixteenth century contains them except as variant readings that have been added to the margins. He mentions that the Syriac, Coptic, Armenian, Slavonic, Ethiopic, and Arabic versions do not contain the verses; neither do the earliest examples of the Old Latin translations nor even the oldest witnesses to the Vulgate. Even in the later Vulgate manuscripts that do contain the passage, there are inner variations, throwing suspicion on the addition. Not one of the Greek fathers quotes the passage, although it would have been very useful to them in the ante-Nicene Trinitarian controversies. Wettstein concludes that the words came into the text as the result of an explanatory marginal comment (gloss) added to a Latin translation of 1 John 5:8, where the spirit, the water, and the blood are seen as veiled references to the Trinity. Near the end of the fourth century, the Spaniard Priscillian quoted the words as part of the text. By the end of the fifth century, Eugenius, bishop of Carthage, included the words in a confession of faith and the clause became widely accepted throughout the Latin church. Wettstein ends his note with a scathing denunciation of Bengel for his support of such an indefensible reading.

Wettstein's treatment of this textual variant serves as a model for several reasons: (1) he brought to bear on the problem all the external evidence (the witnesses); (2) he traced the history of this passage in previous editions of the Greek New Testament and vernacular translations; (3) he cited evidence for the earliest-known reference to the passage as part of the text of 1 John; (4) he gave a rational and convincing explanation for how the passage entered into the textual tradition. The high caliber of Wettstein's work on this passage is confirmed by the circumstance that the text-critical work since his time has added nothing of significance to his analysis of this passage. Nevertheless, since Wettstein chose, for prudential reasons, to print the Textus Receptus, it remained for his successors to harvest the fruit of his labors.

4
THE AGE OF OPTIMISM:
THE NEW TESTAMENT IN THE ORIGINAL GREEK

> Westcott and I are going to edit a Greek text of the N. T. some two or three years hence, if possible. ... Our object is to supply clergymen generally, schools, etc., with a portable Gk. Test., which shall not be disfigured with Byzantine corruptions. (F. J. A. Hort, in a letter written in 1853)

The need to collect, collate, and classify New Testament manuscripts did not come to an end with the publication of Wettstein's Greek New Testament. In fact, the century following Wettstein produced more manuscript discoveries and collations than the previous two centuries combined. For example, J. M. A. Scholz (1794–1852) single-handedly added 616 manuscripts to the list of those previously known (Scrivener 1894, 2:216). As long as new witnesses to the text are discovered, the basic work of comparing and classifying will go on. Nevertheless, the period from the late eighteenth to the late nineteenth century introduced a new era in textual criticism of the Greek New Testament, marked by fundamental advances in methodology as well as a strengthened determination to break free from the Textus Receptus. It was an optimistic age, as progress in science and technology made communication, transportation, medicine, and other services more widely available. This chapter will introduce five textual critics who gave reason for optimism also in the search for a more reliable New Testament text: Johann Jacob Griesbach, Karl Lachmann, Constantin von Tischendorf, Samuel Prideaux Tregelles, and Fenton John Anthony Hort. The next chapter will survey the materials, motives, methods, and models of this age of optimism.

Johann Jakob Griesbach (1745–1812), the son of a pietistic Lutheran minister, came under the influence of Johann Salomo Semler while living in Semler's house as a student at Halle, near Frankfurt (Delling 1978, 7). Semler began preparing Griesbach for an academic career with a focus on New Testament textual criticism. Like Wettstein, Griesbach made a long tour of notable libraries in the Netherlands, England, and France to study and collate manuscripts. At the age of twenty-six, he wrote a treatise on the importance of patristic evidence for the New Testament text, following this up with his first edition of the Greek New Testament in 1774–1775. After obtaining a professorship at the University of Jena (1775), he published two other major editions (1775–1776 and 1796–1806), in which he refined the theories of Bengel, Wettstein, and Semler.

Griesbach has left his mark on the story of the New Testament text for three reasons. First, he sharpened and advanced the theory of textual families that Bengel had initiated and Semler had further developed. Because he had studied so many Greek and Latin manuscripts and patristic quotations, he was struck with the number and variety of textual variants. Although he thought he could identify as many as five or six groups, he eventually settled on the same three as his mentor, Semler: Alexandrian, Western, and Constantinopolitan. He attempted to identify all the major witnesses to each of these groups, including majuscules, minuscules, versions, and fathers. In this, his judgment was remarkably acute, based on the state of the evidence available to him ("unsurpassed in carefulness, caution, and comprehensive knowledge" is the assessment of Zuntz [1953, 5]). Many primary witnesses to these families were not then known or were inadequately known, and some of the minuscules were assigned to both the Alexandrian and Western families because their texts seemed to combine features of both (Kilpatrick 1978, 136). Like Semler, Griesbach believed Origen's quotations gave the earliest evidence for the Alexandrian recension, reasoning that Origen had brought this text with him when he moved from Alexandria to Palestine. Among the Greek manuscripts he assigned to the Alexandrian family are Alexandrinus (A, except in the Gospels), Ephraemi (C), and 33. He identified Bohairic Coptic as the major version representing this group.[1] Codex Bezae (D), the Latin

---

1. I mention for all of the manuscript families only those members identified by Griesbach that have stood the test of time; for a fuller list, see Metzger and Ehrman 2005, 166.

versions and fathers, and the Peshitta (Syriac) were the major witnesses to the Western family, which, like the Alexandrian, could be traced back to the beginning of the third century. Codex A in the Gospels, the hundreds of later manuscripts, and most of the fathers represented the text thought to have derived from the Patriarchate of Constantinople sometime in the fourth century.

Second, Griesbach laid out fifteen "critical rules and observations" for deciding between or among textual variants. Although many of these are drawn from Bengel and Wettstein, it is Griesbach's more detailed statements that have most impressed successive generations of textual critics. The first and most influential canon had been enunciated by Wettstein, but without the scrupulous qualifications given by Griesbach, whose general rule is as follows:

> The shorter reading (unless it lacks entirely the authority of the ancient and weighty witnesses) is to be preferred to the more verbose, for scribes were much more prone to add than to omit. They scarcely ever deliberately omitted anything, but they added many things; certainly they omitted some things by accident, but likewise not a few things have been added to the text by scribes through errors of the eye, ear, memory, imagination, and judgment. (Metzger and Ehrman 2005, 166)

Since Griesbach is often credited (or blamed) for this canon, usually cited simply as *lectio brevior potior* ("the shorter reading is to be preferred"), it is important to see it in the context of the qualifications he added. He gives five conditions under which the shorter reading is to be preferred and six conditions under which the longer reading is to be preferred. Epp summarizes these and observes that many of Griesbach's fourteen other canons are anticipated in these qualifications. Griesbach stipulates:

> (1) that the canon applies only when the reading has some support from "old and weighty witnesses"; and (2) that the originality of a shorter reading is more certain still (a) if it is also a harsher, more obscure, ambiguous, elliptical, Hebraizing, or ungrammatical reading, (b) if the same matter is expressed differently in various codices, (c) if the order of words is inconsistent and unstable, (d) if the reading stands first in a pericope (or church lesson) or (e) if the *fuller reading* shows evidence of a gloss or an interpretation, or is in accord with words in parallel passages, or appears to have been taken from a lectionary. He continues, however, that the shorter reading would *not* have a strong

claim to originality (unless supported by *many notable witnesses*) (1) if the missing portion of the longer reading (a) can be attributed to homoeoteleuton, (b) would have appeared to scribes as obscure, rough, superfluous, unusual, paradoxical, an offense to piety, an error, or inconsistent with parallels, or (d) does not, by its omission, destroy the sense of the word structure, or (2) if the shorter reading (a) is less suitable to the author's character, style, or goal, (b) makes no sense at all, or (c) probably represents an intrusion from a parallel passage or a lectionary. (Epp 1976a, 226)

The third contribution of Griesbach was to move the printed text further away from the Textus Receptus than any previous editor and to show *in the text itself*, not only in the apparatus, his departures from the traditional text. With one eye on the tradition, he chose the 1624 Elzevir edition as the base text, recording in smaller type the variations he preferred.[2] There are essentially two apparatuses in Griesbach's editions: one recording the traditional readings he has rejected and variants of equal or nearly equal value to those in the common text and one containing his critical discussions.

Griesbach's contributions to textual criticism place him in the very highest rank of scholars. Even Scrivener, who rejected Griesbach's theory of three recensions, lauds his "logical acuteness and keen intellectual perception" (Scrivener 1894, 2:226). Epp notes that Griesbach did his work when Wettstein's theory about latinization of all the early Greek manuscripts was the dominant view. Thus, Griesbach's insistence that the oldest manuscripts were the most valuable—the view Bengel had championed—makes his contribution all the more impressive (Epp 1976a, 229).

Nevertheless, Griesbach was unable (or unwilling) to start from scratch and publish a text based solely on his judgment as to the best readings. This may have been partly the result of the sheer magnitude of his other responsibilities and partly an indication of his scholarly reserve. During his career at Jena, Griesbach developed and presented lectures covering the whole field of introduction to and exegesis of the New Testament writings, as well as church history, church dogmatics, and biblical theology (Delling 1978, 8–13). Perhaps the preparation of a completely fresh text was more than he could manage. However, it is more likely

---

2. In the 1,000 passages chosen by Reuss to compare early printed editions, Griesbach's last edition differs from the Elzevir text in 352 places (so Scrivener 1894, 2:225 n. 2).

that he was reticent to commit himself so fully to breaking with tradition. As a scholar, he walked a tight line, for he was regarded by many as a theological liberal and by others as a defender of orthodox dogmatics. For example, he openly rejected the popular belief that the individual words of the New Testament were divinely inspired. At the same time, he defended the apostolic authorship of most of the New Testament, the historicity of miracles, and the importance of biblical theology as the foundation of church doctrine (Delling 1978, 10–12). In the preface to his 1786 *Introduction to the Study of Popular Dogmatics* (*Anleitung zum Studium der populärum Dogmatik*), Griesbach recognized that some readers "will shake their heads suspiciously at supposed heterodoxies," while others "will shrug their shoulders indulgently at the author's attachment to old-fashioned orthodoxy" (Delling 1978, 9).[3] But whatever may have been the limitations of Griesbach's achievements, clearly he emboldened his successors and helped to foster the spirit of optimism that moved them toward a clean break with the Textus Receptus.

Karl Lachmann (1793–1851) was the one who made that break.[4] Like Bentley, Lachmann was a classical scholar and philologist. He is still celebrated for his careful editions of a number of Latin classics and medieval German works. Lachmann was not a theologian and did not take any pains to attract the support of theologians or church officials for his project of editing a New Testament text. He simply went about the job in the same way he edited other ancient texts. Like Bentley and Griesbach, he believed a textual critic should value the oldest evidence above all else in reconstructing a text. Unlike them, however, he did not begin with the Textus Receptus and depart from it where the evidence warranted; he ignored the Textus Receptus and based his edition on a handful of witnesses.

It could be argued that Lachmann intended his edition not to be adopted as a standard "working text" for theological students and clergy but to serve as a demonstration to scholars that it was possible to recover a much earlier text than had so far been put forth.[5] After four years of work,

---

3. Zuntz (1953, 226 n. 1) refers to Griesbach's "half-heartedness which prevented him from reaping the full fruit of his insight."

4. The most detailed account of Lachmann's critical editions of the New Testament is found in Tregelles 1954, 97–117.

5. Gregory (1907, 444–45), refers to it as "a scientific tool" and "a bridge ... across the gap separating us from the true text."

he published an article in the 1830 issue of the most important theological journal of his time, *Theologischen Studien und Kritiken*, describing his forthcoming edition. But when the edition itself came out in 1831, it did not contain the usual preface, with its explanation of the author's critical principles and a comparison of his work to that of previous editors. Instead, at the end of the book of Revelation, Lachmann added a few lines explaining that he had set out his plan "in a more convenient place," namely, the journal article mentioned above. Then he gave the barest outline of his method of operation: (1) He has selected a text in agreement with the custom of the most ancient Eastern churches. (2) Where there was uncertainty about their text, he has given preference to the agreement of Italy and Africa (i.e., to the Old Latin manuscripts). (3) In cases where there was still uncertainty, he has indicated this by brackets in the text and marginal notes on alternative readings. (4) He has completely disregarded the "received readings," but has added these in the closing pages (that is, they did not constitute part of his critical text but were added as a kind of appendix).[6]

Lachmann clearly intended to recover not necessarily the earliest text but what he regarded as the earliest *attainable* text, namely, the text used in fourth-century churches around Constantinople. Disregarding all previously printed editions as well as all minuscule manuscripts, he generally relied on no more than four Greek manuscripts (B, A, C, and T [a fifth-century Greek-Coptic manuscript containing parts of Luke and John]) and often on fewer. For example, Scrivener says that in 165 of the 405 verses of Revelation, Lachmann used only one manuscript (1894, 2:233). To these he added a few Old Latin manuscripts, two codices of the Vulgate, and the quotations of Irenaeus, Origen, Cyprian, Hilary, and Lucifer.

As might have been expected, Lachmann's text was met with a firestorm of criticism. In the first place, it was unheard-of for anyone to publish a critical edition based on such a tiny selection of documents, ignoring hundreds of manuscripts. In the second place, even though his text could not help but be regarded as revolutionary, he had not bothered to offer any explanation of his methodology and its rationale in the place where it would logically have been expected: a preface. Instead, he had referred his readers to a theological journal published a year previously and accessible only to readers of German. Thirdly, he had ignored the sensitivities of the theologians and churchmen, who could not be

---

6. For the Latin text of the notice, see Scrivener 1894, 2:231 n. 1.

expected to embrace a text edited not by a fellow theologian but by a philologist who had taken a notion to encroach on their territory. As we have seen in our story thus far, disagreements about the biblical text were not always expressed in temperate and dispassionate language. The colorful title "Bentley's ape" was just one of the insults hurled at Lachmann, indicating that he was "aping" Bentley in his cavalier attitude toward the Textus Receptus (Metzger and Ehrman 2005, 171).

Not to be deterred, Lachmann issued a second edition (1842–1850), finally offering in the prolegomena of the second volume (1850) an explanation of his methodology. In the first volume, however, he had replied to his critics with the same kind of coarse abuse they had heaped upon him, so his critics were not inclined to accept the new edition.

Historians of textual criticism have, in most respects, vindicated Lachmann's efforts, Zuntz going so far as to assert that the texts of all editions subsequent to Lachmann's, "when contrasted with the *Textus Receptus*, appear to be wellnigh identical"(1953, 7). The most curious decision he made was to print what he regarded as the text of the fourth century, *including even erroneous readings*, so long as those readings were well-attested by the witnesses he was using. This means that his text-critical canons included principles for judging readings based not on their own merits but simply on the basis of documentary evidence. In this, he agreed with his predecessors that preference should be given to readings common to all witnesses. When the witnesses are not unanimous, preference should be given to the reading attested across the broadest geographical range. When the witnesses to variant readings are evenly divided across the regions, documentary evidence cannot produce a secure reading. Although he does not offer principles of internal evidence, his notes occasionally include his judgments about the most likely original reading, and in these judgments he has usually been followed by subsequent editors. Epp credits Lachmann with ushering in "the single most significant fifty-year period in the history of New Testament textual criticism" (1989a, 80). By beginning with a clean page and choosing the earliest witnesses as the basis for his text, he had dealt the Textus Receptus a severe blow.[7] What was needed to complete the job was a com-

---

7. Epp (1989a, 80) likens Lachmann's accomplishment to D-Day in WWII: after Lachmann, it was certain the Textus Receptus would be defeated; the only question was how long until victory was declared.

pelling and convincing account of the history of the New Testament text. Although we have to wait fifty years for that account, our next two movers provide many of the resources to help with the writing of that story.

Lobegott Friedrich Constantin von Tischendorf (1815–1874) earned his place in the story of the New Testament text through his tireless manuscript searches and his production of eight critical editions of the text. A theological student at Leipzig, he was encouraged by his teacher, G. B. Winer, who had edited a famous grammar of the Greek New Testament, to dedicate himself to textual studies. Indirectly, Karl Lachmann also influenced him through his 1830 article in *Theologischen Studien und Kritiken*. In one of the notes to that article, Lachmann had encouraged Parisian scholars to publish the texts of the codices Ephraemi (C) and Claromontanus (D^p).

Tischendorf, newly elected to the theological faculty at the University of Leipzig in 1840, began work on Codex C in Paris that same year and published the New Testament portion in 1843. Thanks to the generous support he received from the governments of Saxony and Russia, he was able to travel widely and to collate and publish editions of scores of both Old Testament and New Testament manuscripts. The manuscript publications alone fill more than twenty volumes (Scrivener 1894, 2:236–37). Most famous is Codex Sinaiticus, which he designated ℵ. The exciting story of the discovery and publication of this manuscript is told in the next chapter.

Tischendorf probably published too many editions of the Greek New Testament. He is said to have been impulsive, changing his judgment on readings from one edition to the next. Although in the main he favored the earliest witnesses, the first volume (the Gospels) of his seventh edition (1859) was marked by a leaning toward the Textus Receptus; he recovered his balance in the second volume, which relies on older witnesses. His great eighth edition, completed in 1873, is a monumental accomplishment, containing the fullest apparatus of readings ever assembled in a single edition. It has been claimed that Tischendorf's successive editions betray the influence of the witnesses he had studied most recently (Kenyon 1951, 290). This tendency is especially evident in his eighth edition, which differs from the seventh in more than 3,000 places, owing largely to the influence of Codex Sinaiticus, which was his major manuscript discovery and publication.

Tischendorf gave less attention to internal canons of criticism than to external criteria. Like Lachmann, he stipulated that the text ought to be founded on the most ancient witnesses, especially Greek manuscripts, but not to the exclusion of the versions and fathers.[8] He referenced four other canons, all of which had been repeatedly invoked by his predecessors. He laid greatest weight on the summary rule of choosing the reading that best explains the origin of the others. Tischendorf died before he could write the prolegomena to his eighth edition. Caspar R. Gregory (1894) prepared a separate volume, *Prolegomena*, to serve this purpose.

Samuel Prideaux Tregelles (1813–1875) was a contemporary of Tischendorf and, like Tischendorf, died of a stroke before he could complete the prolegomena to his work, but in other respects they could scarcely have been more different. Tischendorf's work was heavily financed, his manuscript discoveries celebrated, his name known all over the world. Tregelles was materially poor, he labored in obscurity, and he produced only one edition of the New Testament. Nevertheless, he has a well-earned place in the story of the New Testament text.

Tregelles was born near Falmouth, England, of Quaker parents. He later joined the Plymouth Brethren and finally, late in life, was a lay member of the Church of England. Every other editor we have profiled has had the advantage of a university education, but Tregelles had only three years in Falmouth Classical School before he had to take a job at an iron works to support himself (1829–1835). Both brilliant and industrious, he spent his hours after work learning Greek, Hebrew, and Aramaic (and even Welsh), becoming accomplished enough in Hebrew to publish a series of textbooks. He was a blue-collar scholar who decided to devote himself to the critical study of the Greek text, initially only to lay to rest some of his own questions. By 1838 Tregelles had determined to edit a Greek New Testament, "believing such an undertaking, if entered on in the fear of God, to be really service to Him, from its setting forth more accurately His word" (Tregelles 1854, 154).

In preparation for the task, he set out to examine as many as possible of the major witnesses to the text, traveling to the necessary locations in 1845–1846 and 1849–1850. Tregelles is known for the scrupulously careful manuscript collations he accomplished during these tours as well as for his editing of Codex Zacynthius (Ξ), which is described in the next chapter. Having published, in 1844, a critical edition of the Greek text

---

8. Epp (1989a, 80) cites Tischendorf's "terse and quotable dictum" about witnesses, namely, those "that excel in antiquity prevail in authority."

of the Apocalypse with a new English translation, he revised and republished the translation alone in 1848, appending to it his proposal for a new edition of the Greek New Testament. He first made a careful study of all the previous editions, combining this with an explanation of his own critical principles in his book, *An Account of the Printed Text of the Greek New Testament, with Remarks on its Revision upon Critical Principles, together with a Collation of the Critical Texts of Griesbach, Scholz, Lachmann, and Tischendorf, with that in Common Use.*[9]

Like Lachmann and Tischendorf, Tregelles proposed to use "ancient authorities" alone in constructing his text, disregarding the Textus Receptus altogether.[10] Although documentary evidence alone could take him back only to the fourth century, he believed that he could often recover the original text by applying critical principles to decide among variant readings that had ancient attestation. Unlike Lachmann and other editors, Tregelles determined to include in his apparatus the evidence of all the majuscules, ancient versions, and fathers up to Eusebius both *for* and *against* his preferred readings. He produced his New Testament in fascicles, funded by subscription, beginning in 1857 and concluding in 1872. Disabled by paralysis from a stroke in 1870, he died before he could write the prolegomena. In 1879, F. J. A. Hort and A. W. Streane published a volume of prolegomena, along with a list of additions and corrections. No doubt Tregelles's edition would have been much improved if there had been a reliable collation of Codex Vaticanus (B) and if he had been able to make use of Tischendorf's Codex Sinaiticus (published in 1862) before he issued the Gospels fascicle; nevertheless, Tregelles's efforts produced a text more painstakingly edited and more independent of the Textus Receptus than any other available at that time.

Clearly, Tregelles relied heavily on external criteria, namely, the age and quality of witnesses, for recovering the best text, but he was aware that the witnesses could not be used mechanically because there are many examples where good witnesses differ in their readings. In these cases, "all that we know of the nature and origin of various readings, and of the kinds of errors to which copyists were liable, must be employed" (Tre-

---

9. Much of the substance of this work is accessible in Horne (1856, vol. 4), in which the section on textual criticism of the Greek New Testament is the work of Tregelles.

10. Tischendorf, however, included manuscripts from the fourth to the ninth century as "most ancient"; Tregelles rightly judged this too wide a time span.

gelles 1854, 186). Rather than giving a discrete list of the criteria he used for deciding these difficult cases, Tregelles offered detailed examples of his methodology in solving the textual problems in some two dozen specific passages. Here he is seen to employ the by-now standard internal criteria we have seen above: choose the reading that best explains the origin of the others; reject readings that are best explained as scribal errors; do not quickly reject a reading that seems logically or grammatically incongruous, for further reflection may show it to be more sensible; reject harmonizing readings; reject readings that may have arisen from marginal glosses; reject readings in support of ascetical practices; prefer the harder reading, the shorter reading, and the reading that best agrees with the author's style (summary in Epp 1976a, 233–34).

SUMMARY OF REIGNING TEXT-CRITICAL CANONS OF THE LATE NINETEENTH CENTURY

- Other things being equal, prefer the shorter reading to the longer.
- Prefer the readings of older witnesses to the readings of newer ones.
- Prefer the ungrammatical reading to the smooth.
- Where an Old Testament quotation appears in different forms in the New Testament, choose the reading that least agrees with the standard Old Testament text.
- Reject readings that reflect known liturgical or ascetical practices.
- Reject readings that harmonize the text to parallels.
- Choose the reading that best agrees with an author's style.
- Choose the reading attested across the widest geographical range of witnesses.

Tregelles's edition was especially important for the English-speaking world, because there the Textus Receptus had resisted every attempt to dislodge it. Building on Lachmann's beachhead, Tischendorf and Tregelles wrested even more territory previously held by the Textus Receptus. The analogy is Epp's, who makes Tischendorf a general and Tregelles a brigadier general in the campaign to defeat the Textus Receptus. All three of these receive grateful mention by the "general of the army" and his "first officer" (Epp 1989b, 81), who led the final push and whose story we now tell.

Brooke Foss Westcott (1825–1901) and **Fenton John Anthony Hort** (1828–1892) met at Cambridge University, where Westcott was Hort's tutor in classics. They formed a close friendship, due not only to their professional studies in New Testament but also to their shared interest in the natural sciences. Westcott's father was a botanist and Westcott himself had a lifelong interest in the natural sciences (A. Westcott 1903). Hort also was a botanist, publishing several papers in the field based on observations he made during his many summer alpine treks. Both of them were ordained priests in the Church of England, Westcott becoming canon of Peterborough in 1869 and Hort serving as a parish priest for fifteen years. Westcott became Regius Professor of Divinity at Cambridge in 1870 and Hort was made Hulsean Professor of Divinity in 1878.

In 1853, the two made a plan to replace what Hort called "that vile *Textus Receptus*" (A. Westcott 1903, 1:209) with a revision of the Greek New Testament that would improve upon the editions of Griesbach, Lachmann, and Tischendorf (Westcott and Hort 1881, 2:16–17). The project, which they initially expected to complete within two or three years, occupied them for the next twenty-eight.[11] For the most part they worked through the text independently, discussing their work by correspondence until they reached "agreement or final difference" on each point of discussion (17). In 1870 a committee was formed to undertake a revision of the Authorized Version (kjv) of the Bible. Westcott and Hort were members of the New Testament Company of that committee, so they arranged for the private printing of portions of their Greek New Testament (henceforth W-H), as these became available, for the use of the company. Five days before the Revised Version of the New Testament appeared (May 1881), the first volume of the W-H text was published, followed by a second volume of introductory matter and appendices a few months later.

Westcott and Hort were not overmodest in their choice of a title for

---

11. Both men were engaged in other projects during these years. The long delay in publishing proved beneficial, since they were able to take advantage of full collations of Vaticanus and Sinaiticus as well as the edition of Tregelles and the final edition of Tischendorf.

their text: *The New Testament in the Original Greek*.[12] Hort nuanced this claim slightly in the first sentence of volume 2, subtitled *Introduction, Appendix*: "This edition is an attempt to present exactly the original words of the New Testament, so far as they can now be determined from surviving documents."[13] The two did not, like so many of their predecessors, collate manuscripts and compile an apparatus of variant readings. Instead, they made good use of the collations and apparatuses of the best editors before them. The text appears on the page with only brief references in the side margins to variant readings, which are then discussed in the 140 pages of the appendix in volume 2. Where one of the editors has serious reservations about the text chosen for printing, his counterarguments appear in these "Notes on Select Readings," followed by "H" or "W."

In order to present a text "not disfigured by Byzantine corruptions," Westcott and Hort had to demonstrate that the readings characteristic of that group of witnesses—variously labeled Asiatic (Bengel), Eastern (Semler), Byzantine (Bentley), and Constantinopolitan (Griesbach)—actually were corruptions. They did so by isolating a group of those readings, showing by internal criteria that they had no claim to originality, and thus concluding that the textual witnesses (Greek and Latin manuscripts and patristic works) that exhibited those readings were unreliable for recovering the earliest form of the text of the New Testament. The main witnesses to this Syrian text, as Westcott and Hort called it, were Codex Alexandrinus (A) in the Gospels (but not in Acts and the Epistles), most of the later majuscules (uncials), and almost all the minuscules.

They then gave a fuller description of the two pre-Syrian text-types, the Western and the Alexandrian, than had been previously given. They showed that, although our chronologically earliest witnesses (Marcion, Tatian, Justin, and Irenaeus) exhibit a Western text, this text-type is not, on the whole, a reliable guide to the original text, because the scribes who transmitted this tradition were too free in the ways they handled the text, for example, adding details from oral tradition. Westcott and Hort judged that the Alexandrian text had been transmitted by scribes who carefully

---

12. A photomechanical reprint was issued by Akademische Druck, Graz, Austria, in 1974. Hendrickson (Peabody, Mass.) reprinted vol. 2 in 1988.

13. Hort was the author of vol. 2. Although he made it clear that the editors were jointly responsible for "the principles, arguments, and conclusions," Hort is justly recognized for his clear and comprehensive articulation of their textual theory. Henceforth, where reference is made to that theory, I will credit only Hort.

protected the contents of what they copied but made formal and stylistic changes in keeping with the literary scholarship at home in Alexandria. Thus, the Alexandrian text, although better than the Western, had also been subtly altered.

If neither the Syrian, Western, nor Alexandrian text embodied the original, where was it to be found? Here Westcott and Hort introduced the only real innovation in their theory. They identified a third pre-Syrian text, represented especially by Codex Vaticanus (B) and Codex Sinaiticus (ℵ), which they described as a neutral text, that is, generally free from the alterations that characterized the other three types of text. This neutral text was, for all practical purposes, the original text (with the exception of several passages in the Gospels, which will be treated in the next chapter).

As might have been anticipated, Westcott and Hort's textual theories did not immediately win over all of their contemporaries. Since the W-H text was substantially the base for the newly published Revised Version of the New Testament,[14] the latter became the point of attack for John W. Burgon, dean of Chichester. He published three savage articles against the new revision in the *Quarterly Review*; these were then gathered into a book of more than 500 pages, including material not in the original articles (Burgon 1883). The foundation of Burgon's argument was that God would not have allowed the inspired text to be transmitted by the majority of witnesses over so many centuries if the genuine text was to be found in only a handful of manuscripts. Turning Westcott and Hort's judgment upside down, Burgon declared ℵ and B to be "scandalously corrupt," "two of the least trustworthy documents in existence," "depraved" and "false witnesses." Burgon judged Codex B *"by far the foulest Text that [has] ever seen the light"* (1883, 316). Frederick Scrivener mounted a far more sober, balanced, and informed critique, the center of which was that Westcott and Hort placed far too much confidence in Codex B (Vaticanus), which, said Scrivener, "we have no right to regard … as a second Infallible Voice proceeding from the Vatican" (Scrivener 1894, 2:283). He also charged

---

14. The complete Greek text lying behind the RV was constructed by Edwin Palmer and published at Oxford (by Clarendon) in 1881, the same year the W-H text came out. Palmer used the 1550 text of Stephanus as the basis, putting at the foot of each page the readings in Stephanus that were displaced by the revisers. He was given access to the notes of Scrivener, who had charted every change that could possibly affect the translation.

them with too quickly setting aside some readings of the Syrian text based on internal arguments that Scrivener considered ill supported (287–88).

Although the W-H text met with a good deal of resistance initially, its subsequent influence confirms Epp's judgment that the most important fifty-year period in the history of New Testament textual criticism ended with the W-H text. To observe the old cliché, Westcott and Hort were able to see so far because they were standing on the shoulders of four giants: Griesbach, Lachmann, Tregelles, and Tischendorf. The acquisition of significant new materials made it possible to sharpen the methodology for reconstructing a better text and to motivate these giants to publish better models than their predecessors. The next chapter continues the story of this age of optimism as we look at these materials, methods, motives, and models.

5
The Age of Optimism (Continued): Materials, Methods, Motives, and Models

> All trustworthy restoration of corrupted texts is founded on a study of their history. (F. J. A. Hort in Westcott and Hort 1881, 2:40)

Materials

One cause for the optimism of textual critics of the nineteenth century was the continuing increase in manuscript discoveries, collations, and publications. The New Testament text of Codex Alexandrinus (A) was published in 1786, that of the Gospels and Acts of Codex Bezae (D) in 1793. Tischendorf published the text of Codex Regius (L) in 1846 and of Claromontanus (Dᴾ) in 1852. A transcription of Codex Vaticanus (B) was finally published in 1868. For all of these important majuscules, scholars no longer had to rely simply on collations but had the entire text in print. In addition to publications of known manuscripts, additional witnesses came to light.

Majuscules

א: **Codex Sinaiticus** was the most spectacular manuscript discovery of the century. No other witness to the Greek Bible is as well known as this one, because its story is so exciting that it made its way into the popular press, where it continues to delight and surprise readers.[1] Con-

---
1. See the popularizing account of Bentley 1986.

stantin Tischendorf, who brought the manuscript to light, was the first popularizer of the story.² In one of his many travels in search of biblical manuscripts, he visited the ancient Orthodox monastery of Saint Catherine at Mount Sinai in 1844. Here he claims to have seen in the great hall a basket full of old parchment leaves that were destined to be burned. He quickly determined that they were part of a copy of the Greek translation of the Old Testament (the Septuagint) and asked if he might have them. The authorities of the monastery allowed him to keep about a third of the contents, amounting to forty-three leaves, which he took back to the university library at Leipzig, where they still remain. When he published the text of these leaves in 1846, he was careful not to disclose their earlier location,³ hoping to return and recover the remainder of the manuscript.

He returned to Saint Catherine's in 1853 in search of more leaves from the manuscript, but the monks, their suspicions aroused, did not oblige him, although they permitted him to study other manuscripts in their collection. In a roll of papers, he found a further fragment of the large manuscript, containing eleven lines from Genesis, by which he was convinced that the codex had originally contained the whole of the Old Testament but that the larger part had probably been destroyed. When he came again to the monastery in 1859, his visit was sponsored by the Russian tsar, Alexander II, whose reputation as protector of Orthodoxy around the world probably enhanced the status of Tischendorf. Even so, he was unable to find other portions of the manuscript. Making ready to leave the following day, he was conversing with the steward of the monastery about the Septuagint when the steward mentioned that he, too, had a copy of the Septuagint. When the steward took the book from the red cloth in which it had been wrapped, Tischendorf was astonished to see the manuscript he had been seeking. He was permitted to take it to his room, where he spent the night studying it, discovering that it contained most of the remainder of the Old Testament, the entire New Testament, and two second-century Christian writings, the Epistle of Barnabas and

---

2. Tischendorf gave an address about the discovery at the Conference of the Protestant Church of Germany in 1864; this was later rewritten as a popular tract and translated into several languages, including English (Tischendorf 1934). My account above is summarized from this pamphlet.

3. The text contained part of 1 Chronicles, Jeremiah, Nehemiah, and Esther. Tischendorf named it the Codex Frederico-Augustanus, after Frederick Augustus, the king of Saxony, whose patronage financed so many of Tischendorf's travels.

5. THE AGE OF OPTIMISM (CONTINUED)

much of the Shepherd of Hermas. He later wrote, "I knew that I held in my hand the most precious Biblical treasure in existence—a document whose age and importance exceeded that of all the manuscripts which I had ever examined during twenty years' study of the subject" (Tischendorf 1934, 27–28). Prior to this time, the Epistle of Barnabas was extant only in a Latin translation and no copy of the Shepherd of Hermas was known to exist.

The next day, Tischendorf asked the steward for permission to take the manuscript to Cairo, where a transcription could be made, but the prior of the monastery had departed for Cairo, en route to Constantinople, so permission could not be granted. Tischendorf hurriedly set out for Cairo, where he found the prior and received his permission to have the manuscript delivered to him, after which he transcribed the 110,000 lines of text.[4]

What happened at this point has been much disputed. According to Tischendorf, he suggested to the monks that they present the manuscript to the tsar of Russia, since he was the patron and protector of the Orthodox church worldwide. The monastery, however, was in the process of having a new archbishop (abbot) approved, but the patriarch of Jerusalem refused to ratify the election, so the monks could not give over the manuscript. Eventually Tischendorf persuaded the recently elected archbishop to appeal to the patriarchs, archbishops, and bishops of the church to recognize his authority and, after this was done, Tischendorf received the manuscript "under the form of a loan" (Tischendorf 1934, 31), so that he could take it to Saint Petersburg and have a more accurate copy made. Gregory says the manuscript was a present to the tsar, not a loan, and that it was expected that the tsar would respond with a suitable present, which, in Near Eastern culture, is very much like a purchase price. The gift of the tsar included 7,000 rubles to the monks at Mount Sinai, 2,000 rubles to the monks at Cairo, a number of decorations, somewhat like honorary degrees, to the leading officials at Saint Catherine's, and a silver shrine for that monastery (Gregory 1907, 331–32).

Tischendorf had the text of the manuscript published in 1862 in four volumes, with type and layout designed to match as far as possible the

---

4. C. R. Gregory mentions that the manuscript was turned over to Tischendorf not whole but in sections (quires of eight sheets) and that he was assisted in the copying by two Germans in Cairo who knew some Greek (Gregory 1907, 330).

appearance of the original. He elevated the status of the manuscript by assigning it the first letter of the Hebrew alphabet (א) in the catalog of majuscule manuscripts, even though the letters of the Greek alphabet had not been exhausted.

The codex, dated paleographically to about 350, is in four columns (two columns in the poetic books) on leaves measuring about 15 x 13.5 inches. It is the only majuscule manuscript that contains the entire New Testament.[5] It is a witness to the Alexandrian text-type, frequently agreeing, as we have seen, with Codex Vaticanus (B), but Westcott and Hort also detected some Western readings in it, especially in the Gospel of John (Fee 1968–1969, 23–44; Brogan 2003, 18–19). Tischendorf rated the purity of the text of this manuscript a bit too high, likely because of his personal history with it. Had he lived to see the W-H text, he might well have modified his views (Gregory 1907, 337). In any case, the codex is deservedly celebrated as one of the two most valuable manuscripts of the Greek New Testament in existence, the other being Codex Vaticanus (B).

Other notable majuscules that either came to light or were first published in the nineteenth century include the following.[6]

N. Codex Purpureus Petropolitanus is a sixth-century manuscript originally containing the four Gospels. As the name indicates, this was a copy on purple-dyed vellum; the lettering is silver. It was probably made

---

5. A photographic facsimile edited by Kirsopp Lake was published by Oxford University Press (New Testament, 1911; Old Testament, 1922). After the Russian Revolution, the Soviet Union sold the codex to the British Museum for £100,000. A study of the scribal hands was published by Milne and Skeat in 1938. In 1975 the monks of Saint Catherine discovered in a sealed room an additional twelve leaves and some fragments of the codex. A detailed description of the manuscript, together with a photograph of one page, can be found in Metzger 1981, 76–78. In 2005 the four institutions holding portions of the codex agreed on a collaborative project to digitize the manuscript and make it freely available on the Internet. High-resolution, full-color digital photographs of the entire codex are now available in a searchable database, including a transcription in modern Greek characters. An international symposium on the project was held at the British Library in 2009. At that time the four institutions holding portions of the codex agreed on a statement summarizing the history of the manuscript, a narrative that generally, but not wholly, supports Tischendorf's account. See www.codexsinaiticus.org for the details.

6. I include only manuscripts containing large portions of the New Testament and whose text is largely non-Byzantine or has other features that make it intrinsically interesting. For a complete list and detailed description of witnesses known before the end of the nineteenth century, see Scrivener 1894, vol. 1.

for a person of high rank or status. Now scattered among eight locations, 227 leaves survive; Tischendorf published them in 1846. The text is mainly Byzantine but contains readings of other textual groups.

Ξ. **Codex Zacynthius** is a fragmentary palimpsest manuscript (a manuscript that has had its original text scraped or washed off and been reused) containing most of Luke 1:1–11:33 written in a seventh- to eighth-century hand and overwritten with the text of a Gospel lectionary in the twelfth or thirteenth century (Parker and Birdsall 2004, 117–31, have recently redated the manuscript). It is the oldest-known New Testament manuscript accompanied by a commentary and the only one whose commentary is written in majuscule letters. This catena (from the Latin word for "chain") commentary consists of quotations from the writings of nine church fathers, written in three of the margins surrounding the text. Its text is closely related to that of Codex B (Vaticanus) and it shares a system of chapter divisions otherwise found only in B. Tregelles published the text in 1861.

Ψ. **Codex Athous Laurae** is named for the monastery of the Laura of Athanasius on Mount Athos, where the manuscript was found by C. R. Gregory in 1886. This eighth- or ninth-century codex contains part of Mark and all of Luke, John, Acts, the Catholic Epistles (with James following 2 Peter), and the Pauline Epistles (but lacking one leaf of Hebrews). It is one of a handful of Greek and versional witnesses that contain the so-called shorter (or intermediate) ending of Mark[7] after Mark 16:8, followed by the long ending (16:9–20). It has Alexandrian and Western readings in Mark, largely Byzantine readings elsewhere.[8]

MINUSCULES

Family 13. This designation is given to a group of manuscripts of the Gospels so closely related they must have descended from the same archetype.[9] W. H. Ferrar collated manuscripts 13, 69, 124, and 346 in 1868,

---

7. "And they reported briefly to Peter and those with him all they had been told. And after these things Jesus himself also appeared and sent out through them, from the east even as far as the west, the sacred and imperishable proclamation of eternal salvation. Amen."

8. See Metzger 1981, 98–99, for description of the manuscript and a photograph of one page.

9. An archetype is a model, a copy of a text from which all other copies of that text have descended.

discovering their remarkable likeness to each other. Among other similarities, all of these manuscripts locate the story of the adulterous woman following Luke 21:38, rather than at John 7:53–8:11. This series, now known as the Ferrar Group, has been subsequently expanded to include twelve manuscripts, dating between the eleventh and fifteenth centuries.[10]

81. This manuscript, also known as Codex Augiensis, containing parts of Acts, the Catholic Epistles, and the Pauline Epistles, was copied in 1044. Its text of Acts is particularly valuable as a representative of the Alexandrian type. It was collated by Scrivener in 1859.

VERSIONAL MANUSCRIPTS

With the exception of the Latin, critical study of the early versions was still not well developed by the time of Westcott and Hort (see 1881, 2:15–59), but they did take notice of a recent discovery that promised to shed light on the development of the Syriac tradition.

In 1848 William Cureton, working at the British Museum, identified in a newly discovered codex of the Gospels a version of the Syriac older than the common revision (Peshitta). The codex (now cited as Sy^c) was assigned to the fifth century and its form of text to the second or third. The text, with an accompanying English translation, was published in 1858, well in time for Westcott and Hort to become aware of it; they make brief mention of its great significance (1881, 2:84), although it is apparent that critical study of the manuscript had only just begun.[11]

Although it had been known for some time that the Coptic had existed in at least three dialects, not even the names of the versions were agreed upon in the nineteenth century,[12] but a great many fragmentary manuscripts had been collected.[13] Work was well under way to publish the

---

10. For a photograph of one page of manuscript 124, showing the *pericope adulterae* following Luke 21:38, see Metzger 1981, 120–21. The Ferrar group has been identified with the so-called Caesarean text-type, which had not been proposed in the nineteenth century.

11. Additional parts of what was apparently the same manuscript came to light and were edited in 1872. The definitive publication of all the fragments, with extensive notes and an English translation, is Burkitt 1904.

12. Hort refers to the Memphitic, the Thebaic or Sahidic, and the Bashmuric versions (Westcott and Hort 1881, 2:85–86).

13. For the "state of the question" at the end of the nineteenth century, see Scriv-

5. THE AGE OF OPTIMISM (CONTINUED)

New Testament in Coptic, but truly critical editions of any portion of it were not yet possible.

Many of the important Old Latin manuscripts were already well-known in the eighteenth century but were restudied and published in the nineteenth; others came to light only during that era.

e, known as **Codex Palatinus**, is another "purple codex" with silver ink, dated to the fifth century. It contains the Gospels in the Western order, with a form of text similar to what Augustine used before 400 (Metzger and Ehrman 2005, 102). Tischendorf edited the text in 1847.

f, now known as the **Fleury Palimpsest** because it had once belonged to the Benedictine Abbey at Fleury, in France, is a valuable witness to the African Old Latin because it contains portions of Revelation, Acts, 1–2 Peter, and 1 John. Dating to the fifth century, it preserves a form of text close to that of Cyprian in his quotations from Acts. Although it had been only partially deciphered, Westcott and Hort were aware that it contained portions of the text of Acts (1881, 2:83).

g (gig), **Codex Gigas**, is named for its gigantic size. Not only are the pages huge (20 x 36 inches), but the manuscript contains the entire Bible as well as numerous other works, such that it is said to be too heavy for one person to lift. All of the biblical texts are from the Vulgate except for Acts and Revelation, which exhibit an Old Latin text. The codex was written in the thirteenth century in what was then Bohemia (now the Czech Republic). Its text is valuable because in Acts it agrees with the text quoted by Lucifer of Cagliari in the mid-fourth century. The text of Acts and Revelation was edited and published in 1879.[14] Westcott and Hort knew of the manuscript and its agreement with Lucifer's text (1881, 2:83).

k, **Codex Bobiensis**, is said to be the most important of all Old Latin manuscripts because of its age (ca. 400) and its witness to a form of text at home in Carthage at the time of Cyprian (ca. 250), whose quotations agree with it. Originally containing the four Gospels, it now preserves only portions of Mark and Matthew (in that order). It is the only known witness that concludes the Gospel of Mark with *only* the so-called shorter ending.[15] The manuscript had been twice edited by the mid-eighteenth

---

ener 1894, 2:91–144, which includes a general essay and updated descriptions of manuscripts of the Coptic versions by J. B. Lightfoot, G. Horner, and A. C. Headlam.

14. The manuscript is sometimes called the Devil's Bible because it contains a large representation of the devil, which may be seen in Metzger and Ehrman 2005, 104.

15. All other witnesses that contain this ending also go on to include the long

century (once by Tischendorf) and was known to Westcott and Hort (1881, 2:81).

Of the some 10,000 manuscripts of the Latin Vulgate, only two or three commanded much critical attention during the nineteenth century.

A, or **Codex Amiatinus**, which contains the complete Bible, is generally considered the best manuscript of the Vulgate. Copied in the eighth century in northern England, it was sent as a gift to Pope Gregory in 1716. Tischendorf published the New Testament portion in 1850.

Y, known as **Codex Lindisfarnensis** or the **Lindisfarne Gospels**, is valued both for its text, which is close to that of Amiatinus, and for its beautiful illuminations. An interlinear translation into Anglo-Saxon was added about 950. The text was edited in 1854–1865 and again in 1871–1887.[16]

F, **Codex Fuldensis**, is a sixth-century manuscript of the complete New Testament along with the apocryphal Epistle to the Laodiceans. It was copied for Bishop Victor of Capua in Italy and corrected and signed by the bishop. A curiosity of the codex is its translation of the Gospels in the form of a harmony that Victor traces directly to Tatian's *Diatessaron*.[17] The text was published in 1868. This was the manuscript on which Karl Lachmann largely based the Vulgate New Testament he published in 1842–1850.

PATRISTIC QUOTATIONS

Although quotations from the fathers played a crucial part in enabling Westcott and Hort to demonstrate that the Byzantine text did not exist prior to the fourth century, they did not have the benefit of any critical editions, a circumstance that Hort had lamented a few years earlier.[18]

---

ending (vv. 9–20). For a photograph of the page of Codex k with the ending of Mark, see Aland and Aland 1989, 188.

16. From the huge number of Internet sites referring to the manuscript, a quick link to an image of the first page of Matthew is www.citrinitas.com/history_of_viscom/images/books/lindisfarne.html.

17. Tatian was a scholar living in Syria who produced the first-known "harmony" of the Gospels around 170. This work, called the *Diatessaron*, meaning "through the four," wove the material of the four Gospels into one narrative. It seems to have been the only Gospel that Syrian Christians had for some centuries.

18. See Hort 1876, 5; I am grateful to Gordon Fee for this reference (1992, 250).

In summary, we would have to say that the catalog of manuscripts of the various versions known by the end of the nineteenth century is quite impressive (Scrivener 1894, 2:6–144), but this remained an era more notable for the *collection* of versional materials than for their systematic and thorough use in critical editions of the New Testament. The acquisition of new Greek manuscripts, however, greatly enhanced the efforts of editors to recover a better text, which was at least one of the goals of all the five movers of this era.

Motives

Several complementary motives are evident in the work of these nineteenth-century textual critics we have profiled. The overriding motive was the overthrow of the Textus Receptus. Some combined this with efforts to recover the best possible text of the New Testament to serve scholars and ministers. Others went still further, seeking to edify the faithful by providing a text to serve as a foundation for an up-to-date English translation.

They were agreed that for too long the public had been served by a woefully inadequate text, but there was considerable difference of opinion about the nature of the text it was possible to attain. Although Griesbach insisted against Wettstein that the oldest manuscripts were the most valuable, his base text remained the Textus Receptus. He did strike a blow against it by printing his preferred readings in the body of the text, yet he mitigated the force of that blow by using smaller type for the readings that departed from the Textus Receptus. Lachmann was quite willing to construct the text afresh, using the earliest witnesses as the basis, but his goal was a kind of "halfway house," the text as it existed around Constantinople toward the beginning of the fourth century. One could say a major motive of Lachmann was to encourage his successors to take the next steps toward an earlier form of the text.[19] Griesbach, in effect, asked, "Is there any reason for departing from the received reading?" while Lachmann asked, "Is there any reason for not giving the best attested reading?" (Tregelles 1854, 110). As we have seen, Tischendorf and Tregelles took those next steps, constructing their editions from the best evidence,

---

19. Tregelles (1854, 99) notes that Lachmann considered his text "a basis for criticism." That is, by giving a text based on readings a thousand years older than the Textus Receptus, Lachmann hoped that scholars would be able to work their way back to readings even older than the fourth century.

moving the text even further from the Textus Receptus. Westcott and Hort vigorously stated their intention of undermining the hegemony of the Textus Receptus.

Tischendorf, Tregelles, and Westcott and Hort dared to believe they could recover, in most cases, exactly what the ancient authors had written. Tischendorf paid proper homage to Lachmann by adopting only readings based on ancient authorities. At the same time, he did not rely on external evidence alone, since he judged that some of the readings attested by our most ancient witnesses are the result of critical emendations to the text; he allowed internal evidence to prevail over these primitive emendations. His aim, then, went beyond Lachmann: Tischendorf wanted to recover the original reading wherever possible, but he was aware that sometimes the best one can do is demonstrate the balance of probabilities. Another of his goals was to furnish an apparatus with enough data to enable the critical reader fully to weigh the evidence.

Tregelles took it for granted that "the object of all Textual Criticism is to present an ancient work, as far as possible, in the very words and form in which it proceeded from the writer's own hand" (Tregelles 1854, 174). Thus, Tregelles sought to edit a text of the New Testament that would give those writings "as nearly as can be done on existing evidence, such as they were when originally written in the first century" (174). When he conceived his plan (around 1836) "to form a text on the authority of ancient copies, without allowing the 'received text' any prescriptive right" (152), Tregelles was unaware of the work of Lachmann, but when he became acquainted with it, he readily acknowledged the similarity of his own approach to that of Lachmann. Although Tregelles says in one place that his proposal is to present "the text commonly received in the fourth century," he goes on to make plain that when the data will allow it, we can get "still nearer to the apostolic age" (173). But like Tischendorf, he believed that there are instances in which even the most ancient witnesses agree in citing an erroneous text and that in these cases, internal evidence outweighs external evidence. He distinguished carefully between the age of the *text* of a manuscript and the age of the manuscript itself. That is, he recognized that a scribe in the tenth century might have been copying an exemplar from the fourth century, in which case the *text* of that tenth-century manuscript was a fourth-century text. On this basis, he judged that the text of manuscript 33 (ninth century) "would give it a claim to be admitted as an authority, even though the oldest uncial documents had not been in existence" (176).

5. THE AGE OF OPTIMISM (CONTINUED)

It was Westcott and Hort who made the decisive breakthrough and were audacious enough to entitle their edition *The Original Text of the New Testament*. Although they modestly claimed that their text "makes no pretension to be more than an approximation to the purest text that might be formed from existing materials" (Westcott and Hort 1881, 2:284), they made it clear that the only improvements to their work would likely be in reducing some of the doubts between alternative readings (285). They believed they had advanced beyond the accomplishments of Tischendorf and Tregelles precisely in their ability to reduce substantially the number of such doubtful readings.

But the textual scholars who have moved the story of the New Testament text forward have generally not been interested in pure scholarship. They have done their work for the edification of the faithful. The results have filtered down to the grassroots most directly by means of new translations into the vernacular (see especially Goodspeed 1937, 75–101). In the preface to his first edition, Erasmus expressed a wish that "the gospel and the letters of Paul … were translated into all languages of all peoples" (77). It is well known that Luther, Tyndale, and the other early translators of the Bible into European languages in effect brought the Textus Receptus into common use for preaching, teaching, and devotional reading, but few people are aware that several scholars published English translations based on the text of Griesbach.[20] J. B. Rotherham published a translation based on the text of Tregelles (Rotherham 1872; rev. to the W-H text in 1897). There were even translations of individual manuscripts, including Vaticanus and Sinaiticus (Goodspeed 1937, 85–86). Although not all textual critics sought to disseminate the results of their labors to the general public, Westcott and Hort clearly did. They were members of the New Testament Company of the committee appointed in 1870 to revise the Authorized Version (KJV), and they saw to it that their Greek New Testament was made available to the company section by section, as each was completed. The resulting revision by no means slavishly follows W-H; among others, Scrivener, who was also a member of the New Testament Company, often successfully opposed Westcott and Hort's changes to the

---

20. Goodspeed 1937, 85. Not mentioned by Goodspeed is Alexander Campbell's revision of the New Testament translation of G. Campbell, Macknight, and Doddridge. Among A. Campbell's improvements to this translation were textual emendations based on the Griesbach text; see Thomas 1958.

Textus Receptus.²¹ Even so, the RV put before its readers an English text substantially free of the "Byzantine corruptions" that the two Cambridge scholars had long sought to erase.²²

Methods

We concentrate here on Westcott and Hort, whose work was the culmination and refinement of the best efforts of their predecessors. Although they were not innovators, their genius for organizing and articulating their theory of the development of the text warrants a closer look, particularly with regard to three interrelated elements of that theory: (1) internal evidence, (2) genealogical method, and (3) the neutral text.

Internal Evidence

Westcott and Hort's major weapon against the Textus Receptus was internal evidence, which, as we have seen, deals with this question: Of two or more variant readings, which best explains the origin of the other(s)? That is, which is more probably original? Arguments based on an author's habits have to do with what Hort called intrinsic probability (what the author was likely to have written); arguments based on the habits of scribes derive from what Hort called transcriptional probability (what the copyist made the author *seem* to have written). Westcott and Hort do not offer a list of text-critical canons, but the internal criteria they use in their arguments seem to be those previously articulated by Bengel, Wettstein, and Griesbach.²³ To make good judgments based on intrinsic probability, the critic has to know an author's style, vocabulary, and theology, based on the whole body of that author's work. To make good judgments based on transcriptional probability, the critic has to make some generalizations about "the causes of corruption incident to the process of transcription…,

---

21. Tregelles was also a member of the company, but his health did not permit him to attend the sessions, and he died in 1875. The story of this revision is best told in Schaff 1883, 371–494.

22. By Scrivener's own count, the base text of the RV differs from the base of the AV in 5,788 places (Schaff 1883, 419). One of the best-known of these differences will be treated below under Models.

23. Epp (1976a, 234–35) formulates a list of their implied criteria.

singling out observed proclivities of average copyists" (Westcott and Hort 1881, 2:23).

Westcott and Hort made a careful distinction between internal evidence of readings and internal evidence of documents (Westcott and Hort 1881, 2:19–39). Only two sentences in their second volume are written in uppercase letters. The first is this: "KNOWLEDGE OF DOCUMENTS SHOULD PRECEDE FINAL JUDGEMENT UPON READINGS" (31). Their point was that the textual critic needs to know as much as possible about a textual witness. The date and point of origin of a manuscript are helpful, but usually these cannot be known with certainty.[24] Still, the relative date assigned by paleographers is useful, because of the "presumption that a relatively late text is likely to be a relatively corrupt text" (5), based on the generalization that repeated copying multiplies errors. But when Westcott and Hort refer to "knowledge of documents," what they have in mind especially is the *overall quality of the readings* in that document where there are textual variations with other documents.[25] So, the first step in evaluating the quality of a document is to determine, on the basis of intrinsic and transcriptional probability, whether the document more often gets it "right" or gets it "wrong" where there are variant readings.

The reason internal evidence of documents was so important to Westcott and Hort is that they realized the weaknesses of both intrinsic and transcriptional probability. As to intrinsic probability, authors do not always conform to what we think to be their usual style; they age, change, adapt. Concerning transcriptional probability, Westcott and Hort recognized that we cannot get into the minds of copyists. We can chart their mechanical habits and characteristic mistakes, but we cannot always be certain whether a scribe is perpetuating an older "correction" to the original, or is himself "correcting" what he assumed to be an error in his exemplar. Although in most cases (so Westcott and Hort argued) intrinsic and transcriptional probability reinforce each other and enable the critic to identify what the author originally wrote, there are many

---

24. The earliest Greek New Testament manuscript with a date inscribed on it was copied in 949 (Metzger 1981, 110).

25. This is probably what Hort means when he writes, "documentary attestation has been in most cases allowed to confer the place of honour as against internal evidence" (Westcott and Hort 1881, 2:17). Curiously, it is in large part the cumulative effect of internal evidence that enables Westcott and Hort to judge where a document fits in the history of the text.

examples where we cannot distinguish with certainty between what the author wrote and what a copyist made the author seem to write. What do we do then? The answer is that we fall back on the internal evidence of documents. That is, once we have decided that a textual witness preserves a relatively "pure" (not corrupted) text, we will prefer the reading in that witness over witnesses that differ from it in cases where internal evidence of readings yields an uncertain result.

Genealogical Method

Their next step was to group together those witnesses that had a similar character of readings, under the principle that "identity of reading implies identity of origin" (Westcott and Hort 1881, 2:46). The assumption was that scribes do not often make the same alteration to a text independently of each other; if one manuscript exhibits the same pattern of readings as another, they must both derive from a common ancestor, such that a "family tree" could theoretically be constructed. This "genealogical tree of transmission" (46) would show how closely each group of documents was related to the original text. Therefore, the second principle to be written in uppercase letters is as follows: "ALL TRUSTWORTHY RESTORATION OF CORRUPTED TEXTS IS FOUNDED ON A STUDY OF THEIR HISTORY" (46). But it is crucial to realize that history here refers not to the literal historical origins and travels of a document but, rather, to its relative place in the transmission of the text.

Westcott and Hort used genealogical method as a way to confirm Bengel's dictum that "manuscripts must be weighed, rather than counted." They give the following example: Imagine that there are ten copies of an original text. An editor, noticing that nine of these manuscripts agree in their support of a variant reading against the other one, might be tempted to favor the reading supported by the nine. Another editor, making a more detailed study of all ten manuscripts, becomes convinced that nine of them share so many characteristics in common that they must all be descendants of the same parent manuscript, now lost. The editor can virtually restore this lost manuscript by careful study of the readings of the nine descendants. The result is that he is left with only two ultimate witnesses to the text: the tenth manuscript, which he has before him, and the "restored" ancestor of the other nine. Thus the value of the nine manuscripts is reduced to one (Westcott and Hort 1881, 2:40–42).

5. THE AGE OF OPTIMISM (CONTINUED)

It is important to notice that Westcott and Hort did not, as far as we know, actually attempt to trace the historical genealogy of any manuscript back through the generations, so as to produce what classical textual critics call a stemma, that is, a family tree. They showed what such a stemma might look like (Westcott and Hort 1881, 2:54), but this was a theoretical construct only.[26]

A complicating factor in the efforts to trace the genealogy of a document is the presence of "mixture" that occurs when a copyist has before him two exemplars with different types of text and he combines features of both in his copy or copies part of his manuscript from one exemplar and part from another. Westcott and Hort believed, however, that the skilled critic can compensate for the problem of mixture.

Westcott and Hort applied their weapon of internal evidence against one class of mixed readings in an effort to demonstrate conclusively that the Byzantine text (which they called Syrian) was a late, corrupt branch of the original text. They pointed this weapon against conflate readings, that is, readings in which two variant forms of the text have been combined into a third form. They used eight examples of such conflate readings from the Gospels.[27] One example will show their method at work.

Mark 9:49 contains a curious statement from Jesus (with reference to the fire of Gehenna) that occurs in three variant forms in the textual witnesses:

1. "For everyone will be salted with fire" (πᾶς γὰρ πυρὶ ἁλισθήσεται, *pas gar pyri halisthēsetai*).
2. "For every sacrifice will be salted with salt" (πᾶσα γὰρ θυσία ἁλὶ ἁλισθήσεται, *pasa gar thysia hali halisthēsetai*).
3. "For everyone will be salted with fire, and every sacrifice will be salted with salt" (πᾶς γὰρ πυρὶ ἁλισθήσεται, καὶ πᾶσα θυσία ἁλὶ ἁλισθήσεται, *pas gar pyri halisthēsetai, kai pasa thysia hali halisthēsetai*).

Westcott and Hort explain the second variant as arising from a copyist's adjustment of the text to conform to Lev 7:13, where the Greek translation of the Hebrew text reads: "Every gift of your sacrifice you will salt with

---

26. See the penetrating critique of Colwell 1947.
27. The examples are from Mark 6:33; 8:26; 9:38; 9:49; Luke 9:10; 9:54; 12:18; 24:53.

salt" (πᾶν δῶρον θυσίας ὑμῶν ἁλὶ ἁλισθήσεται, *pan dōron thysias hymōn hali halisthēsetai*). But the third variant form can only be explained as a conflation of the other two. Obviously, the conflate reading must be later than the other two forms. It happens that this third form is supported by Byzantine witnesses, while the other two forms are supported by earlier text-types. Moreover, the same thing is true of the conflate readings of all the other seven examples.

Westcott and Hort did not rest their case on these eight examples alone, but they pointed to them as typical of the character of the Syrian (Byzantine) textual family. Based on detailed study of the manuscripts, versions, and patristic quotations that make up this family, they describe the Syrian text as "conspicuously a full text ... [delighting] in pronouns, conjunctions, and expletives and supplied links of all kinds, as well as in more considerable additions" (Westcott and Hort 1881, 2:135). Its most obvious qualities are "lucidity and completeness" (134).

Westcott and Hort identified as witnesses to this text the majuscule manuscripts A (in the Gospels) E F G H S V Y, most minuscules, the Peshitta (Syriac), and quotations of the Antiochian church fathers. In seeking to date the origin of this textual family, they point out that no church father prior to Chrysostom (d. 407) quotes this type of New Testament text. Thus, the Syrian text in its full and final form is not known before the fourth century. The conclusion of Westcott and Hort is that, based on internal evidence of readings (smooth, full, interpolated, conflated), internal evidence of documents (the witnesses that have this characteristic pattern of readings), and external evidence of date (this pattern of readings unattested prior to the fourth century), "all distinctively Syrian readings may be set aside at once as certainly originating after the middle of the third century, and therefore, as far as transmission is concerned, corruptions of the apostolic text" (Westcott and Hort 1881, 2:117). With this bombshell, Westcott and Hort demolished the foundation on which the Textus Receptus had stood for 365 years.

What, then, were the sources of the Syrian text? Westcott and Hort claimed that the answer was to be found in the two previously proposed textual families, the Alexandrian and Western, "and a third" (Westcott and Hort 1881, 2:116). In a detailed analysis, they traced the origins of the Alexandrian and Western[28] texts to the second century, claiming, in fact,

---

28. They point out that Western is not a fitting designation, since readings

that the Western text contains the earliest-known readings (from Marcion, Justin Martyr, Tatian, and Irenaeus). Greek manuscript witnesses to the Western text are those previously identified (the bilinguals, especially Bezae [D] and Claromontanus [D^p]). Versional evidence includes the Old Latin and the Curetonian Syriac (Sy^c). Despite the antiquity of the Western text, they rejected most of the characteristically Western readings as inauthentic because of internal evidence of readings.[29] They describe these readings as harmonistic, involving "a love of paraphrase" and a "fondness for assimilation" (123–25).

They describe the Alexandrian text as preserving a relatively incorrupt form of the New Testament, but with grammatical and stylistic editing, which they see as "the work of careful and leisurely hands ... [which] not seldom display a delicate philological tact which unavoidably lends them at first sight a deceptive appearance of originality" (Westcott and Hort 1881, 2:131–32). To this family they assigned Greek witnesses C L 33, the Coptic Sahidic and Bohairic versions, and the quotations of Clement of Alexandria and Origen.

The Neutral Text

But the surprising development in Westcott and Hort's reconstruction of the transmission of the New Testament text was hinted at in the reference above to "a third" pre-Syrian text. This third text appears in parentheses in the table of contents and section headings as "(neutral)" (Westcott and Hort 1881, 2:xii, xiv, xv, 93, 107, 115). The parentheses are dropped at page 126, where we find "*The neutral text and its preservation*" as a heading. Westcott and Hort begin to mainstream the term at page 170, but they never give it a capital letter, which would allow it to stand alongside the Western and Alexandrian texts as a family or type. This is because they do not detect in the representatives of the neutral text evidence of either editorial revision or scribal freedom, which are characteristic of the variant readings of the other three kinds of texts. Rather, the neutral text

---

characteristic of this type are also found in the East "and probably to a great extent originated there" (Westcott and Hort 1881, 2:108).

29. They made an exception for a small group of readings they dubbed "Western non-interpolations," which will be discussed below.

is pre-Syrian, but neither Western nor Alexandrian (31); it is, precisely, neutral, that is, as close to the autographs as we are likely to get.[30]

They described only one Greek manuscript that fits this profile, namely, Codex B (Vaticanus), the text of which had finally become available in a printed edition in 1868. A slightly less-pure representative of the neutral text is Codex Sinaiticus (ℵ). Westcott and Hort judge these two manuscripts to derive from different exemplars, both of which go back to "a common original ... the date of which cannot be later than the early part of the second century, and may well be yet earlier" (Westcott and Hort 1881, 2:233). This "common original" preserves a remarkably pure form of the text. The text they published as *The New Testament in the Original Greek* bears out their belief "(1) that readings of ℵB should be accepted as the true readings until strong internal evidence is found to the contrary, and (2) that no readings of ℵB can be safely rejected absolutely, though it is sometimes right to place them only on an alternative footing, especially where they receive no support from Versions or Fathers" (225).

The decisive importance of internal evidence to Westcott and Hort is especially apparent in a set of readings to which they give the awkward name "Western non-interpolations." At these nine places (Matt 27:49; Luke 22:19–20; 24:3, 6, 12, 36, 40, 51, and 52) the Western text is notably shorter (by anywhere from two words to as many as thirty-two) than the Syrian, Alexandrian, or neutral text (except that the Syrian text joins the Western at Matt 27:49). Although there are other examples where the Western text is shorter, Westcott and Hort hold that these other examples almost always yield "a clearer and more vigorous presentation of the sense" than the original intends to convey (1881, 2:175).[31] That is not the case with these nine texts. Rather, "the original record has here, to the best of our belief, suffered interpolation in all the extant Non-Western texts" (ibid.). But why do Westcott and Hort not refer to these nine passages as "neutral interpolations"? Here they fall back on a question-begging explanation so confusing that it is not worth the trouble to summarize (127,

---

30. I have not seen this difference mentioned in other treatments of Westcott and Hort, including that of Metzger, who refers to the "Neutral," rather than the "neutral," text (Metzger 1968, 179). I believe Westcott and Hort's usage is a matter of principle, not simply of typography.

31. Westcott and Hort list an additional eighteen passages (including examples from all four Gospels) in which the Western text may have a claim to originality over against the other three text-types (1881, 2:176).

176–77). It is probably the case that they simply could not bear to describe their neutral text as an interpolated one.

I have described Westcott and Hort's methodology in some detail because their work has been so influential on the discipline. Their identification of a neutral text was the greatest weakness in their theory, as subsequent study has shown. Their greatest strength was in their generally clear, cogent, and detailed argumentation for the development of the text of the New Testament. Above all, they broke the stranglehold of the Textus Receptus for all time.

Models

The textual variants involving the largest gross amount of text in the New Testament are Mark 16:9–20 and John 7:53–8:11. Because of their long use in the church and deep familiarity from preaching, teaching, and devotional use, any attempt to relegate these texts to the margin was bound to meet with steep resistance. But the accumulation of evidence against the authenticity of these passages reached critical mass in the nineteenth century. Griesbach, Lachmann, Tischendorf, Tregelles, and Westcott and Hort all rejected them as part of the original text. It will be useful to see how the first of these texts was handled in three publications.[32]

In his *Account of the Printed Text of the Greek New Testament* (1854), Tregelles devotes fourteen pages (246–61) to Mark 16:9–20. He defends three propositions: (1) many church fathers attest to the absence of these verses from copies of the Gospel; (2) from as early as the second century, some fathers cite portions of the text of these verses; (3) the most ancient and reliable manuscripts, combined with arguments from style, confirm that Mark did not write these verses.

Tregelles performs a somewhat delicate operation. On the one hand, he gives extensive quotations from patristic sources in support of his first two propositions and cites the Greek and versional manuscript evidence in great detail, defending Codex Vaticanus (B, which does not contain these verses) against its detractors. Based on these supports, he gives as his opinion "that the *book of Mark himself* extends no further than ἐφοβοῦντο γάρ [*ephobounto gar*, for they were afraid], xvi. 8" (Tregelles

---

32. As for John 7:53–8:11, the history of the manuscript tradition of the *pericope adulterae* is given in Keith 2009, 209–31.

1854, 258). On the other hand, he accepts Mark 16:9–20, "by whomsoever written," as an authentic part of the Gospel and thus as canonical (258). How does he reach this conclusion? He accepts the argument that the text contains so many difficulties that, unless it had been recognized from an early age as containing authentic tradition about Jesus, it would have been rejected, rather than widely copied. He therefore concludes that the section is "an authentic anonymous addition to what Mark himself wrote down from the narration of St Peter" and should be received as part of the Gospel (259). Tregelles then goes on to assure his readers that inspiration does not depend on authorship by apostles (or close associates of them), since "the true and potential author was God, and not the individual writer, known or anonymous" (260).

In their edition of the text, Westcott and Hort place double brackets around Mark 16:9–20 (and around the so-called shorter ending, which is given in their text following vv. 9–20) with a marginal note to see the appendix. The appendix explains that double brackets are used to mark "specially important interpolations," earlier described as "stray relics surviving from the apostolic or subapostolic age" (Westcott and Hort 1881, 2:296). Aside from Mark 16:9–20 and John 7:53–8:11, double brackets are used only to mark the Western non-interpolations and three other noteworthy interpolations (Matt 16:2–3; Luke 22:43–44; 23:34). All such readings are, by definition, "noteworthy rejected readings," that is, judged not to be part of the original text (295).

The appendix of "Notes on Select Readings" runs to 140 pages, of which twenty-two are given over to the discussion of the two rejected endings of Mark's Gospel. Such a detailed treatment no doubt reflects the contentious debate about this text by the New Testament Company of the Revision Committee, since we know that Scrivener strongly supported the authenticity of the long ending (Scrivener 1894, 2:337–44). Without question, the discovery of Codex Sinaiticus (ℵ) by Tischendorf had strengthened the case for the authenticity of the ending at Mark 16:8, although the patristic evidence, and much of the versional, was already well known, as summarized by Tregelles in 1854. Westcott and Hort note also that the earliest examples of the Eusebian canons (an ancient system for numbering parallel sections in the Gospels) has no provision for numbering Mark 16:9–20. They also make the shrewd point that the manuscripts that contain the shorter ending (now sometimes called the intermediate ending) are, in fact, also witnesses to a text ending at verse 8, since the shorter ending was obviously composed to rectify that problematic ending. Moreover, they call

5. THE AGE OF OPTIMISM (CONTINUED)

attention to statements of Eusebius and Jerome that seem to indicate that most of the manuscripts known to these fathers ended at verse 8. They thus counter the argument that the only Greek manuscripts that end at verse 8 are Sinaiticus (ℵ) and Vaticanus (B).

As to internal evidence, they find no persuasive arguments for anyone's deliberately excising Mark 16:9–20, had they been original; on the other hand, they admit that the fit between verses 8 and 9 is so problematic that they cannot imagine anyone having written verses 9–20 expressly to repair an unsatisfactory ending. Instead, some early copyist or editor must have attached "unchanged a narrative of Christ's appearances after the Resurrection which he found in some secondary record then surviving from the preceding generation" (Westcott and Hort 1881, 2:51 Notes). Their conclusion is that we do not have the actual ending of the Gospel. Either the author was somehow prevented from concluding the work, or the ending may have been accidentally lost from the autograph, but the form of text ending at verse 8 is the earliest attested. Their decision not to relegate the long ending to the margin but to print it with the text, albeit in double brackets, shows what a powerful hold the tradition still had on them.[33]

Vernacular translations of the Bible model text-critical work for the benefit of ordinary readers of the Bible. How did the committee charged with updating the Authorized Version (KJV) deal with the textual variants at Mark 16:9–20? They included these verses, in the same type size and style as the preceding material, but left a space between verses 8 and 9. The following note is given in the lower margin: "The two oldest Greek manuscripts, and some other authorities, omit from ver. 9 to the end. Some other authorities have a different ending to the Gospel."

As we will see, Bible translation/revision committees have had great difficulty in communicating text-critical decisions to their public. Textual scholars do not need the information found in the footnote of the Revised Version because they have access to the data firsthand. On the other hand, ordinary readers do not glean enough information from the marginal

---

33. It is surprising how long-lasting has been the attempt to rescue the ending of Mark for the church while, at the same time, denying its authenticity as a part of the original text. Richard Simon laid out all the essential arguments against it as early as 1678 but then insisted that 16:9–20 contained truth as old as the rest of the Gospel and that the passage has continued to be read in the churches generally; see Delobel 1994, 100–101.

note to do them any good. Questions relating to this problem have been raised again and again, with no consensus in sight: (1) Should the editors ever retain in the translation material they have judged to be later additions to the text? (2) If so, how should they decide which material gets in and which is excluded? (3) Should the material excluded from the text be physically present in a footnote, or only alluded to? (4) How should the textual data be written up in the footnote?[34]

The period from Griesbach to Westcott and Hort saw more progress in New Testament textual criticism than any other comparable period. In fact, the general soundness of Westcott and Hort's textual theories is attested still today. But the optimism and self-confidence that greeted the twentieth century soon began to shade into doubt, even as our textual resources became richer. We turn next to this period of mixed blessings.

---

34. Even the first editions of the KJV contain notes referring to variant readings; Metzger 1968, 144, lists thirteen such notes in the New Testament section.

6
THE AGE OF THE PAPYRI: A HARVEST OF RICHES

> The discovery of the famous Chester Beatty biblical papyri …
> has added so much to our knowledge of the history of the text
> and the way in which it was produced … that a new piece of
> evidence, however small, is of quite peculiar interest. (C. H.
> Roberts 1935, 11–12)

Without question, Westcott and Hort had delivered to their readers a vastly improved text. In general, they had made good on their plan to edit a text "not disfigured with Byzantine corruptions." Although the Textus Receptus continued in use in clergy education for decades to come, the W-H text eventually acquired the status of a *new* "received text" and has remained the essential foundation for the most widely used hand editions until the present time. The beauty of Westcott and Hort's project was its elegant simplicity. When interrogated by these two scholars, the textual witnesses suggested that the text of the New Testament had been subjected in the second century to competing processes: The Western text resulted from the work of freewheeling scribes who added local color, made harmonistic corruptions, and inserted bits from oral tradition. The Alexandrian text was the result of scholars who made small philological improvements to already good texts. The Syrian revisers combined readings from these two traditions to produce a full, smooth, conflated text. Meanwhile, the original text had escaped editorial corruption in a handful of witnesses, chiefly codices Vaticanus and Sinaiticus, and often only the former. Here was to be found the neutral, that is, unedited, text.

But the ink was scarcely dry on the Westcott and Hort project before new textual discoveries called into question their reconstruction of the history of the textual tradition. They had argued that the chief versional witness to their Syrian (Byzantine) text was the Peshitta (Syriac), which they recognized as the last stage of a revision process (i.e., one could find pre-Syrian readings in the Peshitta itself). The Old Syriac manuscript recently published by William Cureton exhibited in fuller form this pre-Syrian text of the Gospels. By the time the second edition of W-H was published (1896), F. C. Burkitt was able to draw upon the evidence from another Old Syriac manuscript of the Gospels (the Sinaitic Syriac) published in 1892 to suggest some modifications to Westcott and Hort's characterization of the Syrian text (Westcott and Hort 1896, 2:330).

Burkitt's modifications were the harbingers of a vast outpouring of publications that have called into question the adequacy of the W-H text as a new Textus Receptus. In place of their elegantly simple account, their successors have written a story of mind-boggling complexity. In the next three chapters I will trace the outlines of that story, beginning in this chapter with the astonishing gains that have been made in the acquisition of ancient witnesses to the text, the materials. The following two chapters will describe the search for better methods, the expansion of motives, and the publication of new text-critical models.

Materials

Papyri

Textual critics have sometimes referred to the twentieth century as "the age of the papyri,"[1] in the same way that the nineteenth century was the age of the majuscules. The two great majuscules, Vaticanus and Sinaiticus, dwarfed all other textual witnesses in the opinion of Westcott and Hort, but papyrus manuscripts are nowhere to be found in their discussion. Tischendorf had published the first New Testament papyrus in 1868,[2] and four others had been published before 1898, but all were highly fragmentary and none of them older than the fourth century (Epp 1989b, 269–70).

---

1. Eldon Jay Epp (1989b, 262) traces this usage to a comment alleged to have been made by Theodor Mommsen in 1902. Mommsen apparently designated the nineteenth century as the age of inscriptions, but for New Testament textual critics, the nineteenth century is the era of the great majuscule manuscripts.

2. Now designated as P^{11} and containing portions of about forty verses from 1 Cor 1–7.

The stage was set for a major change in 1897, when the "big bang" of New Testament papyrus discoveries occurred at Oxyrhynchus (modern Behnesah), south of Cairo, Egypt. Here Bernard Grenfell and Arthur Hunt, of the Egypt Exploration Fund, found a leaf from an apocryphal Gospel (later identified as the Gospel of Thomas) containing sayings of Jesus and another leaf with portions of the first chapter of Matthew. The Matthew fragment, dating to the third century, is now labeled P^1 and heads up the standard catalog of New Testament manuscripts. Soon the rubbish heaps of several ancient Egyptian sites began to yield large numbers of papyrus fragments, including classical works, governmental and personal documents, private letters, and theological writings.[3] Over the next century, the work at Oxyrhynchus alone resulted in the publication of more than 5,000 manuscripts, of which forty-seven are from the New Testament (Epp 2004, 12).[4] These include portions of Matthew, Luke, John, Acts, Romans, 1 Corinthians, Galatians, Philippians, 1–2 Thessalonians, Hebrews, James, 1 John, Jude, and the Apocalypse of John.[5] Other sites in Egypt (ancient Aphroditopolis, Coptos, Medinet Madinopolis) also yielded New Testament papyri.

New Testament scholars were slow to appreciate the importance of the papyri for textual criticism. Of the forty-two New Testament papyri edited and published before 1930, almost all were fragments containing, at most, sixty to ninety verses of text. Their first editors dated few of them prior to the fourth century, the era of ℵ and B. Compared to these large and elegant majuscules, the worn and scrappy bits that early Christians had discarded along with their old letters and receipts were not impressive (Epp 1989b, 270). It was also not easy to classify and evaluate the character of text found on even the largest fragments. After all, the division of the textual tradition into three groups, Alexandrian, Western, and Byzantine (with its alternate names) had gained a firm place in New Testament textual studies, and Westcott and Hort's neutral category was vying for a seat at the table. It must have seemed natural to try to fit the papyri into these

---

3. Deissmann 1910, 24–50, is an early, semipopular account of these discoveries. A more scholarly account is E. Turner 1968, 25–41.

4. See Egypt Exploration Society 1898–. The series now numbers more than seventy volumes. The website may be accessed at www.papyrology.ox.ac.uk/POxy/papyri/the_papyri.html.

5. Eleven New Testament parchment majuscules were also found there (Epp 2004, 12).

categories. It was customary—and still is to a large extent—to describe the type of text witnessed by these various papyri as Alexandrian, neutral, אB type, Western, or mixed (276–79). (My use of these terms below is a concession to this convention, although I will show reasons why we should abandon this practice.)

It would take older manuscripts with much larger portions of text to do for the twentieth century what the great majuscules had done for the nineteenth. Such manuscripts were not being uncovered by archaeological teams working in the piles of used-up and discarded texts in Egyptian town dumps. They were much more likely to be brought to antiquities dealers by native treasure hunters poking in the ruins of ancient buildings and cemeteries. So it was that in 1930–1931, several early New Testament papyrus manuscripts preserving large quantities of text became available for purchase by a private collector. Other large-scale finds came to light in the 1950s and 1960s and finally, about seventy years after the publication of the W-H text, the importance of the papyri for textual criticism began to be appreciated on a wide front. Meanwhile, the fragmentary discoveries continued (and continue still) to be identified, so that at the time of this writing, the number of New Testament papyri in the Gregory-Aland catalog stands at 124. The following list describes some of the more important of these manuscripts. Except for a few that are of special interest in New Testament studies, I concentrate on those papyri with multiple pages surviving.[6]

P^4, P^{64}, P^{67}. Fragments of the same manuscript sometimes end up in different collections and are edited and published separately. P^4, containing portions of four leaves with material from chs. 1–6 of the Gospel of Luke, had been used as part of the binding of a codex containing two works of Philo. It was excavated by a French expedition to Coptos (Qift), Egypt, in 1889. P^{64}, consisting of fragments of a single leaf with portions of Matt 26, was purchased by a private collector in 1901. P^{67} consists of two fragments containing portions of Matt 3:9, 15; 5:20–22, 25–28; these were purchased by a different collector at an unstated time and location. All are dated to the late second/early third century. P^4 is housed in the National Library in France, P^{64} at Magdalen College, Oxford, and P^{67} at

---

6. Compare Metzger and Ehrman 2005, 53–61. Complete transcriptions of the texts of sixty-nine New Testament papyrus manuscripts, along with many photographs and paleographic descriptions, are found in Comfort and Barrett 2001; see also the continuing series of New Testament papyri edited by Wachtel and Witte 1986–.

the Fundación San Lucas Evangelista, Barcelona, Spain. In a 1977 lecture, C. H. Roberts, who originally edited P64, gave his opinion that all three papyri (P4, P64, and P67) were from the same codex (Roberts 1979, 13). T. C. Skeat supported Roberts's opinion and, after further study, concluded that the fragments were part of a second-century codex of the four Gospels in a two-column format with marginal marks to indicate section divisions (Skeat 1997, 1–24). Although Skeat's proposal that these three papyri belonged to a four-Gospel codex has attracted considerable support, it has not gone unchallenged (Head 2005, 450–57).

The manuscript is important not primarily for the character of its text[7] but because its two-column format, careful handwriting, and organization of text mark it out as probably the work of a professional scribe. Stanton (2004, 73) has suggested that the codex was likely produced for public reading in worship, but Hurtado argues that the compact page size (about 5 x 6.75 inches) more likely indicates that it was commissioned for a wealthy private reader (Hurtado 2006a, 169).

P38 and P48 are treated together because of their contents and textual character. P38 consists of a single leaf purchased in Cairo in 1924 and dated by its editor to the third century. It contains portions of Acts 18:27–19:6, 12–16, with a characteristic pattern of readings agreeing with Codex Bezae (D), seen as the best representative of the Western text in Acts. P48 is also a single leaf from another third-century codex of Acts, with portions of 23:11–17, 25–29. This Oxyrhynchus fragment is important, despite its smallness, because it also witnesses to a text best represented by Codex Bezae.

In 1930–1931 Chester Beatty, a collector of ancient books, purchased from a private dealer twelve manuscripts, eight of them with texts from the Old Testament, three with New Testament writings, and the other containing apocryphal texts and some sermons of Melito of Sardis. These were the first biblical papyri with extensive texts to come to light. Although the location of the find is not certain, Frederic Kenyon, who edited the New Testament manuscripts, conjectured that they formed part of a Christian library in the Fayum,[8] west of the Nile, where the collection

---

7. Only P4 has a substantial enough body of text to be useful for comparison with other manuscripts. Using Westcott and Hort's categories, the text is Alexandrian, agreeing closely with Codex Vaticanus in its readings against the Textus Receptus.

8. The Fayum is an oasis southwest of Memphis; see map in Pestman 1990, 305–6.

had probably been hidden in jars for safekeeping during the persecution by Diocletian (303–313).[9] The New Testament manuscripts were numbered P[45], P[46], and P[47].

P[45]. This codex, dated by Kenyon to the first half of the third century, originally had about 220 leaves and contained the four Gospels and Acts. Only two partial leaves of Matthew and two of John survive; Mark is represented by six leaves, Luke by seven, and Acts by thirteen.

As soon as it was published, P[45] presented problems for those seeking to relate its text to the standard groupings.[10] Even the latest revision of Metzger's handbook shows how problematic it was (and is) to use the W-H nomenclature to provide reference points. The book refers to a new local text, dubbed Caesarean, which Metzger uses to describe the text of Mark in P[45]. We then meet the description "intermediate between the Alexandrian and Western" to characterize the text of the other Gospels. Finally, the text of Acts is said to be "decidedly nearer the Alexandrian [with] none of the major variants characteristic of the Western text of this book, though it has some of the minor ones" (Metzger and Ehrman 2005, 54).

P[46]. This manuscript was sold piecemeal, with Chester Beatty eventually acquiring fifty-six leaves and the University of Michigan thirty leaves of a codex originally made up of 104 leaves.[11] The eighty-six extant leaves contain Epistles traditionally treated as Paul's, in the following order: Romans, Hebrews, 1–2 Corinthians, Ephesians, Galatians, Philippians, Colossians, and 1 Thessalonians. The original contents are still debated; although the missing pages at the beginning would have contained Rom 1:1–5:16,[12] what the manuscript would have included on the pages missing at the end is uncertain (Epp 2002b, 495–502).

---

9. See Kenyon 1933–1937. In addition to critical introductions, full-size color plates and transcriptions of all manuscripts are included.

10. These efforts, extending from around 1935 to 1949, are summarized in Klijn 1949, 132–46; cf. Epp 1989b, 278–79.

11. We know the original size because fourteen pages (seven leaves) are missing from Romans, which is surely the first epistle in the collection; thus fourteen pages must be missing from the end, since this is a single-quire codex. For a full-color image of one page, see www.katapi.org.uk/BibleMSS/P46.htm.

12. The first extant page begins in the middle of Rom 5:17; by counting the average number of letters per line and lines per page, paleographers determine how much text is missing.

As the earliest manuscript of the Paulines (dated around 200 C.E.), P46 drew a great deal of critical attention. The position of Hebrews following Romans is unusual (but not unique); its inclusion in the Pauline canon shows how highly it was esteemed in the East (Kenyon 1937, 74). The manuscript is unique in placing the doxology in Romans (which occurs in six different locations among textual witnesses) following 15:33.[13] The text of P46 was evaluated in light of the Westcott-Hort groupings and was generally recognized as siding with their neutral text. But a classicist, Günther Zuntz, produced a study that went from the other direction, beginning with P46 as the standard and evaluating other witnesses to the Pauline corpus against the Beatty papyrus. He found P46 to be "a uniquely important manuscript … giving the true wording, sometimes alone or with few and unexpected allies, more often in numerous but not uniform company" (Zuntz 1953, 56).

P47 added critically important evidence for the text of Revelation, which is poorly attested. Prior to the discovery of this manuscript, Codex Sinaiticus was the oldest Greek witness to the Apocalypse. Kenyon dated P47 to the second half of the third century. The manuscript contains ten leaves of a codex (with the text of 9:10–17:2) that was probably thirty-two leaves long originally. It proved to be related to the same text-group as Sinaiticus.

P52 has probably been seen by more students of the New Testament than any other manuscript, for its photograph appears on many dust jackets or book covers.[14] This tiny scrap (about 2.5 x 3.5 inches) from the Gospel of John (18:31–33, 37–38) is, by a wide consensus, the oldest known fragment of any part of the New Testament, dated by several paleographers within the first half of the second century. When C. H. Roberts identified the piece in 1934 while examining unpublished papyri at the John Rylands Library in Manchester, England, he thought it so important that he published a small book devoted to the find (Roberts 1935). Since the Gospel of John is generally thought not to have been written until 85–100 C.E., to have a manuscript of it that was in use perhaps no more than twenty-five to fifty years later, in a place far removed from Ephesus,

---

13. For the other locations and discussion of the doxology, see Metzger 1994, 470–73.

14. I can quickly put my hands on four such books on my own shelves.

where the Gospel was likely written, makes the document all the more important.[15]

The next discoveries of New Testament papyri with extensive portions of text occurred in 1952, when Martin Bodmer, a book collector from Geneva, purchased three codices subsequently numbered P[66], P[72], and P[75]. All had apparently been found in the ruins of an ancient monastery near Dishnā, in Upper Egypt (Robinson 1986, 2–26).

P[66] originally contained the Gospel of John in a codex of 156 pages, of which 104 remain, preserving the text from 1:1 to 14:26 almost complete (6:11–35 are missing) and 14:29–21:9 in fragmentary condition.[16] Its editor dated it to around 200; most other paleographers who have examined the codex have concurred. Because of its beautiful calligraphy, coupled with the widespread corrections to the text that have been made against a second copy, Colwell suggested that P[66] may have been copied in a scriptorium (Colwell 1965, 382). The manuscript contains more than 400 singular readings, nearly half of them the result of carelessness in copying, and most of them corrected by the scribe himself.[17] It is the oldest known witness that does not contain the pericope of the adulteress (John 7:53–8:11).

Metzger's comment that "the text of P[66] is mixed, with elements that are typically Alexandrian and Western" (Metzger and Ehrman 2005, 57) is in line with the general assessment of textual critics. In fact, by the time P[66] was published, it was becoming clear that none of the large papyri had a "pure" text, a fact that was raising a number of questions about the history of the New Testament text as reconstructed by Westcott and Hort and their early successors.

P[72] was edited by Michel Testuz (1959). Textual critics have been interested primarily in the fact that this manuscript contains the earliest known copy (third century) of Jude and 1–2 Peter, but the additional writ-

---

15. See a color image of the verso of the fragment at www.kchanson.com/ANCDOCS/greek/johnpap.html. Black-and-white photographs of both sides, with description, are found in Metzger 1981, 62–63.

16. The *editio princeps* was published by V. Martin in 1956. An additional thirty-nine fragments were later published by Martin in 1962. These volumes include black-and-white photographs of the entire manuscript.

17. See Metzger 1981, 8, where a plate showing John 11:30–31 reveals a half-dozen corrections. The most thorough study of scribal habits in the early papyri is Royse 2008. Royse devotes pp. 398–540 (!) to P[66].

ings contained in the codex make it of interest for other reasons as well. The contents include, in this order: Nativity of Mary, Apocryphal Correspondence of Paul and the Corinthians, the eleventh Ode of Solomon, the Epistle of Jude, Melito's Homily on the Passover, a hymn fragment, the Apology of Phileas, Pss 33 and 34, and the two Epistles of Peter. Moreover, as many as six scribes copied these writings, which were assembled into a composite codex in the early fourth century (Haines-Eitzen 2000, 96–104). Because of the small page size (about 6 x 5.75 inches), Testuz judged that the codex was produced for a wealthy individual for his own, rather than public, use. The codex has obvious implications for the history of early Christian devotion, including issues related to canon formation (Epp 2002a, 491–93).[18] The text of 1 Peter is said to have affinities with the Alexandrian group, especially Codex Vaticanus (B; Kubo 1975, 152) and Codex Alexandrinus (A; Metzger and Ehrman 2005, 58). Its text in 2 Peter and Jude is mixed.

P^{75} (in connection with P^{66}) put the papyri solidly on the text-critical map. The two "gave the Bodmer and all early papyri a new status" (Epp 1989b, 283). The manuscript apparently came from the same monastic library as P^{66}. It is a single-quire codex of the Gospels of Luke and John, originally containing seventy-two leaves (144 pages) in a tall, narrow format (about 10.25 x 5.125 inches), written between about 175 and 225, making it the earliest known copy of Luke and possibly the earliest known of any considerable part of John. The surviving 102 pages contain the greatest portion of Luke and about half of John.[19]

As soon as it was published, P^{75} surprised the text-critical world because its text is remarkably similar to that of Codex Vaticanus; in fact, P^{75} and B are more closely related than any other early New Testament manuscripts (Royse 2008, 616–17). They share some readings not known from any other witnesses. Not long after the W-H edition, several scholars had

---

18. The composite nature of the codex is not apparent to the casual reader of secondary literature, because the contents were published as *Papyrus Bodmer V* (1958), *Papyrus Bodmer X–XII* (1959), *Papyrus Bodmer VII–IX* (1959), *Papyrus Bodmer XIII* (1960), *Papyrus Bodmer XX* (1964), this last edited by Victor Martin.

19. See Martin and Kasser 1961. Like P^{66}, this edition contains photographic facsimiles of each page. For a full-color image showing the end of Luke and the beginning of John go to www.earlham.edu/~seidti/iam/tc_pap75.html. For additions to the *editio princeps*, see Lakmann 2007, 22–41; I am grateful to Parker 2008, 320, for this reference.

Five Important Papyrus Manuscripts				
Siglum	Name	Date	Contents	Importance
P45	P.Chest.Beatty I	third century	portions of all three Gospels and Acts	intermediate between Alexandrian and Western
P46	P.Chest.Beatty II+P.Mich.222	third century	portions of most of the Paulines	age and amount of text contained
P47	P.Chest.Beatty III	third century	Rev 9:10–17:2	text agrees closely with Sinaiticus
P66	P. Bodmer II	third century	about two-thirds of Gospel of John	quality and quantity of text
P75	P.Bodmer XIV–XV	third century	large portion of Luke and about half of John	text almost identical with Vaticanus

argued that the B-type text—Hort's neutral text—was actually the result of a fourth-century recension of the text in Alexandria. The discovery of P75 thus pushed the origin of the B-type text back into the second century and raised the question whether this was a recension (a revised text) at all.[20] P75 also shares with some witnesses of the Coptic version a few otherwise unique readings, including at John 10:7 Jesus' words "I am the shepherd [ὁ ποιμήν, *ho poimēn*] of the sheep," where most witnesses read "I am the door [ἡ θύρα, *hē thyra*] of the sheep." The most often-remarked agreement with the Coptic is at Luke 16:19, where, when the man who ignored Lazarus is mentioned, the text of P75 reads "a rich man *named* Νευῆς [*Neuēs*]," here agreeing with the Sahidic, which reproduces a tradition of the Coptic church that the man's name was Nineveh.[21] In 2006 P75 was purchased by

---

20. Calvin Porter opened the question (1962, 363–76); Carlo M. Martini dealt with the issue more fully and directly (1977); see also Fee 1974, 19–45.

21. Both of these examples are taken from Metzger and Ehrman 2005, 59. Metzger explains that the scribe intended to write *nineuēs* but accidentally omitted the initial *ni*; see the discussion of other possibilities in Royse 2008, 687–90.

the Vatican Library, perhaps because the text of P⁷⁵ is so closely related to that of Codex Vaticanus (B).

Majuscules

Some manuscripts are worth knowing about for their artistic merit and what they tell us about the social and economic status of some persons in the medieval church, as well as for the place of these manuscripts in the history of the text. Codex Purpureus Petropolitanus (N) was profiled in the last chapter. Other similarly ornamented manuscripts were published in the late nineteenth or early twentieth centuries. Among the finest examples are the three below, all of which have also been drawn into the discussion over the proposed Caesarean text, later to be discussed.

O, which is known as **Codex Sinopensis** from its place of acquisition, Sinope in Asia Minor, was purchased in 1899. Dated to the sixth century, it is one of several surviving manuscripts written with gold ink on purple vellum, similar to Codex Purpureus Petropolitanus (N), which was written with silver ink. The codex contains forty-three leaves of the Gospel of Matthew and five miniature illustrations. It is housed in the National Library in Paris.

Σ, known as **Codex Rossanensis**, containing the Gospels of Matthew and Mark, is another purple manuscript with silver lettering (gold in the first three lines of each Gospel). The sixth-century codex is ornamented with seventeen miniatures in watercolor.²² The text is said to agree closely with that of Codex N.

Φ, **Codex Beratinus**, is another sixth-century purple vellum with silver ink. Like Σ, it was probably a four-Gospel manuscript but now contains only Matthew and Mark. Its chief interest for textual critics is a lengthy addition to Matt 20:28, which is also found in Bezae (D) and a few versional witnesses to the Western text. The addition, which has to do with not seeking a prominent place when invited to dine, is explained by Metzger as "a piece of floating tradition, an expanded but inferior version of Lk 14.8–10" (Metzger 1994, 43).

W is undoubtedly the most important majuscule New Testament manuscript in the United States. Purchased by Charles W. Freer in 1906,

---

22. For a black-and-white example of an illustration portraying Jesus before Pilate, see Metzger and Ehrman 2005, fig. 14. Photographic reproduction with color plates was published in Muñoz 1907.

it is known as **Codex Freerianus** or **Codex Washingtonianus** (**Washingtonensis**), from its location in the Freer Art Gallery of the Smithsonian Institution in Washington, D.C. This fourth/fifth century codex has 187 leaves containing the four Gospels (lacking only Mark 15:13–38 and John 14:25–16:7) in the Western order (Matthew, John, Luke, Mark).

The text represents a remarkable example of block mixture. Using the conventional categories, Matthew and part of Luke (8:13–24:53) exhibit a Byzantine-type text; Mark 1:1–5:30 is Western; Mark 5:31–16:20 is of that Western/Alexandrian mixture that would come later to be called Caesarean; Luke 1:1–8:12 and John 5:12–21:25 are Alexandrian. Since the codex also exhibits variations in its method of paragraphing, its first editor thought the ancestor of W had been patched together from fragments of several Gospel manuscripts.

Codex W is famous also because it is the only Greek manuscript that adds, near the end of the Gospel of Mark (after 16:14), the following words, attested in part by Jerome:

> And they excused themselves, saying, "This age of lawlessness and unbelief is under Satan, who does not allow the truth and power of God to prevail over the unclean things of the spirits. Therefore reveal thy righteousness now"—thus they spoke to Christ. And Christ replied to them, "The term of years for Satan's power has been fulfilled, but other terrible things draw near. And for those who have sinned I was delivered over to death, that they may return to the truth and sin no more; that they may inherit the spiritual and incorruptible glory of righteousness which is in heaven."[23] (Metzger and Ehrman 2005, 81)

In recognition of the centennial of the acquisition of Codex Washingtonianus, the Society of Biblical Literature included a special section on the Freer Collection in its 2006 Annual Meeting in Washington, D.C. The papers from that meeting were published that same year (Hurtado 2006b).

Θ, known as **Codex Koridethi** from having resided in a church at Koridethi, in the Caucasus near the Black Sea, contains the four Gospels. The codex is now in Tbilisi, in the Republic of Georgia. Because of its eccentric style of handwriting, it is difficult to date, but its original edi-

---

23. For a plate of Codex W containing this "Freer Logian," see Metzger 1981, 83. For color images of the entire manuscript, go to www.scntm.org-/manuscripts/GA032/.

	Five Important Majuscule Manuscripts				
Siglum	Name	Date	Contents	Importance	
ℵ 01	Sinaiticus	fourth century	complete NT	only complete copy of NT in majuscule	
A 02	Alexandrinus	fifth century	most of NT	in Gospels, oldest manuscript with Byzantine text	
B 03	Vaticanus	fourth century	NT except Heb 9:14–end, Timothy, Titus, Philemon	earliest Alexandrian manuscript with most of NT	
D 05	Bezae	fifth century	Most of text of Gospels and Acts	best representative of Western text	
W 032	Washingtonianus	fourth/fifth century	Gospels	contains examples of four text-types in block mixture	

tors assigned it to the ninth century. Metzger opines that the scribe was a Georgian not accustomed to writing Greek (Metzger 1981, 100–101, with plate).

The manuscript is celebrated chiefly for its text of Mark, which has been found to be closely related to Family 1, Family 13, and the minuscules 28, 565, and 700, all members of an ancient text-type later to be named Caesarean (Lake and Blake 1923, 267–86). The codex also shares with a group of minuscules the reading at Matt 27:16–17 where Barabbas is named Jesus Barabbas. As we saw in chapter 2, several other manuscripts have a marginal note attesting that in some ancient manuscripts, Barabbas is called Jesus; Origen also comments on the variant reading, which confirms its antiquity.

Minuscules

Of the roughly 2,800 minuscule New Testament manuscripts known to exist today, between 900 and 1,000 of these were known at the end of the nineteenth century, but relatively few had been completely collated and their texts made available in printed form. Westcott and Hort lamented "this large amount of present ignorance respecting the contents of cursives," noting that "valuable texts may lie hidden among them" (Westcott and Hort 1881, 2:77). Not only have nearly 2,000 New Testament minuscules come to light since Westcott and Hort, but collations and editions of several important ones have been published, and progress has been made in identifying the distinctive texts of related groups of minuscules. Some of these minuscules and groups most likely to be encountered in popular hand editions of the Greek New Testament are mentioned here.[24]

565 is a ninth-century purple parchment codex of the Gospels, written in gold ink. Its text in Mark is close to that of Θ. The text of Mark and collations of the other Gospels were published in 1885.

579 is a thirteenth-century codex of the Gospels with an Alexandrian text that often agrees with B, ℵ, and L in Mark, Luke, and John and with a late Byzantine text in Matthew. An edition of the Alexandrian portions was published in 1903.

614 is a thirteenth-century manuscript of Acts and the Pauline and General Epistles. It is noteworthy for its pre-Byzantine readings, many of which agree with Codex Bezae. The text of Acts was published in 1934.[25]

700, another Gospels codex of the eleventh century, has a text distinctively different from the Textus Receptus, including 270 unique readings. Metzger notes that it shares with only one other Greek manuscript the reading in Luke 11:2, "May your Holy Spirit come upon us and cleanse us," in place of "May your kingdom come," agreeing with Marcion and Gregory of Nyssa in this curious variant (Metzger and Ehrman 2005, 90). A collation was published in 1890.[26]

---

24. For others and for bibliographical information, see Metzger and Ehrman 2005, 86–92, from which I have drawn much for this section. For three synopses and tables showing which Greek manuscripts appear in the apparatuses of several Greek New Testaments, see J. Elliott 1987.

25. For a photograph of a page of 614, see Aland and Aland 1989, 149.

26. For a photograph of the page containing Luke 11:2–8 and description of the manuscript, see Metzger 1981, 122–23.

1241, dating from the twelfth century, contains the entire New Testament except for Revelation in a form of text agreeing often with Alexandrian readings but more heavily Byzantine in Matthew and Mark.

1582, a Gospels codex written in 948, has recently been shown to exhibit in the Gospel of Matthew a text and marginal notes related to the text Origen used in the third century.

1739, known as the **Von der Goltz Codex**, is a remarkable tenth-century manuscript discovered in 1879 by E. Von der Goltz in the Laura at Mount Athos. It contains Acts and the Pauline and General Epistles in "a relatively pure form of the Alexandrian type" (Metzger and Ehrman 2005, 91). Since it contains marginal notes taken from Irenaeus, Clement of Alexandria, Origen, and Basil (329–379) but none of the later fathers), students of the manuscript have concluded that it was copied from a fourth-century majuscule exemplar. Von der Goltz published the text in 1899.[27]

Family 13. Brief attention was given in the last chapter to the Ferrar Group of minuscules (13, 69, 124, and 346). Further studies have added several other manuscripts to this group, which Kirsopp Lake designated Family 13 (Lake and Lake 1941; Geerlings 1961a).

LECTIONARIES

Lectionary manuscripts have been, and still remain, the most neglected of witnesses to the New Testament text (Osburn 1995, 61–74). Although many editions of the Greek New Testament from Wettstein on have made sporadic use of lectionaries, no major edition until recent years has attempted regular and systematic citation of lectionary evidence.[28] In 1932 E. C. Colwell inaugurated a project at the University of Chicago with the aim of producing a critical lectionary text.[29] A series of PhD projects, master's theses, and shorter publications appeared over the next thirty years (Wikgren 1963), greatly enhancing our knowledge of the lectionary text

---

27. For a photograph of one page and description of the manuscript, see Metzger 1981, 112–13.

28. The volumes on the Gospels of Luke (1984, 1987) and John (1995–) in the International Greek New Testament Project (IGNTP) make selective but systematic and rational use of lectionary manuscripts; see Osburn 1995, 69.

29. See Colwell and Riddle 1933. The articles in this short volume lay out the terminology and methodology for future research.

Five Important Minuscule Manuscripts

Siglum	Name	Date	Contents	Importance
33	queen of the cursives	ninth century	NT except Revelation	mostly Alexandrian text-type
Fam. 1	(mss 1, 118, 131, 209, 1582)	twelfth–fourteenth century	Gospels	influential in development of Caesarean text hypothesis
614		thirteenth century	Acts and Epistles	contains many Western readings
1739	Von der Goltz Codex	tenth century	Acts and Epistles	copy of a fourth-century manuscript of Alexandrian type
2053		thirteenth century	Revelation	one of the best witnesses to early text of Revelation

and its history; the aim of publishing a critical text, however, was not met. Still debated are the origins of the lectionary system, the precise relationship of the lectionary text to the running text of the New Testament, and the extent to which the lectionary text has introduced variant readings into the running text.

Versional Manuscripts

The publication of the Gospels in the Curetonian Syriac manuscript confirmed Westcott and Hort's surmise—held also by Griesbach and J. L. Hug—that an Old Syriac text had once existed. In 1892, the year of Hort's death, another Old Syriac manuscript came to light.

Sinaitic Syriac (Sy^s) is the name given to a palimpsest manuscript discovered by Agnes Smith Lewis in Saint Catherine's Monastery on

Mount Sinai. From a codex originally containing 166 leaves, 142 survive, preserving in the underwriting a fourth-century copy of the Gospels in a version agreeing remarkably with the Curetonian and perhaps representing a slightly older form of the Old Syriac.[30] F. C. Burkitt was able to bring its evidence to bear in an appendix to the second edition of the W-H text (1896).[31] These two Old Syriac manuscripts undergirded Hort's argument that the Peshitta reflected not "a true representation of its original text" but a revision made to conform to later Greek manuscripts (Westcott and Hort 1881, 2:84; cf. 156, 159). Predictably, defenders of the Textus Receptus turned this argument on its head, arguing that the Curetonian and Sinaitic Syriac manuscripts represented a later, degenerate form of the Syriac, but this counterargument was impossible to sustain.[32]

No other Old Syriac New Testament manuscripts are known, either for the Gospels or for any other part of the New Testament. Scholars have attempted to recover remnants of an Old Syriac text of Acts and the Epistles by studying the quotations of Syriac patristic writers[33] and the Armenian version of the New Testament, which may derive from a Syriac base (Metzger 1977, 164–69).

Many scholars have turned to Tatian's **Diatessaron** (ca. 170 C.E.) as the earliest version of the Syriac Gospels, but this is still a much-debated issue and is connected with the question whether the original language of the *Diatessaron* was Syriac or Greek (Metzger 1977, 25–48). A small fragment generally thought to be from a Greek copy of Tatian's *Diatessaron* dating from before 257 was unearthed in 1933 at Dura-Europos on the Euphrates,[34] but the connection of this ancient harmony with Tatian has been challenged (Parker, Taylor, and Goodacre 1999, 192–228). In relation to the studies of the history and textual complexion of the Syriac

---

30. For a photograph of a page of Sy^s, see Aland and Aland 1989, 195.
31. The definitive edition of the manuscript is Lewis 1910.
32. For a fascinating account of this development, see North 1999, 10–16.
33. For one example, see Baarda 1995, 101–3, where Baarda attempts a hypothetical reconstruction of the Old Syriac form of 1 Cor 1:27 and Heb 5:7. The relevant literature consists of three collections, all dated to the fourth century: the Demonstrations of Aphrahat "the Persian Sage," the prose and poetry of Ephrem of Nisibim and Edessa, and the ascetical writings under the title *Liber Graduum*; see Brock 1995, 224–36.
34. See Kraeling 1936. For the text of the fragment, see Metzger and Ehrman 2005, 133. The fragment carries the Gregory-Aland number 0212.

Bible, Diatessaronic studies are probably the most vexing and demanding of all subspecialties (Petersen 1994).

Although there are many editions of the Peshitta (Syriac) in print, a critical edition of the complete Syriac New Testament in its later and earlier attestation will require careful sifting of all the Syriac patristic evidence.[35] A critical edition of the Gospels can be found in the work of G. A. Kiraz (1996).

As to Coptic versions, Westcott and Hort judged both the Bohairic (which they called Memphitic) and the Sahidic (which they also called Thebaic) to be "founded on a very ancient Non-Western text" (Westcott and Hort 1881, 2:157).[36] They thought the Bohairic to be slightly the earlier of the two,[37] just the reverse of the current consensus. The Sahidic manuscripts available at that time were highly fragmentary and none earlier than the eighth century (Metzger 1977, 23; see the detailed list in Scrivener 1894, 2:110–44). Since the Bohairic survived to become the official version of the Coptic church, many more manuscripts of this dialect were available, although most were quite late.[38] No doubt the Westcott-Hort textual theories were in part responsible for an interest in compiling the known Coptic witnesses and searching out others.

George Horner published utilitarian editions of both the Bohairic (Horner 1898–1905) and the Sahidic (Horner 1911–1924). His method was to print as the base text the oldest manuscript of each portion of the New Testament (Gospels, Acts, etc.) and to register the variants of other manuscripts in the apparatus. Although they are not critical editions,

---

35. For a survey of the later revisions and the manuscripts and editions that exhibit them, see Metzger 1977, 48–80. One can see facsimiles of some Syriac manuscripts in Vogels 1929, plates 42–45. The INTF in Münster is in process of publishing a complete edition of the text of the Harklean Syriac; see B. Aland 1986; Aland and Juckel 1991–2002.

36. Subsequent studies have confirmed that both the Sahidic and Bohairic in general reflect an Alexandrian text, although Metzger points out that in the Gospels and Acts, the Sahidic "has many Western readings" (Metzger 1977, 110).

37. They also knew a third version, the Fayyumic, which they called Bashmuric. Although there is still some disagreement about the variety of dialects in which Coptic translations were made, NA[27] refers to the following: Akhmimic, Subachmimic, Bohairic, Middle Egyptian (two variant forms), Proto-Bohairic, and Sahidic; see introduction to NA[27], 68.

38. Evidence from the Coptic had been cited in the editions of Fell and Mill; a complete edition of the Bohairic was published as early as 1716.

Horner's publications supplied a kind of "working text" for several generations of students who would be attracted into Coptic studies. His edition of the Bohairic included the elements of a Coptic grammar as well as detailed descriptions of many of the manuscripts. The twentieth century has seen a rich outpouring of Coptic manuscript discoveries[39] and critical studies, some of the most important of which are summarized below (Wisse 1995, 131–41).

MS. PPalau Rib. Inv.-Nr. 181, 182, and 183 refers to a fifth-century manuscript containing Mark, Luke, and John in Sahidic, now housed in Barcelona. Its editor compared the readings of this codex to MS 569, a ninth-century manuscript of the Gospels in the Pierpont Morgan Library in New York, and two manuscripts in the Chester Beatty Library (Quecke 1972a, 1972b, 1984).

Chester Beatty Manuscripts A and B are complete codices of, respectively, the Pauline Epistles and the book of Acts with the Gospel of John following. These were purchased for the Chester Beatty Library in 1924–1925. Dating from around 600, they are the earliest Coptic witnesses to Acts and the Paulines with "a complete and homogeneous text" (Metzger 1977, 114).[40]

Manuscript Q designates a codex containing a nearly complete copy of the Gospel of John written in the sub-Akhmimic dialect (closely related to the Sahidic), probably in the late fourth century. The papyrus codex was found wrapped in a rag, deposited in a broken crock, and buried in a cemetery near a village in Egypt, possibly because it had become worn from church use. Because of its early date and the importance of its location, the manuscript was published as a large-format complete photographic facsimile with the transcription of each page facing the original and an English translation following (Thompson 1924).

The **Crosby Codex (Mississippi Codex)**, part of the papyri collection at the University of Mississippi, is a single-quire codex containing an unusual assortment of writings, among which is a complete copy of 1 Peter in Sahidic, dating to the third/fourth century (Willis 1990, 135–216).[41]

---

39. Several hundred manuscripts are already catalogued in the ongoing series by Schmitz and Mink 1986–1991.

40. For published edition, see Thompson 1932.

41. The other writings include part of 2 Maccabees, Jonah, and Melito's Homily on the Passion.

The **Scheide Codex**, written in Middle Egyptian and dating to around the end of the fourth century, contains one of the earliest complete copies of the Gospel of Matthew in existence in any language (Schenke 1981).

The **Glazier Codex** (G^{67}), acquired at the same time as the Scheide Codex and written on pages exactly the same size, contains the text of Acts 1:1–15:3 in Middle Egyptian dating to the fifth century and now housed in the Pierpont Morgan Library. Although the beginning of Acts is extant, the manuscript contains no title and ends at 15:3, with the next page left blank and the following one painted with a miniature (Metzger 1977, 118–19; for critical edition, see Schenke 1991). The manuscript is especially valuable as a representative of the Western text (Epp 2003, 118–23).

Papyrus Bodmer III is noteworthy as the oldest known manuscript in Bohairic with a substantial portion of text (fourth century). This papyrus codex contains most of the Gospel of John and about three chapters of Genesis. Its editor, Rodolphe Kasser, described the language as proto-Bohairic (Kasser 1958).

There has been no appreciable increase in manuscript evidence for the New Testament in Latin in the twentieth century, but enormous progress has been made in the publication of critical texts (Petzer 1995, 113–30). Pierre Sabatier pioneered efforts to publish critical editions of the Old Latin text in the mid-eighteenth century (Metzger 1977, 319). Sabatier's work has been honored and advanced by the establishment of the Vetus Latina Institute in connection with the Benedictine Archabbey in Beuron, Germany. Since 1949 the Institute has published a series of volumes presenting a critical edition of portions of the Old Latin Bible (*Vetus Latina* 1949–).[42] For each book of the New Testament, the editors print the Nestle-Aland Greek text, the Old Latin text in the various forms exhibited in the available manuscripts (as well as Vulgate manuscripts to the ninth century), and all patristic quotations up to 1000 c.e. This series is the current standard for the critical text of the Old Latin Bible.[43] The Institute for New Testament Textual Research has published an edition of the Old

---

42. For history of the Institute and its work, see http://erzabtei-beuron.de/kultur/vetus_latina.php.

43. The series for the entire Bible is projected to run to twenty-seven volumes, with eleven devoted to the New Testament. As of this writing, the fascicles on Ephesians, Philippians and Colossians, 1–2 Thessalonians, 1–2 Timothy, Titus, Philemon, Hebrews, Catholic Epistles, and Revelation have been published. Annual research reports can be accessed at www.vetus-latina.de.

Latin Gospels without a critical apparatus but with the variants of known manuscripts listed (Jülicher, Matzkow, and Aland 1963–1976). Among editions of the Latin Vulgate, the most serviceable is available through the American Bible Society as a companion to the UBS Greek text (Fischer et al., 1983).

CHURCH FATHERS

Westcott and Hort relied heavily on patristic quotations to demonstrate the presence of different forms of the Greek text at various times and places during the first four centuries of the church, but they were aware of the difficulty of recovering the Greek text behind the citations and allusions of all the fathers (Westcott and Hort 1881, 2:110–15). Even to the present, the citation of patristic support for variant readings in popular hand editions of the New Testament is not always reliable (Fee 1995, 194). The primary reason is that editors of these texts often do not have critical editions of the fathers but must work from collections of the data that have not been rigorously controlled. Fortunately, textual scholars working today have a growing number of reliable tools to help in recovering the patristic texts (Fee 1995, 191–207; North 1995, 208–23; Brock 1995, 224–36). The major resources in this toolkit include the following.

Clavis patrum graecorum (*CPG*; 1974–1987) is "the absolutely indispensable guidebook to the Greek Fathers and their works" (Fee 1995, 195). There is a companion key to the Latin fathers, *Clavis patrum latinorum* (*CPL*; 1961). These resources list the works of each of the fathers and the critical editions of their writings, along with other bibliography.

Biblia patristica indicates its usefulness by the subtitle: *Index des citations et allusions bibliques dans la littérature patristique* (1975–1991). Here one can find indexed by book, chapter, and verse the Old Testament and New Testament quotations and allusions of all the fathers of the second and third centuries, as well as selected fathers of the third and fourth centuries.

The happiest development has been the publication of critical editions of many of the fathers. A noteworthy series devoted to offering reliable texts of the Greek fathers began publication in 1991 under the title The New Testament in the Greek Fathers.[44] The ultimate aim of these

---

44. Edited from 1991 to 1998 by Bart Ehrman, from 1998 to 2009 by Michael

efforts is to produce a more accurate critical apparatus to the Greek New Testament.[45]

Textual critics prior to the nineteenth century were hampered by a dearth of textual witnesses in critical editions. Tischendorf, Tregelles, and Westcott and Hort had the benefit of working with more and better materials than their predecessors, but the sheer number of witnesses to the text was already becoming a problem. Today's textual critic is faced with an embarrassment of riches, including, especially, the papyri, none of which were used in creating the W-H text. During much of the twentieth century and beyond, the most difficult challenge has been to organize and evaluate the data. One would expect, given the increase in material witnesses, that textual scholars would also have been able to produce a better edition of the New Testament text than Westcott and Hort were able to edit. But, as we shall see, this is a question still up for debate.

Holmes, and from 2010 to the present by Roderic L. Mullen (Atlanta: Society of Biblical Literature).

45. For suggestions of how best to evaluate the data and his example of what such an apparatus might look like, see Fee 1995, 201–4.

7
The Age of Consensus, the Age of Doubt

> Our dilemma seems to be that we know too much to believe the old, but we do not yet know enough to create the new. (E. C. Colwell 1947, 83)

As we saw in the last chapter, discoveries of papyrus fragments of New Testament documents older than the great majuscules began to surface in Egypt even before the deaths of Westcott and Hort. But it was only in the second quarter of the twentieth century that papyri with considerable portions of text became available. As important as these new discoveries were, to say nothing of the additional witnesses surveyed above, they did not immediately result in a sea change in New Testament textual criticism.

For better or worse, Westcott and Hort staked out the territory that would occupy New Testament textual critics for a very long time. The two principles they expressed in uppercase letters provide convenient markers by which to trace the movements of the discipline in the twentieth century. Here they are once more, this time embedded in their original sentences:

> The first step towards obtaining a sure foundation is the consistent application of the principle that KNOWLEDGE OF DOCUMENTS SHOULD PRECEDE FINAL JUDGMENT UPON READINGS. ... It may be laid down ... emphatically, as a second principle, that ALL TRUSTWORTHY RESTORATION OF CORRUPTED TEXTS IS FOUNDED ON THE STUDY OF THEIR HISTORY, that is, of the relations of descent or affinity which connect the several documents. (Westcott and Hort 1881, 2:31, 40)

Reduced to the essentials, these two dicta (in reverse order) emphasize the twin responsibilities of (1) studying documents in all their historical relationships and (2) judging the quality of readings within these documents. In classical text-critical language, the first task is *recensio*, establishing the relationship of extant copies to each other such that one could draw a family tree (stemma) back to the original (Maas 1958). The second task is *examinatio*, making rational judgments from among variant readings as to which is the original in a given variation unit.[1]

Movers, Methods, Models

It is possible to organize and track much of the development of New Testament textual criticism in the twentieth century in relation to these two tasks (Birdsall 1970, 308–77). But, as we will see, each of these responsibilities has to be adapted to the particular challenges presented by the number and character of the witnesses to the text; each responsibility entails an extremely complex set of skills and operations, and each raises new questions in every generation. Since the number of witnesses to the text has increased dramatically since Westcott and Hort, an important contribution to the registration system should first be noted.

A Better Reference System

When Wettstein devised his reference system for New Testament manuscripts, he had only twenty-two majuscules to deal with; by the time of Tischendorf's eighth edition, eighty-eight majuscules were known, to say nothing of minuscules and lectionaries (Parker 1995, 26–27).[2] By 1900 the reference system had become so confusing and unwieldy that a major revision was needed. In 1908 Casper René Gregory devised a plan that is still in use.[3] In his system, papyri are referred to by a Gothic or Old English 𝔓 prefixed to a supralinear number ($𝔓^1$, $𝔓^2$, $𝔓^3$). Majuscules are identified by Arabic numerals with a zero prefixed (01, 02, 03); in deference to custom, Gregory retained the capital letters for majuscules

---

1. The third operation in classical textual criticism, *emendatio*, will be touched upon in the next chapter. For the term "variation unit," see Colwell 1964, 253–61 and Epp 1976b, 153–73.
2. Parker points out that two of these majuscules were papyri and eleven were lectionaries.
3. Gregory (1908, 1–30) details how he arrived at the system; for a clear explanation of the system, see Aland and Aland 1989, 73–75.

through 045, so that ℵ (01) or 01 (ℵ) may be seen with reference to Codex Sinaiticus, A (02) or 02 A for Alexandrinus, and so on. Minuscules are identified by simple Arabic numerals (1, 2, 3). Lectionaries have a cursive letter ℓ prefixed to an Arabic numeral (ℓ 1, ℓ 2, ℓ 3). Although the system is not altogether rational—papyri and lectionaries are separated not by handwriting but by other criteria—it has proved to be serviceable.[4] The ongoing registry of New Testament manuscripts (sometimes called the Gregory-Aland list) is maintained by the Institute for New Testament Textual Research (Institut für neutestamentliche Textforschung) at the University of Münster in Germany.[5] During the twentieth century, textual critics devoted a great deal of energy to trying to work out the relationships among the witnesses in this registry.

History of Documents: "Relations of Descent or Affinity"

Two factors make it impossible to draw up a family tree of New Testament manuscripts. In the first place, there are simply too many documents to deal with (and not enough known about their history). In the second place, the presence of mixture within documents is so pervasive as to make it impossible to trace all the "family relations." To use a different analogy, if a stream issues from an underground source and divides into several branches, it is relatively easy to trace all the branches back to their source. But if all those branches subsequently empty into the same river, each may contribute some unique mineral or vegetable content to the river, but it will be extremely difficult to separate these contents and assign each to its parent stream. As is well known, Westcott and Hort wrote much about genealogical relations of manuscripts, but their application of genealogical principles was theoretical, as shown by their model stemma in volume 2, where they explain: "Let us suppose that the extant descendants [of a single lost original] are fourteen, denoted as *abcdefghiklmno*" (Westcott and Hort 1881, 2:54). Although they (and their predecessors back to Bengel) had assigned textual witnesses into groups, such group-

---

4. Gregory did not include the versional and patristic evidence in his system. The current generally accepted reference system for the versions and Fathers is detailed in NA^{27}, 63*–76*.

5. On 11 February 2009, the Institute's website (http://www.uni-muenster.de/NTTextforschung/) yielded the following numbers: papyri through P^{124}, majuscules through 0318, minuscules through 2882, and lectionaries through ℓ 2436.

ings were rough-and-ready, based on readings they shared in common against a standard text of some kind. What was needed was a more reliable way of grouping manuscripts.

As we saw in the last chapter, there are some small groups of manuscripts that agree so remarkably in their readings, age, and history that they can be traced back to the same place of origin (Family 13, for example). But is it possible to classify and group the whole mass of witnesses to the New Testament text, based on shared readings? Hermann Freiherr von Soden (1852–1914) attempted to do this in his edition of the Greek New Testament published in 1902–1913. Thanks to the assistance of a wealthy patron, Elise König, he was able to hire forty-five assistants to help him collate and edit manuscripts, his aim being to examine every known witness to the New Testament text. Von Soden created a new reference system designed to indicate the contents, age, and text-type to which he assigned each witness. The system is so complicated that it requires the reader to consult three different apparatuses and to interpret a variety of new symbols that might as well be "meaningless hieroglyphs" (Metzger and Ehrman 2005, 187), unless the reader consults a detailed key.[6]

Based on comments by Jerome, von Soden was convinced that the text of the Greek Bible (Old Testament and New Testament) had been transmitted in three editions (Metzger 1963a, 3–4). He referred to the most widespread of these as the Koine text (Westcott and Hort's Syrian), attributed to Lucian of Antioch and designated by the siglum K. A second text-type, represented by Sinaiticus, Vaticanus, a few minuscules, Sahidic and Bohairic Coptic, and some Egyptian fathers, he traced to Alexandria—this would be Westcott and Hort's Alexandrian and neutral texts rolled into one—and attributed these to a little-known figure Jerome cites named Hesychius. This is the H text. Von Soden identified the remainder of the witnesses, including Codex Bezae (D), the Koridethi Codex (Θ), and many minuscules with a mixed text as representatives of Jerome's Palestinian codices, which Origen had supposedly edited and Eusebius and Pamphilus published. Von Soden preferred the name Ierosoluma (Jerusalem) and designated this the I text. In passages where all three text-types agree, we have the I-H-K text, which, with minor exceptions, constitutes the earliest attainable text, the lost archetype attested first by Origen.

---

6. For an explanation of the system, a photographic plate of a page, and an interpretation of the sample page, see Aland and Aland 1989, 40–47.

Where two of the types agree against the third, the two represent (with some exceptions) the earliest form.[7] Although von Soden's textual reconstruction has been thoroughly discredited, he succeeded in classifying 1,260 minuscules, identifying many subgroups of minuscules in each of the K and I text-types. His demonstration that the late medieval text (the K text) was not uniform but had been progressively modified stylistically and verbally was groundbreaking. The resulting subgroups have formed the basis for all subsequent attempts to classify the formidable mass of minuscule manuscripts (Epp 1967, 27–29). Nevertheless, von Soden's published text was widely judged to be far less reliable than that of Tischendorf, which he was attempting to replace, as well as that of Westcott and Hort. Except for his multiple K groups, von Soden's subgroups have generally not proved helpful.

Other scholars, rather than attempting to organize the entire body of witnesses to the text, sought to make incremental improvements in Westcott and Hort's genealogical method. One way was to isolate other small groups of manuscripts such as the Ferrar Group, which was identified in 1868. Scholars subsequently added eight more manuscripts to the original four of this group. In 1902 Kirsopp Lake published a study of four minuscules (1, 118, 131, 209) so closely related that they appeared to constitute a distinct group, especially in the Gospel of Mark (Lake 1902).[8] Lake suggested the name Family 1 for this group and Family 13 for the Ferrar Group. Moreover, Lake showed that these two groups are related to each other (perhaps we might think of cousins). But, curiously, their disagreements with the Textus Receptus fell into odd patterns: although each group had its own distinctive array of readings, the two groups together shared some readings with Hort's neutral witnesses, other readings with Old Latin and Old Syriac witnesses, and still others with Western witnesses. Although Westcott and Hort would probably have cited all these readings simply as evidence of the mixture characteristic of late medieval manuscripts, Lake noted that a few other minuscules (22, 28, 565, and 700), not themselves members of either Family 13 or Family 1, agreed with both groups in their strange alignments with the text-types Westcott and Hort had identified. How was one to explain these phenomena?

---

7. For a clear and succinct overview of von Soden's complicated theory of textual development, see Kenyon 1937, 179–86.

8. Lake subsequently added manuscript 1582 to the group.

The Koridethi Codex (Θ) came to the rescue. Although in Matthew, Luke, and John its text is generally Byzantine, in Mark it frequently departs from the Byzantine witnesses to agree with 565, Family 1, Family 13, 28, and 700. For example, at Matt 27:16–17, manuscripts Θ, 1, 118, 209, 700, and 1582 all give the name of Barabbas as Jesus Barabbas. Kirsopp Lake and Robert P. Blake pointed out the pattern of readings Koridethi shared with the minuscules and minuscule groups above. They were convinced they had identified a new text-type, distinctive from those in the Westcott-Hort system (Lake and Blake 1923, 267–86). Burnett Hillman Streeter (1874–1937), working independently from Lake and Blake, also believed he had uncovered a new text-type; it was he who gave it the name Caesarean.

In 1924 Streeter published an imaginative reconstruction of the origins of the four Gospels (Streeter 1924). He suggested that not only was each of the Gospels produced in a major church center (Mark–Rome; Matthew–Antioch; Luke–Achaea [Corinth?]; John–Ephesus), but when the four Gospels were all in circulation, distinctive local texts of these would have developed in each of the great episcopal sees. Streeter identified Hort's neutral and Alexandrian texts as, respectively, an earlier and later form of the text standardized at Alexandria; the Western text represented the ancient Roman text as standardized in forms recognized in the African and European Old Latin (one form standardized in Carthage, the other in Ephesus). He identified the Old Syriac as a translation of the text fixed in Antioch. Where, then, did the text represented by the Koridethi Codex and its associates fit in? Streeter believed the answer lay in the Markan quotations of Origen after he moved from Alexandria to Caesarea (231 C.E.). Studies of variant forms of the text of Mark quoted by Origen led Streeter to the conclusion that prior to this move, Origen quoted the Gospel of Mark from an Alexandrian text; after the move, he used a text agreeing with manuscript Θ and its allies, a text Streeter described as "the old text of Caesarea" (Streeter 1924, 100). These local texts all contributed to the revised text promulgated by Lucian of Antioch around 310, which became the Byzantine standard text.[9]

Support for Streeter's reconstruction of the history of a Caesarean text quickly began to erode, owing to more careful study of Origen's New

---

9. See the two charts in Streeter 1924, 26, comparing his theory of local texts with that of Hort; see the chart on p. 108, where primary and secondary textual witnesses are assigned to each local text.

7. THE AGE OF CONSENSUS, THE AGE OF DOUBT   137

Testament quotations while in Alexandria and Caesarea, more sophisticated evaluation of variant readings, and the publication of P^{45}, which appeared to exhibit a Caesarean text in an Egyptian manuscript dated to the third century, a text that probably went back to the second century (Metzger 1963a, 42–72). Shortly, one began to read of a prerecensional or a pre-Caesarean text. By the 1940s, the Caesarean text was "disintegrating" (67). There had been difficulty from the beginning in defining the precise character of the text represented by Family 1, Family 13, Θ, and the minuscules associated with them, since what united them was not readings unique to their group but a distinctive *selection* of Alexandrian (or neutral) and Western readings. Was the Caesarean text really a neutral text corrected by Western readings, or a Western text corrected by neutral readings? Was it a *process* defined by mixture, or a distinct *edition* made at some place and time?

THE SEARCH FOR BETTER METHODS OF GROUPING: THREE NOTEWORTHY EFFORTS[10]

Even as the connection of the Koridethi group (for want of a better term) with Caesarea was growing tenuous, so also was the theory that the established text-types (Alexandrian, Western, Byzantine) all resulted from deliberate editorial revisions in discrete geographical locations. By the 1960s, we had papyri dating from the third century, all from Egypt, representing all of the proposed textual groups except the Byzantine. Moreover, the text of P^{75} was so close to that of Vaticanus (B) that, as noted above, it pushed back the idea of an Alexandrian recension to the mid-second century and even called into question the whole notion of early textual recensions. Clearly, if Hort's genealogical method was going to survive, work would be needed on both the methodology of grouping witnesses and the terminology for referring to these groups (Colwell 1947).

Prior to the twentieth century, there were no quantitative standards for determining how to place a manuscript within a group. The typical practice was simply to count up the number of times a certain manuscript agreed with, say, the quotations of Origen when that father disagreed with a chosen standard, usually the Textus Receptus. Left out of consideration was the question of how often the manuscript *failed* to agree with Origen

---

10. See further Ehrman 1987a, 2–45.

in his differences from the Textus Receptus, as well as how often each of the witnesses *agreed* with the Textus Receptus. The usual method was based on agreement in variation from a standard, rather than agreement or variation in total text.

In a series of studies, Ernest C. Colwell (1901–1974), with contributions from Ernest W. Tune and Merrill M. Parvis, developed a three-step method for classifying textual witnesses into definable groups (Colwell 1959, 1961, 1965). Step one was to draw up a list of places where there are multiple (at least three) variant forms of the text and see how a textual witness aligns with others in support of those variations.[11] Having identified the group the witness most closely resembles, Colwell moved to step two, determining whether the witness in question supports the *distinctive* readings of the group (one of Colwell's "essential criteria" for identifying members of a text-type is that all members of the group must contain some readings that are peculiar to this group when compared to other text-types). Step three was to establish that the witness agrees with the other members of the group in a *large majority* of all readings (at least 70 percent) where the evidence is divided and that it is separated from its nearest neighbor group by at least 10 percent of its readings (Colwell and Tune 1963, 28–29). Since not every textual witness can be collated against every other textual witness, Colwell and Tune identified as representative of "the majority of manuscript groupings known today" (ibid., 28) the following manuscripts: TR P^{45} P^{66c} P^{75} ℵ ℵ^c A A^c B D W W^c Θ Ψ Ω Cr 565. Each of these sources would be collated against each of the others.

In a demonstration study, Colwell and Tune selected a portion of text large enough to offer hundreds of places of variation, namely, John 11. When they removed common scribal errors and singular readings from consideration, they were left with one hundred places in which at least two witnesses agree against the others. Colwell and Tune recorded in a table the percentage of agreement of each manuscript with each of the other manuscripts (Colwell and Tune 1963, 30–31). They confirmed an identifiable Beta text-type (Westcott and Hort's neutral plus Alexandrian), with members agreeing ± 70–92 percent and an identifiable Alpha text-type (Westcott and Hort's Syrian), with members agreeing

---

11. Colwell was building upon and refining E. A. Hutton's method of "Triple Readings" in Hutton 1911. In Colwell's scheme, each of the variant forms had to be supported by previously established groups, one of the ancient versions, or a manuscript widely recognized as distinctive (Colwell 1959, 758–59).

± 70–93 percent. The Delta (Westcott and Hort's Western) and Gamma (the putative Caesarean) groups did not emerge as distinctive text-types, at least in John 11.[12] Were a person to compare the readings of a newly discovered manuscript in these hundred places of variation in John 11, it should be possible to confirm whether that new manuscript belonged to one of the four groups above (or at least whether it belonged to the Beta or Alpha groups).

There are obvious shortcomings in Colwell's practice of quantitative analysis, especially its inability to overcome the presence of block mixture, which often results from the use of two or more exemplars to produce a new copy.[13] Nevertheless, Colwell's studies marked a major advance in the methodology for identifying the quantitative relationship among textual witnesses. This has been confirmed, for example, by Gordon Fee's use and refinement of Colwell's method in his analysis of Codex Sinaiticus (א) in the Gospel of John (Fee 1968–1969, 27–38), among other studies (Wisse 1982).

Any attempt to group and classify New Testament manuscripts must reckon with the enormous mass of minuscules, far too large to permit complete collations. Although von Soden did manage to classify almost 1,300 minuscules and assign them to various subgroups of his K and I texts, he did not develop a consistent and systematic method of collation. Both the achievements and limitations of von Soden's method became apparent when two of Colwell's students, Paul McReynolds and Frederik Wisse, were asked to classify 1,385 minuscule manuscripts of the Gospel of Luke. Their purpose was to obtain a representative sample of minuscules to include in the critical apparatus of Luke being prepared by the International Greek New Testament Project (IGNTP). Since the base text for the IGNTP was the 1873 Oxford edition of the Textus Receptus, McReynolds and Wisse were directed to select manuscripts for the apparatus based on their variations from the Textus Receptus, as determined by quantitative analysis.

Their study of von Soden's K and I groups disclosed distinctive patterns in the combination of readings these groups shared in relation to

---

12. That is, the witnesses to these two putative text-types did not meet the 70 percent/10 percent standards Colwell had set. L. Richards (1977) demonstrated the weakness of prescribing a set percentage of agreement among witnesses to a text-type. Colwell adopted the group symbols Alpha, Beta, Gamma, and Delta from Frederic Kenyon (Aland and Aland 1989, 106).

13. See this and other criticisms in Ehrman 1987b, 468–71.

the Textus Receptus. McReynolds and Wisse decided that when two-thirds of the members of one of these known groups shared the same distinctive pattern of variations from the Textus Receptus, the *profile* of the group was visible. In order, then, to see where a previously unclassified manuscript belongs among these groups, it need only be compared in those readings that disclose the profile of the group. Five members of the IGNTP committee, including McReynolds and Wisse, decided that the group profiles for Luke should be based on variants in chapters 1, 10, and 20 (i.e., the beginning, middle, and end of the Gospel), so as to mitigate the possible effects of block mixture. Application of the method facilitated the selection of 128 minuscules to be represented in the apparatus of the IGNTP volumes on Luke. Obviously, the Claremont Profile Method is not a substitute for a complete quantitative analysis of textual witnesses; its value lies in the possibility of making a quick, if rough-and-ready, decision about how to classify and group a previously uncollated document.[14]

The methods outlined above classify manuscripts within traditional textual groups or subgroups (e.g., Alexandrian, Western, K^i, K^r) based on shared readings. Kurt and Barbara Aland developed a classification system for the Institute for New Testament Textual Research without reference to the traditional groupings. Convinced that local texts (i.e., text-types) did not develop before the fourth century, they rejected the use of the traditional terms to describe the second- and third-century manuscripts that had come to light in the twentieth century (Aland and Aland 1989, 50–71). Rather, they argued, these early copies (which were mostly papyri) represent a "living text," free from editorial control. These papyri exhibit a spectrum of copying tendencies in relation to their fidelity to the parent text: some were copied very carefully, some less carefully, some wildly, and some paraphrastically. From these copies arose a strict text, a normal text, a free text and a paraphrastic text. Manuscripts containing a strict text are judged to have transmitted most faithfully the original text. Although the Alands do not explain their criteria for identifying the original text, their strict text is roughly equivalent to Hort's neutral text (Petzer 1994, 32).

The Alands then created five categories within which all textual witnesses can be divided. Category one includes all manuscripts before the

---

14. See the critique of Ehrman (1987b, 471–86), where he advocates and illustrates what he calls "the comprehensive profile method."

third/fourth century. Their age alone gives them a special quality. Here all the early witnesses to what eventually came to be called the Alexandrian text-type are placed. Category two includes manuscripts that also have a special quality and are useful for establishing the original text even though they contain "alien influences (particularly of the Byzantine text)" (Aland and Aland 1989, 106). Category three contains manuscripts "of a distinctive character with an independent text" (ibid.). These witnesses are important for reconstructing the history of the text but also may contribute to establishing the original text. Manuscripts related to Codex Bezae (i.e., sharing its readings) make up category four. Category five consists of manuscripts "with a purely or predominantly Byzantine text."[15] By comparing a previously uncollated manuscript to the readings of 1,000 test passages (*Teststellen*) from the New Testament, the Alands are able to place the witness in one of the five categories.

The purpose of this classification system is not, as with the other two, to group manuscripts based on their genealogical relationship (except perhaps for categories four and five). Rather, it is to decide which manuscripts are useful for (1) establishing the original text or (2) contributing to the history of the text. A major function of the system is the negative purpose of recognizing which manuscripts (those with D-type and strictly Byzantine readings) can be excluded from the textual apparatus of the NA^{26} text (which the Alands, as a "working hypothesis," identify with the "ancient text" or the "original text"; Aland and Aland 1989, 333). The circularity of the process has often been commented upon: one dismisses manuscripts that do not support the original text, which is most nearly represented by the NA^{26} text; at the same time, one constructs the NA^{26} text on the basis of manuscripts that contain the original text.

CAN WE DISPENSE WITH LOCAL TEXTS?

From Bengel to Streeter, local texts reigned. Whereas Bengel had identified two (African and Asiatic), Streeter had construed as many as five (Alexandria, Antioch, Caesarea, Italy/Gaul, and Carthage). But by the late nineteenth century it was already clear that text-types could not be

---

15. Ibid. Descriptive lists of the papyri, all the majuscules, and 175 minuscules, with their category assignments, can be found in Aland and Aland 1989, 96–138. More detailed descriptions of the categories appear on 335–36.

so neatly traced back to discrete geographical locations. As early as 1901 Frederic Kenyon had proposed a system of identifying text-types without reference to geography: the Greek letters *alpha* (α), *beta* (β), *gamma* (γ), and *delta* (δ) represented, respectively, the Byzantine, Alexandrian, Caesarean, and Western text-types (Kenyon 1912, 315–63). After numerous New Testament papyri had been discovered dating to a period before any official recensions of the text would have appeared, it seemed anachronistic to classify these manuscripts according to their agreement with the texts of the later majuscule manuscripts. Colwell adopted Kenyon's terminology on the basis that it made no claims about the text and that it was memorable (Colwell 1958, 73 n. 2). The Alands, as we have seen, abandoned the local/genealogical approach and instituted their own system.

At a 1988 conference, Eldon Jay Epp suggested replacing the conventional terms Alexandrian text, Western text, and others with "textual group" or "textual cluster," since "these terms lack the offensive implications of a rigidly fixed form or a tightly integrated character and … they avoid the attribution to textual groups of an officially conveyed status" (Epp 1989c, 85–86). In his published paper he proposed to use symbols that are arbitrary and at the same time connected with past research, taking the roman alphabet, rather than the Greek, to represent the four textual clusters A, B, C, D. Cluster (or group) A calls to mind the "average" or "accepted" text that became the majority text, best represented by Codex Alexandrinus (A). Group B includes those textual witnesses that display the text associated with P^{75} and Codex Vaticanus (B). Epp introduces group D next, a cluster including P^{38}, P^{48}, and P^{69} and representing a text later found in Codex Bezae (D). Group C represents the text found in P^{45} and parts of Codex Washingtonianus (W), inaccurately labeled by some as Caesarean. The letter C reminds us that this textual cluster is described as related to both the B and D texts. Once a person has understood the significance of C as representing an in-between textual group, it can take its proper place in the sequence A, B, C, D. Of these four, only group A will be acknowledged by all to be a distinct entity, a genuine text-type that came into existence sometime in the fourth century. In the remainder of the article, Epp identifies the closer and more distant members of each textual cluster, using Colwell's benchmark of 70 percent agreement among members of the group and a gap of about 10 percent from neighboring groups, but acknowledging that only P^{45} and W come near 70 percent agreement in the C cluster (Epp 1989c, 97).

Beyond the "Historical-Documentary" Method of Westcott and Hort?

In reading such a quick and condensed survey of efforts to group and classify witnesses to the New Testament text, it is possible to forget the purpose of this immense and creative effort, namely, to improve upon Westcott and Hort's reconstruction of the text of the New Testament and its history. The gains in our material evidence for the text—more and earlier manuscripts—and our methodological advances in grouping and classifying witnesses are strikingly evident. But it can be—and has been—argued that neither the critical New Testament texts that have been published nor the textual histories that have been attempted have advanced us significantly beyond Westcott and Hort (Epp 1974, 386–414). Some scholars have therefore proposed that we focus more on individual readings of the witnesses than on the historical-genealogical relationships of manuscripts.

Westcott and Hort distinguished between internal evidence of *readings* and internal evidence of *documents*, but the difference was not as great as one might suppose. The internal evidence of readings has to do with which of two readings makes the best sense contextually, grammatically, and stylistically (intrinsic evidence) and which reading a scribe was most likely to have changed to make it more agreeable to the reader (transcriptional evidence). Internal evidence of documents has to do largely with which manuscripts consistently furnish better readings than other manuscripts: "Where one of the documents is found habitually to contain these morally certain or at least strongly preferred readings, and the other habitually to contain their rejected rivals, we can have no doubt, first, that the text of the first has been transmitted in comparative purity, and that the text of the second has suffered comparatively large corruption" (Westcott and Hort 1881, 2:32).

When we have identified a manuscript that has transmitted the text "in comparative purity," we will prefer the reading of that manuscript where there is a variation difficult to decide on intrinsic and transcriptional grounds. So Hort's first principle called upon the reader not to make a final judgment upon a variant reading without first considering which of the supporting manuscripts had the best "batting average," so to speak.

But some scholars have argued that the value Westcott and Hort placed upon Codex Vaticanus (B) as the manuscript that "far exceeds all other documents in neutrality of text" (Westcott and Hort 1881, 2:171) resulted in a "cult of the best manuscript," that is, a tendency to rely too much on the documentary support for a reading rather than the internal grounds for that reading (J. Elliott 1972, 339–40). In place of "the best manuscript," they have argued, we should think only of the best reading. In J. K. Elliott's pithy phrase, "the cult of the best manuscripts gives way to the cult of the best readings" (J. Elliott 1992, 28).

The Preference for Internal Evidence of Readings: "Thoroughgoing Eclecticism"

In a series of notes on the Gospel of Mark published during the 1920s, C. H. Turner introduced the principle, "Knowledge of an author's usage should precede final judgment," thus turning Hort's famous dictum on its head (C. Turner 1923–1927, 25:377). In case after case, Turner decided between variant readings based largely on Markan style. His methods have been refined and expanded by two Oxford scholars, G. D. Kilpatrick (1910–1989) and Kilpatrick's student J. K. Elliott, both of whom have concentrated exclusively or primarily on individual readings rather than external evidence in deciding textual variants. This approach has been described variously as "rational criticism,"[16] "rigorous eclecticism" (Kilpatrick 1943, 36), and "thoroughgoing eclecticism" (Elliott's preferred term; see J. Elliott 1995, 321).

Eclecticism implies selection from among possibilities—but what possibilities? Thoroughgoing eclectics choose readings based on the context, the author's style, usage, and theology, and the fitness of one reading to account for the origin of the other(s). The resulting eclectic text will contain readings deriving from a variety of witnesses, even from a single Greek or versional manuscript.[17] Thoroughgoing (or rigorous) eclectics argue that all significant textual corruption occurred before the end of the second century, that is, before almost all of the manuscripts we possess were copied. Therefore, not only is it impossible to recover an archetype of the New Testament text from documentary evidence, it is not really important, because the original reading might have survived anywhere within the tradition. Responding to criticism that thoroughgoing eclectics

---

16. From the title of M.-J. Lagrange's *La Critique Rationnelle*, vol. 2 of his *Critique textuelle* (1935).

17. See Metzger and Ehrman 2005, 225, for the list of readings adopted by Kilpatrick in his *Greek-English Diglot*.

are not interested in history, Elliott replies that they are interested in "a history of textual variation" rather than "a history of documents" (J. Elliott 1992, 37).

Although Kilpatrick and Elliott have been unyielding in their commitment to internal evidence as the basis for establishing the text, they have had few followers.[18] But they have influenced the discipline to the extent that by midcentury, most New Testament textual critics seemed to have embraced a kind of eclectic criticism, though not thoroughgoing or rigorous eclecticism.

The twentieth-century debate over method has resulted in the near consensus that the only kind of text we are capable of producing is an eclectic text. For example, F. C. Grant claimed that the translation committee of the RSV chose each reading from the Greek text "on its own merits" and not by following one type of text (Grant 1946, 41). The Greek text behind the NEB is even more eclectic than that of the RSV (see Tasker 1964). Although it is not claimed that the UBS Greek text is eclectic, Metzger (1994, 10*–14*) clearly indicates that eclectic criteria were used to construct the text. The question is not *whether* an eclectic text, but rather, to use the title of an essay by Gordon Fee, "Rigorous or Reasoned Eclecticism—Which?" (Fee 1976).

The manifold increase in early manuscripts and the massive efforts to chart their interrelationships led scholars to hope that they would be able to reconstruct the history of the text, but this has not occurred. Does this mean, then, that all New Testament manuscripts are equally important simply as repositories of readings? Most textual critics have not thought so. Rather, the consensus tends toward a reasoned eclecticism, that is, a judicious use of both external and internal criteria in making textual decisions.[19] Reasoned eclectics continue to appeal to the age of the witnesses that support a reading, as well as the geographical distribution of these

---

18. But see, for one example, Ross 1998, 59–72, who argues the case for sixteen textual variants on the basis of intrinsic evidence alone.

19. Epp defines the eclectic approach as "a method (1) that treats each text-critical problem … separately and largely in isolation from other problems, (2) that 'chooses' or 'selects' (*eklegomai*) from among the available and recognized text-critical criteria those that presumably are appropriate to that particular text-critical situation, and (3) that then applies the selected criteria in such a way as to 'pick' or 'choose' (*eklegomai*) a reading from one or another manuscript and thereby arrive at a text-critical decision for that particular variation-unit" (Epp 1976a, 212).

witnesses. They believe that the general quality of manuscripts can be judged, that some preserve better readings more often than others do. At the same time, readings that commend themselves because they are supported by good witnesses must also be shown to be superior by intrinsic and transcriptional probability—internal evidence.[20]

In a paper read in 1975 for the Textual Criticism Section of the Society of Biblical Literature, Eldon Epp raised a key question about the eclectic method: Is it a solution or a symptom (Epp 1976a)? That is, can it enable us to produce the best possible New Testament text, or is it only a symptom of our continuing inability to reconstruct the earliest history of the text on a documentary basis? In a widely quoted survey article in 1956, K. W. Clark clearly saw the eclectic method as "a secondary and tentative method ... suitable only for exploration and experimentation." He went on to say, "The eclectic method, by its very nature, belongs to a day like ours in which we know only that the traditional theory of the text is faulty but cannot yet see clearly to correct the fault" (Clark 1956, 37–38). In 1989 Epp reiterated his earlier judgment that the eclectic method was, indeed, a symptom of our continuing inability to reconstruct the history of the text in the second and first centuries: "Many of us share [the] hope that the eclectic method can be replaced by something more permanent—a confidently reconstructed history and a persuasive theory of the text—and we are working actively toward that goal" (Epp 1989a, 102).

REHABILITATING HORT

In 1968 Colwell wrote a programmatic article pleading for a resuscitation of Hort and a revision of Hort's methodology. Concerned about the drift away from the historical reconstruction of the text and an overemphasis on internal evidence, he laid out a five-step program designed to improve upon Hort by incorporating all the new textual evidence into text-critical methodology. (1) Begin with readings, including not only Greek manuscripts but also the versions and fathers, gaining such a knowledge of scribal habits as to enable "a series of compendia of corruptions" to be drawn up (Colwell 1968, 143). (2) Characterize individual scribes and

---

20. "Central to this approach is a fundamental guideline: the variant most likely to be original is the one that best accounts for the origin of all competing variants in terms of both external and internal evidence" (Holmes 2002, 79).

manuscripts by identifying the habits of a scribe well enough to enable the researcher to discard singular readings. (3) Group the manuscripts according to the principles Colwell had laid out in his earlier work. (4) Construct a historical framework, adjusting Hort's reconstruction by the recognition that *"the story of the manuscript tradition of the New Testament is the story of progression from a relatively uncontrolled tradition to a rigorously controlled tradition"* (148). The early uncontrolled tradition is best seen in the Delta (Western) text, which is not so much a text-type as an assortment of provincial readings. The Beta (Alexandrian) and Alpha (Byzantine) emerge as text-types in the fourth century. The Caesarean text is a process (not a text-type) of exercising local control over the Western readings. (5) Make final judgment on readings, using Hort's canons of internal criticism to the full but also giving precedence to the manuscripts when intrinsic and transcriptional probability do not coincide.

Colwell's emphasis on making progress by going back—studying individual manuscripts and scribal habits—was based in part on his 1965 comparative analysis of P^{45}, P^{66}, and P^{75} (Colwell 1965), but he was also influenced by the extraordinary study of P^{46} by Günther Zuntz published in 1953. Zuntz may almost be said to have illustrated Colwell's program before Colwell articulated it.[21]

Zuntz, a philologist, applied classical text-critical methods in an attempt to recover the archetype of the Pauline corpus, beginning with the oldest-known manuscript of the Paulines, P^{46}. But because the textual tradition of the New Testament is so contaminated by mixture that it is impossible to work back to the archetype by constructing a stemma, Zuntz instead sought to isolate the oldest reading or readings at each point of variation in the text, without regard to the textual tradition (Byzantine, Western, Alexandrian, Caesarean) in which the reading was attested. His aim was to breach the "barrier of the second century," to "bridge the gap between the originals and the earliest extant evidence" (Zuntz 1953, 11). Zuntz looked at the variant readings in 1 Corinthians and Hebrews attested by P^{46}, decided (on the basis of internal criteria) where that manuscript contained the original text, and noted which textual groups and manuscripts within those groups sided with P^{46}.[22] He concluded that

---

21. For Zuntz's methodology, see Holmes 2006, 89–113; Birdsall 1992, 169–71. Birdsall comments: "to illustrate what Colwell in his final text-critical essay was urging upon his fellow labourers, we may take Zuntz as the prime example" (171).

22. These agreements are shown on charts in Zuntz 1953, 143–49; cf. 61–68.

although in a few instances P[46] preserves the original reading almost alone, the papyrus is supported in various places by one or more members of every recognized textual group, including Byzantine. That is, good readings might be found in any textual tradition; one could not depend on genealogical relations to establish the best text.[23]

Zuntz compared the second-century text of the Pauline corpus to a great reservoir, from which flowed two main branches, an Eastern and a Western. Individual manuscripts "may … be likened to samples of water drawn from a large stream at different places" (Zuntz 1953, 264). Although the Western stream has more "muddy" samples than the Eastern (whose main channel is the "pure" Alexandrian tradition), some original readings lost to the Alexandrian channel are preserved in the Western tradition (and in certain channels of the Eastern stream). The main characteristic of the Alexandrian channel of the Pauline corpus is a concern for "trustworthy manuscripts, the establishment of a pure text, and the arrangement of the whole according to some guiding principle, without addition or omission" (278). Zuntz hypothesized that in Alexandria, prior to 200 C.E. (i.e., around the date of P[46]), Christian scholars with philological know-how applied "filters or sluices" to the stream of tradition, "checked the unprincipled tendencies of the preceding age and finally sent forth the 'Euthalian' standard edition" of the late fourth century (280).

As Holmes points out, Zuntz made "a lasting and substantial contribution" to text-critical methodology by showing clearly that reasoned eclecticism is not a "temporary method or stopgap measure; it is our best and only way forward" (Holmes 2006, 99). Although the "proto-Alexandrian" and Alexandrian witnesses more often preserve the right than the wrong reading, they have sometimes erred by correcting the original reading, which survived in Western and Byzantine witnesses. Only by assessing each reading on its own merits can the textual critic bridge the gap between our earliest manuscripts and the text.

Advocating for the Majority Text

A radically different approach to the recovery of the original text surfaced in the mid-1950s and continues to be defended by a small cadre of

---

23. Even so, Zuntz found that the group P[46] B 1739 Clement Origen Sahidic Bohairic has a higher proportion of original readings than other groups where there are variants attested.

advocates. There are very few credentialed and experienced textual critics among them.[24] Even so, the major voices in this movement exercise considerable influence in some circles, including groups of missionaries and Bible translators in Africa, Asia, and Latin America. Taking their cue from John Burgon, who defended the traditional text against Westcott and Hort, they hold that the original text of the New Testament is found in the majority of manuscripts (Wallace 1995, 297–320).

The Majority Text position is self-consciously based on a commitment to plenary verbal inspiration of the Bible and several corollaries and inferences that flow from this doctrine: (1) that God has providentially preserved the true text in every age; (2) that textual corruption is largely the work of heretics; (3) that based on statistical probability, the greatest number of surviving manuscripts are more likely to contain the original text than a minority of manuscripts would do; (4) that the reason early Byzantine manuscripts cannot be found is because the faithful wore them out from usage; (5) that arguments from internal evidence are too subjective to be reliable (Wallace 1995, 297–320).

Advocates of the Byzantine text form fall into two camps. One group accepts the Textus Receptus (often referred to simply as "the traditional text") and vernacular translations based upon it (typically, the KJV/AV) as best representing the original text (W. Pickering 1980; Hills 1956; Fuller 1975). The other group recognizes that the majority text is not identical with the Textus Receptus; it is the former they support as the original text (Hodges and Farstad 1985; Pierpoint and Robinson 1991).[25] Advocates of both positions insist that, absent major disruptions in the transmission history, the earliest reading is the one most likely to persist in the majority of manuscripts. But, as Metzger points out, there have been several such major disruptions in the transmission process of the New Testament documents, most notably the destruction of Christian books under Diocletian in the fourth century and the waning of the Christian population under the sway of Islam in the seventh century (Metzger and Ehrman 2005, 220). Moreover, we know from patristic references that some textual

---

24. Edward Hills and Maurice Robinson come to mind. Harry Sturz, who was a recognized textual critic, supported the Byzantine text as just as early and valuable as the Alexandrian and Western, but Sturz was not a "card-carrying" member of the Majority Text fraternity.

25. Wallace (1995, 306) notes that the Textus Receptus (1825 Oxford ed.) and the Majority Text differ in 1,838 places.

readings that are available to us today in only a handful of witnesses were at one time in the majority of manuscripts known to a particular father.[26]

The Majority Text theory has attracted virtually no support from working textual critics for several reasons (Wallace 1995, 310–15). First, the Byzantine text is not found in any Greek manuscript prior to the fourth century and was not the majority text until the ninth century.[27] Second, none of the versions contains a Byzantine text prior to the Gothic text of the late fourth century. Third, none of the church fathers prior to Asterius of Antioch (fourth century) uses a distinctively Byzantine text. Fourth, witnesses to the Byzantine text have hundreds of variant readings among themselves where no majority prevails. If internal evidence is out of court, no reliable decisions can be made in these cases. Fifth, the Majority Text theory is founded upon a theological apriority, not a reasoned methodology that can be publicly defended within the guild of scholars (see also Fee 1993, 183–208).

This chapter confirms that, while there was a broad consensus that Westcott and Hort had delivered a vastly superior text and had broken the stranglehold of the Textus Receptus, the twentieth century presented a new set of challenges. The increase in early textual witnesses called into question the tidy division of text-types that had marked the methodology of the previous two centuries. Although there were enormous efforts devoted to reorganizing the data and creating new methodological models, it was a fair question whether these efforts had brought us closer to the original text. In the W. H. P. Hatch Memorial Lecture delivered at the SBL Annual Meeting in 1973, Eldon Jay Epp described the twentieth century as an "interlude in New Testament Textual Criticism" (Epp 1974), but the foundations of the discipline were about to be shaken, as the question of the essential goals of textual criticism came to the fore. Maybe the original text was not the point, after all.

---

26. Zuntz (1953, 84) calls attention to the reading χωρις, *chōris*, in Heb 2:9, which is attested today in Greek in only the tenth-century manuscript 1739 but which was the predominant reading known to third-century church fathers.

27. Sturz (1984) identifies some 150 readings characteristic of the Byzantine text that are also found in early papyri; most of these, however, have support from other non-Byzantine texts; moreover, no papyrus manuscript has the distinctive Byzantine *pattern* of readings.

8
New Directions: Expanding the Goals of Textual Criticism

> The legitimate task of textual criticism is not limited to the recovery of approximately the original form of the documents, to the establishment of the "best" text, nor to the "elimination of spurious readings." ... The various forms of the text are sources for the study of the history of Christianity. (D. W. Riddle 1936, 221)

In chapter 2 I quoted A. E. Housman's famously succinct definition of textual criticism as "the science of discovering error in texts and the art of removing it" (Housman 1961, 131). But I went on to point out that removing error is not the only aim of textual critics. After all, if the original text is all that matters, then variations from this text can simply be discarded. Hort claimed that "textual criticism is always negative, because its final aim is virtually nothing more than the detection and rejection of error" (Westcott and Hort 1881, 2:3). Of course, most errors were simply that: unconscious scribal mistakes. Hort reassured his readers that, with the exception of Marcion's excisions from the text, "there are no signs of deliberate falsification of the text for dogmatic purposes" (282–83).[1] But, as we have seen above, several of the pioneers of New Testament textual criticism came under fire because they relegated to the apparatus some

---

1. To be fair to Hort, he acknowledged (Westcott and Hort 1881, 2:282) that scribes sometimes altered the text in ways that present-day scholars might attribute to dogmatic motives, but Hort saw these not as "deliberate falsification of the text" but rather as attempts to correct the errors of predecessors, to make explicit implied information, or to clarify texts open to misconstrual. See further Miller 1999.

theologically significant textual variants. Burgon's savage attack on the W-H text was focused precisely on the "scandalously corrupt" manuscripts underlying the RV.

One of the most distinctive developments in New Testament textual criticism in the postmodern era and beyond is a broadening of its focus beyond the recovery of the original text to the history, motives, and effects of textual variation. This chapter will survey some of the movers, motives, and models that characterize this new direction.

Or perhaps it is not so new. As long ago as 1904, Kirsopp Lake devoted his inaugural lecture at the University of Leiden to doctrinal modifications of New Testament texts (Lake 1904; cf. Conybeare 1902). Other short studies dealt with a variety of theologically significant textual variants, but not in any systematic fashion (W. Howard 1941). Textual critics were slow to investigate thoroughly the relationship between the history of the church and the history of its text, perhaps wary of upsetting the faithful. Hort's comment that "substantial variation ... can hardly form more than a thousandth part of the entire text" (Westcott and Hort 1881, 2:2) has been repeatedly quoted in handbooks (for example, Kenyon 1951, 6–7). Kenneth Clark pointedly observed that this estimate "must have been rhetorical rather than mathematical, for a tenth of one per cent would amount to merely twenty lines in Nestle" (Clark 1966, 3). The disputed endings of the Gospel of Mark alone take up more than twenty lines in Nestle-Aland.

In 1908 Rendel Harris called for more systematic study of theological variation, insisting that the history of the text should be read alongside the history of the church, with particular attention to the doctrinal debates of the various parties (Harris 1908). The history department of the University of Chicago was a pioneer in emphasizing the social world of early Christianity. Scholars there began in the 1930s to explore the relationship between textual criticism and Christian dogma. In 1936 Donald W. Riddle suggested that the history of theology can be more or less reconstructed from a study of textual variation (Riddle 1936). In 1951 C. S. C. Williams published his *Alterations to the Text of the Synoptic Gospels and Acts*. Around the same time, in Germany, Erich Fascher suggested that during the period from 50 to 125 C.E., interpretation of the New Testament text had already begun to be reflected in the alterations copyists made to the texts before them (Fascher 1953). In the 1953 publication of his Schweich Lectures, Zuntz went so far as to suggest to his readers that he would "quote to you some instances where the correction of a pronoun, a particle, or even of a single letter affects, or even cancels, some traditional tenet of New Testament theology" (Zuntz 1953, 3).

In 1966 M. R. Pelt presented a wide-ranging PhD dissertation to Duke University entitled "Textual Variation in Relation to Theological Interpretation in the New Testament." That same year Eldon Jay Epp's Harvard dissertation was published under the title *The Theological Tendency of Codex Bezae Cantabrigiensis in Acts*. Epp's thesis was that there was an anti-Judaic bias in the Western text of Acts, represented most fully in Codex Bezae (D). His study was the catalyst for a burst of interest in research on theological textual variation in the second half of the twentieth century (Epp 2005, xxvii–xxx). In addition to more studies on the text of Codex Bezae,[2] smaller-scale investigations of theological tendencies in manuscripts appeared from the 1970s to the present (see Eshbaugh 1979; Globe 1980; Parsons 1986; Head 1993). But in 1968, Colwell had warned against "the current enthusiasm for manuscript variations as contributions to the history of theology," insisting that we must first know the history of theology at the time and place of a particular manuscript before we can attribute theological motivation to those responsible for its variants (Colwell 1968, 133).

In 1993 Bart Ehrman rose to Colwell's challenge in his groundbreaking study *The Orthodox Corruption of Scripture*, subtitled: *The Effect of Early Christological Controversies on the Text of the New Testament*. Focusing on the christological debates of the second and third centuries as these are recounted by such heresiologists as Justin, Irenaeus, Tertullian, and Hippolytus, Ehrman treats some 180 units of textual variation that he believes to be related to these christological issues. His thesis is that orthodox (or "proto-orthodox") scribes altered the text of the New Testament in order to combat three major heresies (as they saw them): adoptionism, the teaching that Christ was human only, having been "adopted" as Son of God at his baptism; separationism, the teaching that the divine Christ descended upon the human Jesus at the time of his baptism and departed from him prior to his death on the cross (thus, the divine/human natures were real, but separate); and docetism, the teaching that Jesus was fully and only divine, although he seemed (from the Greek δοκεῖν, *dokein*, "to

---

2. Two more PhD dissertations were written on the text of Codex Bezae (Rice 1974 and Holmes 1984).

seem, to appear") to be human and to suffer and die.³ A major strength of Ehrman's approach is that he begins with the writings of the heresiologists, locating the varieties of christological belief in specific times and places, and then traces the history of selected textual variants to those respective times and places. Whether or not one agrees with Ehrman's judgment about theological motivation in the specific cases he considers, it is clear that Ehrman has demonstrated convincingly the importance of other motives for doing textual criticism than simply dismissing erroneous readings and recovering original ones. Ehrman is interested in scribal activity "as a kind of hermeneutical process," analogous to what everyone does when ascribing meaning to the texts we read: "we 'rewrite' them ... we explain them to ourselves 'in our own words.'" Ancient scribes, concerned to make the *meaning* of texts unambiguous sometimes really *did* rewrite them, not in their minds, but on the page (Ehrman 1993a, 29–31). At the same time, it is clear that Ehrman is interested in the original text, because he argues again and again that scribes have altered the original in support of orthodoxy. One cannot detect the alteration unless one can identify the original.

Ehrman's book appeared at a time when critical biblical studies and related disciplines had begun to emphasize variety over consensus, multivalence over uniformity in early Judaism and Christianity.⁴ A year before Ehrman's book came out, J. Neville Birdsall reflected on "the malaise which affects all aspects of textual criticism," wondering if the uncertainties of the discipline did not have their roots "in the philosophies of the twentieth century, which in various ways have cast doubt upon the possibility of a unified understanding of things, and even upon the possibility of knowledge of things" (Birdsall 1992, 188). In short, Ehrman's book (and its popularized successor, *Misquoting Jesus* [2005]) helped to make New Testament textual criticism relevant to a postmodern readership. At the same time, the book capitalized on the reawakening of interest by biblical scholars in the social world of early Christianity.

---

3. Ehrman also devotes a short chapter to patripassionism ("modalism"), the teaching that the Christ was actually a "mode" of the Father's being and that the Father himself suffered in the Son.

4. It was in the 1980s that I first began to see references to "Judaisms" and "Christianities."

The Text as "Window"

Good historical study has always been interested in "the world behind the text," but textual critics have too often solved textual problems without a plausible reconstruction of the history of the text.[5] In 1995 Ehrman made reference to a number of studies showing that New Testament manuscripts can throw light not only on the theological controversies of the early church but on the social history of early Christianity broadly, including Jewish-Christian relations, the role of women, and the use of magic and fortune-telling (Ehrman 1995; Metzger and Ehrman 2005, 280–99).

It was in part the rise of feminist studies on Scripture that drew renewed attention to some variants in Codex Bezae in Acts that might be interpreted as deemphasizing the prominence of women in early Christianity (Witherington 1984, 82–84).[6] Even more controversial has been the discussion over the "women's silence" text in 1 Cor 14:34–35, which, more than a century ago, was labeled a non-Pauline interpolation into the text.[7] Recent studies have somewhat strengthened this argument, as will be shown later in this chapter.

Colwell had warned against attributing theological motivation to variant readings unless scholars could first demonstrate a sure knowledge of the history of theology at the time of the witness or witnesses attesting to the variant in question. The same requirement attaches to other aspects of the social world that might be reflected in textual variants having to do, for example, with Christian asceticism in relation to sexual practices. All such studies demand a carefully controlled and sophisticated methodology; happily, recent literature provides some good examples of this kind of research (Kloha 2008, 85–108).

---

5. Colwell observed in 1968 that "Kurt Aland is able to solve finally the problem of one Western Non-Interpolation after another without reconstructing the history of the manuscript tradition" (Colwell 1968, 133).

6. For example, Witherington cites Bezae's references in Acts 17:4, 12 to some of Paul's Thessalonian converts as "wives of prominent men" where most other witnesses read "prominent women." For a more nuanced study, see Holmes 2003, 183–203.

7. Although no textual witness omits the passage, a number of manuscripts place it after 14:40 and Codex Fuldensis (545 C.E.) puts it both following 14:40 and also in the margin after 14:33.

What about the Original Text?

The sketch above suggests that there has been a major shift of emphasis away from the goal of recovering the original text of the New Testament. Already in 1966 Kenneth W. Clark observed that early Christian scribes handled the text so freely "that the gospel text was little more stable than the oral tradition, and … we may be pursuing the retreating mirage of the 'original text'" (Clark 1966, 15). More recently, Eldon Epp explored the larger question of what we mean by "original text" (Epp 1999). After surveying dozens of handbooks on textual criticism, he concluded that, although many of them stipulate the recovery of the original text of the New Testament as the goal of textual criticism, few of them define explicitly what they mean by "original text." Is the original text the autograph? Or is it just something as close to the autograph as we can get—the most likely original text? Epp points out that even such qualifiers as "the earliest attainable or recoverable text" serve as little more than quotation marks around the word "original" in the phrase "original text" (254). Recent studies indicate to Epp an emerging new use of "original text" to include lost predecessor forms of the text. Possible examples include: (1) because of the so-called minor agreements of Matthew and Luke against Mark, it has been suggested that Matthew and Luke used a form of the Gospel of Mark earlier than the final composition of this Gospel, thus, an "original" before the "original"; (2) the phrase "in Ephesus" is lacking from Eph 1:1 in our earliest manuscripts of this letter; since the context seems to require the name of a destination, it has been suggested that the letter was originally issued in several copies, each to a different location, before the final "original" edition was published as a "catholic" letter to all the churches (255–63).

More surprising—and troubling to many—will be the question whether a scribal revision or reordering of a published text can qualify as a new original when it is the only form known to its readers. Is it possible to treat not only prepublication forms of the text as original, but also postpublication forms?[8] For example, the text of Acts is extant in two major

---

8. Josep Rius-Camps has proposed that the pericope of the adulterous woman was part of the original Gospel of Mark (appearing after 12:12), was picked up by Luke (at 20:19), and was subsequently removed from both Mark and Luke, only to be added later by some manuscripts at various locations (Rius-Camps 2007, 379–405). For response to Rius-Camps, see Keith 2009.

forms, one of them roughly 8 percent longer than the other. One theory is that Luke wrote and published a short version, then later a longer version intended to replace the earlier one. Since both editions survived and most readers would probably have known only one of these, should both forms of the text be treated as original?[9] J. K. Elliott conjectured that the opening verses of Mark's Gospel (1:1–3) are a later addition, the original beginning having probably been lost "within the first 50 years of its composition and publication" (J. Elliott 2000, 584–88). Elliott's conjecture fits well with the suggestion that the original ending of Mark's Gospel has also been lost; if copied onto a single-quire codex, the loss of the outside sheet of papyrus would have affected both the beginning and the ending of the Gospel.

Some scholars have argued that the Pauline correspondence has been widely interpolated.[10] Should these suggested interpolations be considered original, having occurred so early that by the time the Gospels and the Pauline letters were collected, the interpolations had become canonical, in the sense that most readers of the text were completely unaware of earlier forms? Even to ask the question is to indicate that the issue of canonicity is related to literary-critical and text-critical concerns. In fact, however, one of the problems with interpolation theories is that in many cases there is seldom much, if any, manuscript evidence to support the proposed theory (Wisse 1990, 172–78). Epp suggests, therefore, that it may be legitimate to regard proposed "*preformulations* or *reformulations*" of texts as legitimate subjects of text-critical analysis "*if such an exploration is initiated on the basis of appropriate textual variation or other manuscript evidence*" (1999, 268).

Has the search for the original text been surrendered as the major goal of New Testament textual criticism? For some scholars it has, but most textual critics in their papers and articles still write as if they assume there is an original reading. As Moisés Silva astutely points out, although

---

9. For summary and bibliography, see Parker 2008, 297. The possibility of two forms of the same text emerging from the same center would not surprise textual critics of the Old Testament, because the Qumran manuscripts exhibit a longer text and a shorter text of a half-dozen books of the Old Testament. Did the community accept both forms as original, or was that even a question the readers would have entertained? See further Ulrich 1999, 34–78.

10. This position has been most vigorously set forth in recent years by William O. Walker in a stream of articles. See especially Walker 1987, 610–18; other articles are noted in Epp 1999, 268 n. 89.

some readers have appealed to Ehrman's *Orthodox Corruption* "in support of blurring the notion of the original text, there is hardly a page in the book that does not in fact mention such a text or assume its accessibility" (Silva 2002, 149). But, however much the original text may be important to Ehrman, the original readings have been marginalized, because Ehrman is more interested in the changes in the text that witness to theological concerns of Christian scribes and their readers during the first three centuries.

At least one contemporary New Testament textual critic appears to doubt not only the possibility of recovering the original text but even the desirability of doing so. In 1997 David C. Parker published *The Living Text of the Gospels*. The book offers a brief introduction to the materials and practice of textual criticism generally but with special attention to the Gospels, which, as he correctly observes, offer a different set of challenges than other parts of the New Testament. The heart of the book is a detailed examination of the Lord's Prayer in Matt 6:9–13 and Luke 11:2–4 and of Jesus' sayings on marriage and divorce in Matt 5:27–32; 19:3–9; Mark 10:2–12; and Luke 16:18.

By looking carefully at variations in manuscripts, versions, and patristic quotations, Parker shows that the Lord's Prayer circulated from very early times in several different forms; moreover, some forms of the text would be unknown to us were it not for the fortuitous survival of one or two manuscripts (Parker 1997, 69–71). Not only is it impossible to reconstruct a single form of the Lord's Prayer that lies behind both the Matthean and the Lukan versions (that is, to get behind the texts to the truth), but ancient commentators (Origen in particular) willingly embraced the truths within the variant traditions they knew.

The textual transmission of Jesus' sayings on marriage, divorce, and remarriage presents an even more complex set of problems than we find in the Lord's Prayer. Because early Christians (just as modern ones) turned to these texts to solve critical social and moral questions, they wanted to find a uniform, authoritative teaching from Jesus. But we cannot extract from the textual tradition a single teaching of Jesus that gave rise to all of the Gospel texts, nor can we reconstruct with confidence the earliest reading in each of the four texts in the Gospels. We see evidence of harmonization of texts and more subtle reworking of words and phrases that amount to "a collection of interpretative rewritings of a tradition." What are the implications for the church? Just this: "Once this is acknowledged, then the concept of a Gospel that is fixed in shape, authoritative, and final as a piece of literature has to be abandoned" (Parker 1997, 93). For Parker, this is not a counsel of despair, for once the distinction between *scripture* and *tradition* has been cleared away (because scripture is available to us only in its variant forms in manuscripts, i.e., only as tradition), the church is freed from the necessity of recovering *the* original text: "The question is not whether we *can* recover it, but why we want to" (209). This does not mean that textual critics should give up on the search for the earliest forms of the text. Reconstruction of the textual history is important, but not because the earliest forms of the text are necessarily more authoritative for the church than later forms. After all, scribal changes are living testimony to the continuing interaction of tradition (the scribe working on behalf of the church) and scripture (the text being copied; 204).

In his more recent book, *An Introduction to New Testament Manuscripts and Their Texts*, Parker adopts terminology that may prove to be more serviceable, as well as more accurate, than "original text." He alludes to the criterion that the reading to be preferred at a point of variation is the one that best accounts for the origin of all the others, but he makes it clear that the preferred reading is not necessarily the *original* text; it is simply the earliest form of text known from the available witnesses. He names this the initial text, playing on the meaning of the German *Ausgangstext*, the term used for the text printed in the *Editio critica maior* (Parker 2008, 180–81). The adoption of the term initial text might help us cut through some of the confusion suggested by Epp's survey of multivalent meanings of the term original text. Even so, it should be clear to the reader that interest in multiple meanings and ambiguity in textual variation has become a major characteristic of postmodern text-critical studies.

To be sure, the confident and optimistic climate that ushered in Westcott and Hort's *New Testament in the Original Greek* has long since vanished. There is considerable doubt about the possibility of reconstructing *the* original Greek text in all its particulars. Nevertheless, efforts to edit and publish better editions of the Greek New Testament remain a major goal of textual critics. The following examples are representative models.

Models

Of the many editions that followed W-H, we have space here to profile only the two major hand editions that are the current workhorses for students of the Greek New Testament and the two major editions designed to replace Tischendorf.[11] Following this discussion, we will focus on a model treatment of a significant textual variant.

In 1898 Eberhard Nestle published a hand edition based on a comparison of the texts of Tischendorf (1869–1872), Westcott and Hort (1881), and Weymouth (1892; after 1901 the text of Weiss [1894–1900]). Where two of the three agreed, this was the text Nestle printed, with the reading of the third composing a sort of apparatus. Beginning with the thirteenth edition, Eberhard's son Erwin became editor. From this point, a truly critical apparatus of variant readings and their major supporting witnesses accompanies the text. Kurt Aland became associate editor for the twenty-first edition (1952) and editor for the twenty-fifth edition (1963). The text constructed under his editorship is a truly critical text, no longer the "mean" text of three nineteenth-century editions. The twenty-sixth and twenty-seventh editions (1979, 1993) contain a much-improved and expanded apparatus. By means of an ingenious set of symbols, the apparatus is able to convey an enormous amount of information in a very small space. NA^{27} is the hand edition most widely used by working textual critics (B. Aland et al. 1993a).

In 1966 five Bible societies published an edition for the use of Bible translators and students. An international team of scholars began with the W-H text, compared several other editions, and decided textual variants on the basis of majority vote. The apparatus is generally limited to variant readings that directly affect translation, but more evidence per variant is cited than is customary in hand editions. The editors assign ratings (A, B, C, D) reflecting their relative degree of certainty for each of the variants selected for the text. Beginning with the third edition (1975, edited by Kurt Aland, Matthew Black, Bruce Metzger, and Allen Wikgren), the text conforms to that of the twenty-sixth edition of the Nestle-Aland text, so that, except for some variations in punctuation, paragraphing, and orthography, only the apparatuses differ. With the fourth edition (1993), Black and Wikgren were replaced by Barbara Aland and Carlo M. Martini; Johannes Karavidopoulos was added to the team (B. Aland, et al. 1993b). In 1970 Bruce Metzger edited a companion volume, *A Textual Commentary on the Greek New Testament* (2nd ed., 1994), that discusses the major

---

11. For more detailed surveys, see Metzger and Ehrman 2005, 83–94; Aland and Aland 1989, 19–47, 222–67; Silva 1995, 283–96. For a working introduction to critical editions, see the chapter on "editions and how to use them" in Parker 2008, 191–223.

variant readings and gives the rationale for the committee's decisions. The UBS text is probably the hand edition most widely used by seminary and theological-school students, Bible translators, and church ministers.

It might have been expected that the discovery of a large number of New Testament manuscripts since W-H, particularly early papyri, would have resulted in editions of the New Testament differing from W-H in numerous places. This has not occurred. To be sure, the new evidence, particularly of the papyri, has greatly expanded the apparatuses of our critical editions.[12] In a 1973 lecture, Eldon Epp lamented "The Twentieth Century Interlude in New Testament Textual Criticism," citing studies showing that the most widely used Greek New Testaments in the mid-twentieth century, including NA[25] and UBS, exhibit very few significant variations from the W-H text (Epp 1974, 388–90). But perhaps this is more a testimony to the remarkable judgment of the two Cambridge scholars than to the failure of their successors.

There are two major critical editions currently underway, although only portions of text have thus far been produced, despite the fact that the first of these efforts began more than sixty years ago.

In 1949, committees of British and American scholars were organized in order to produce a comprehensive apparatus of the Greek New Testament in which the witnesses were collated against the 1973 Oxford edition of the Textus Receptus. The first fruit of that project is *The Gospel according to St. Luke* (1984, 1987), which includes the largest apparatus ever assembled for any part of the New Testament. The text of the Textus Receptus is printed one verse at a time, with apparatus for that verse following, including full quotations from the fathers rather than references only. In some cases an entire page is devoted to a single verse.[13] Work is well under way on the Gospel of John, with the goal of producing not simply an apparatus but a critical text (Parker 2003a, 21–43). Two volumes of preliminary studies have already been published (W. Elliott and Parker 1995; Schmid et al. 2007).

In 1997 the first fascicle of a massive new edition appeared, sponsored by the Institute for New Testament Textual Research, in Münster, under the general title *Novum Testamentum graecum: Editio critica maior*.[14]

---

12. This is traced sequentially through the Nestle editions in Comfort 1990, 16–22.
13. Silva 1995, 293, observes that it takes nine pages to cover Luke 2:1–14.
14. The first portion to be published is vol. 4, edited by B. Aland, containing the Catholic Epistles (1997).

Unlike the IGNTP, the German project was intended from the beginning to result in a new critical text and not only an apparatus. A series of preliminary studies, including complete collations of a great number of manuscripts, was published in preparation for this edition.[15]

The sheer mass of textual witnesses has presented the greatest challenge in preparing a truly critical text of the New Testament. Ideally, complete collations of all witnesses, at least those in Greek, should be completed, but this has heretofore proved impossible to undertake. We surveyed above some of the efforts to group and classify the witnesses for the purposes of editing comprehensive editions. Since there is not enough room in even the largest apparatus for citing the evidence of every witness, editors have to decide for each portion of the canon (Gospels, Acts, Paulines, Catholic Epistles, Revelation) which manuscripts are so important they should be cited as "constant witnesses." The most ambitious and comprehensive attempt in this regard is represented by the volumes in the Text und Textwert series produced for the *Editio critica maior*. One of the most promising developments for the future is the use of electronic databases by both the IGNTP and the Institute at Münster. For more than a decade the two projects have been developing a joint system for making electronic transcriptions of manuscripts (Parker 2008, 100–102, 200–201). They are also collaborating in assessing ways of analyzing manuscript groups (Parker 2003a, 21).

Luke 22:19–20 from Westcott-Hort to Ehrman

In keeping with previous presentations of specific models, we will now look at a model treatment of a significant textual variant during the period from the late nineteenth to the late twentieth century. One of the most contentious textual problems in the New Testament concerns the Lukan version of the Last Supper, which has been transmitted in two major forms.[16] The longer version has Jesus offering the Twelve a cup (vv. 17–18), bread (v. 19), and another cup (v. 20). In this form of the text, the bread saying ("this is my body") includes the words "that is given for

---

15. These appeared under the general series title Text und Textwert der griechischen Handschriften des Neuen Testaments in fourteen volumes, from 1987 to 1999.

16. Four additional forms of the text are efforts to reconcile the two larger textforms; see the convenient chart in Metzger 1994, 149.

you. Do this in remembrance of me.'" Then we read of a second cup: "And the cup likewise after supper, saying, 'This cup is the new covenant in my blood that is poured out for you.'" The shorter version lacks verses 19b–20; thus, it has the cup saying (vv. 17–18) followed by verse 19a: "And taking bread, giving thanks, he broke and gave it to them saying, 'This is my body.'" These words are immediately joined to those of verse 21: "But behold the hand of the one betraying me is with me on the table."

The short form, which is attested only by Western witnesses (Codex Bezae and five Old Latin manuscripts) was judged by Westcott and Hort to be a Western non-interpolation, that is, a place where, contrary to its usual expansionist tendencies, the Western text preserves the pristine, shorter text against the majority. According to Hort, the shorter reading is difficult only because of the inversion of order of the bread and the cup; the longer reading, however, is difficult both because of the mention of two cups and because Jesus' declaration that he would "from now on" not drink from the cup until the kingdom of God would come is not related, as in Matthew and Mark, to the institution of the Lord's Supper but is attached to "rites preparatory to the Supper" (Westcott and Hort 1881, 2:64 Notes). They also judged that the long text appears to be an adaptation of Paul's account in 1 Cor 11:23–25. In their edition of the Greek New Testament, Westcott and Hort placed double brackets around Luke 22:19b–20 as a "noteworthy rejected reading."

The RV of 1881 did not follow W-H at Luke 22:19–20 (nor did the revisers adopt any of the other Western non-interpolations), but the short text was adopted in *The Twentieth Century New Testament* (1902) and *The New Testament: An American Translation* (1923). Within fifty years of W-H, the commentaries on Luke by Plummer (1896), Zahn (1913), Easton (1926), Klostermann (1929), and Creed (1930) all held for the short text. The RSV (1946) gave wide popular exposure to the short text, demoting 22:19b–20 to the margin. In the popular multivolume *Interpreter's Bible* (1952), except for a brief reference in the introduction, the commentary on Luke does not even note the problem of the two text-forms but assumes the short text as original. The NEB (1961) also translates the shorter text.[17] From the first edition of

---

17. Both the RSV and the NEB claim to have used an eclectic text, but the latter pays far less attention to external evidence than the former. The Greek text inferentially underlying the NEB was edited and published by R. Tasker (1964).

the Greek text of Nestle (1898) through NA[25] (1963), the shorter text is preferred. The first edition of UBS (1965) prints the long text, but with double brackets around verses 19b–20, showing that the passage is not authentic. Thus, for about half a century, critical studies in general favored the short text.

By the late 1930s scholars of the stature of Hatch, Kenyon, Legg, and Benoit had mounted defenses of the longer text (Williams 1951, 47–50). The tide began to move even more strongly in favor of the longer text in a number of publications around the middle of the century (Schürmann 1955; Jeremias 1966, 145–59). The change of opinion was heavily influenced by the publication of P. Bod. XIV–XV (P[75]), in which the Gospel of Luke has the longer reading, thus carrying evidence for this form of the text back to 175–225 C.E. (K. Aland 1967b, 155–72). NA[26] (1979) and NA[27] (1993) prefer the longer text, as do UBS[2] (1968), UBS[3] (1975), and UBS[4] (1992). Moreover, the degree of certainty of the editorial committee was raised from a C in UBS[3] to a B in UBS[4]. This reversal of the W-H judgment is reflected in the second edition of the RSV (1971), where the preface notes that Luke 22:19b–20 has been "restored to the text ... with new manuscript support." Other recent English-language translations favoring the long text include the NIV (without even a footnote), New American Standard Version, NAB, TEV, Jerusalem Bible, Contemporary Standard Version, and NJB.

There is not enough space here to detail the debate on this significant textual variant, but much of it is summarized in Ehrman's discussion in his *Orthodox Corruption of Scripture* (1993a, 199–209, 223–31). Ehrman identifies the longer text as an example of what he labels "Anti-Docetic Corruptions of Scripture." He argues that the original text of Luke 22:19–20 was altered by "proto-orthodox" scribes to emphasize the importance of the atoning significance of the death of Jesus ("my body, *which is given for you*"), an emphasis missing in the short form.

Ehrman begins with the external arguments, showing, first, that documentary evidence has to be weighed, not only counted. Since the Western text is characteristically expansive in comparison to the Alexandrian/neutral text, Western readings that are shorter than Alexandrian/neutral ones deserve to be taken very seriously. Second, the acquisition of P[75] has not materially tipped the scales in favor of the reading already attested in most witnesses. This is because Hort had already argued that both the neutral and the Western traditions had emerged by the second century; thus, even though no second-century Greek manuscripts were available to Westcott and Hort, they assumed their existence.[18] Moreover, they argued that in a small number of instances, the neutral tradition had been interpolated very early in its history. Ehrman also notes that the rightly celebrated papyri that have come to light in the twentieth century are all from Egypt and thus are evidence only of the kind of text available there; they do not necessarily reflect text-types available in other parts of the Mediterranean world.[19]

As to intrinsic probabilities (what Luke would most likely have written), Ehrman points to a number of non-Lukan features of vocabulary and style in verses 19b–20 but lays greater emphasis on Luke's careful avoidance of atonement theology in his references to the death of Jesus. Ehrman argues that not only does Luke himself not describe the death of Jesus as a sacrifice for sin, but Luke "has actually gone out of his way to *eliminate* just such a theology from the narrative he inherited from his predecessor, Mark" (Ehrman 1993a, 199). Thus, Luke's citation of Isa 53, a classic vicarious-atonement text in early Christianity (see Mark 10:45), does not include those verses that refer to the sufferings of the Servant of the Lord as being "for our transgressions" or "for our iniquities" or as "an offering for sin" (see Acts 8:32–33). Ehrman references other speeches in Acts in which the death of Jesus is represented as the act of a martyr, unjustly condemned but vindicated by resurrection, rather than as an act of atonement for sin (Acts 2:22–36; 3:12–16; 4:8–12; 7:51–56; 13:26–41). The shorter text in Luke avoids the Markan reference to "my blood of the covenant, which is poured out for many" (Mark 14:24) and is thus more in tune with Luke's theology.

A decision between or among competing textual variants requires a clear description of transcriptional probabilities. In this case, would a scribe have been more likely to add verses 19b–20 to a text originally lacking the words or to remove them from a text originally containing

---

18. Colwell had written that "there is nothing in [the agreement of P^{75} and Codex Vaticanus] that is novel to Hort's theory. Hort did not possess P^{75}, but he imagined it" (1969, 156).

19. This is a problematic argument, because the discovery of these papyri in Egypt tells us nothing about their original provenance. As has been shown, the New Testament documents could have originated anywhere in the Mediterranean world and been carried to Egypt in a matter of days or weeks (Epp 1991, 56). More precisely, seven New Testament papyri have been discovered elsewhere than Egypt, although these are fragmentary and none earlier than the sixth century; see Epp 2007, 396 n. 17.

them? It has been frequently argued that the short text arose because the mention of two cups would have been thought so confusing that a scribe eliminated the reference to the second cup, but, as Hort showed in 1881, it is improbable that a scribe would have omitted the most familiar form of the words of institution (very similar to 1 Cor 11:24–25) and would have retained "the vaguer, less sacred, and less familiar words, in great part peculiar to Lc." (Westcott and Hort 1881, 2:63). Ehrman also asks the obvious question of why the scribe in question would not have eliminated the first cup, instead of the second. Whatever occasioned the change in the text, the mention of two cups is not a sufficient cause. Another possibility for how the shorter form could have occurred is by accidental omission, but Ehrman rightly points out that it is difficult to account for precisely these thirty-two words having dropped out of the text for no discernible reason.[20] He concludes that it is much easier to account for the addition of these traditional words than for their omission.

Ehrman then suggests that this scribal interpolation is but one of a considerable number of alterations to the text made by "proto-orthodox" Christians in order to counter the teaching of their Docetic opponents, who taught that Christ only *seemed* to be a flesh-and-blood human. He quotes Tertullian, who cites the language of 1 Corinthians and Luke against Marcion, concluding, "Thus from the evidence of the flesh, we get a proof of the body, and a proof of the flesh from the evidence of the blood" (*Marc.* 4.40). Ehrman concludes that the scribes who thus altered the text of Luke did so out of concern that Luke's account "did not prove as serviceable for later Christians who wanted to emphasize the atoning merits of [Jesus'] death, a death that involved the real shedding of real blood for the sins of the world. … In changing the text this way, these scribes were part of a much larger phenomenon that has left its abiding mark throughout the manuscript record of the New Testament" (1993a, 209).

My point in profiling Ehrman's treatment of the text-critical problems in Luke 22:19–20 as a model is not to declare myself on one side of the debate but to illustrate the range and variety of analytical procedures, historical knowledge, and theological implications of textual criticism, as well as their embodiment in popular English translations of the New Tes-

---

20. We do know of manuscripts in which larger portions of text have been accidentally omitted, but these can usually be explained by homeoteleuton, that is, the omitted section and its surrounding text share words with the same ending.

tament of the twentieth century.[21] Ehrman's approach stands as a marker of the far-reaching reassessment of the discipline of New Testament textual criticism that began mid-century and has accelerated during the postmodern era. To the major indications of that reassessment we turn in the final chapter.

---

21. A serious problem with Ehrman's book is his casual reference to the way "scribes" altered the text for tendentious reasons. As we will see in the next chapter, there is minimal support for the notion that scribes in general edited their texts in such dramatic fashion as Ehrman suggests. The popularized version of his work, *Misquoting Jesus: The Story behind Who Changed the Bible and Why* (2005) also attributes theological changes in the texts to copyists of the second and third centuries, but it may well be that such changes derive from private owners who annotated their texts, which were then copied by others, as the next chapter will suggest.

9
Reassessing the Discipline

> As New Testament textual criticism moves into the twenty-first century, it must shed whatever remains of its innocence, for nothing is simple anymore. (Eldon Jay Epp 1999, 280)

In 1977, Eldon Jay Epp, then chair of the New Testament Textual Criticism Section of the Society of Biblical Literature, presented a paper lamenting "the growing lack of concern and support for New Testament textual criticism in America," as witnessed especially by the demise of graduate programs in the discipline and the difficulty of recruiting students into the field (Epp 1979). There were good reasons at that time for Epp's gloomy assessment of the future of the discipline.[1] Indeed, the serious decline in the teaching of the classics and the decreasing opportunities for Greek and Latin studies in secondary and tertiary institutions in North America and the United Kingdom are worrisome signs even today.[2]

Nevertheless, during the thirty-three years of my seminary teaching career, I have witnessed a rebirth of interest in New Testament textual criticism. Fortunately, the technological advances in acquiring and managing data make it easier than ever for students to have access to ancient texts, even if these students have no intention of specializing in textual

---

1. Epp acknowledges in a note added in 2004 to the reprint of the published paper that the original paper reflected his twin frustrations at the difficulty of attracting new participants to the New Testament Textual Criticism Section of the SBL and the slow progress of the IGNTP. He notes that, nearly thirty years later, prospects are brighter.
2. See Metzger 2003, 201–3. Metzger reports that only six hundred of the more than one million BA degrees awarded in the United States in 1994 were granted to classics majors. See also the assessment of Hurtado 2006a, 7–11.

criticism. To paraphrase what has been observed about many specialized studies, textual criticism is too important to be left to textual critics. Students and practitioners of exegesis, theology, church history, religious education, preaching, and Bible translation all have a stake in the work of textual criticism. Moreover, the field is moving in promising new directions.[3] I will sketch out these new directions in this chapter, this time combining motives and movers, again reminding the reader that valuable contributions of other movers are found in the notes.

Materials

In 1975 reports appeared that several complete or nearly complete New Testament manuscripts had been discovered in a storage room at Saint Catherine's Monastery on Mount Sinai (Politis 1980, 5–17). From this find, twelve new majuscules, four minuscules, and forty-five lectionaries have been added to the Gregory-Aland list (Metzger 2003, 204). Unfortunately, however, these texts have still not been made available for study.

Most of the manuscripts described in previous chapters contain sizeable portions of text, but fully two-thirds of all known papyri and majuscules contain only one or two leaves, and many of these manuscripts have only a fragment or two of a single leaf. Most New Testament manuscript "discoveries" made nowadays come by way of identifying previously unread fragments from the Oxyrhynchus finds or other collections or among those purchased from antiquities dealers.[4] During the past decade more than twenty papyri from the Oxyrhynchus collection have been identified as New Testament manuscripts.[5] Included are portions of

---

3. In addition to the essays in Black 2002, cited at several places in previous chapters, see Hurtado 1999, 26–48.

4. To give just one example, in the 1980s Macquarie University in Sydney, Australia, purchased from a dealer a number of Greek papyrus fragments thought to be from the Hellenistic era, among which was later identified the earliest-known fragment of Acts (third century). Now bearing the Gregory-Aland number P[91] and the Macquarie catalogue number P.Macquarie Inv. 360, the fragment (published in 1986) was found to be contiguous with another fragment held in Milan (P. Mil. Vogl. Inv. 1224) and published in 1982. Together, the fragments contain portions of Acts 2:30–37, 46–47; 3:1–2.

5. See Head 2000, 1–16. Images of all these papyri and others identified since Head's article can be seen on the Oxyrhynchus website at http://www.papyrology.ox.ac.uk/POxy/.

text from the Gospels of Matthew (seven new manuscripts), Luke, and John (seven new manuscripts), Acts, Romans, 1–2 Corinthians, Hebrews, James, and Revelation. All of these new finds are fragmentary; nevertheless, they are invaluable for the additional information they yield about scribal practices, the history of the church in Egypt, and early Christian liturgical practice (Hurtado 2006a, 4–14). Here and there they offer support for noteworthy variant readings. A case in point is the reading ὁ ἐκλεκτός (*ho eklektos*) in P[106] (P.Oxy. 4445) at John 1:34, where John says about Jesus, "I have seen and testified that this one is the *elect* of God" instead of "the *son* [υἱός, *hyios*] of God." "The son" is the reading of the vast majority of witnesses, although P[106] now provides third-century support for the reading of Codex Sinaiticus, some later minuscules, some Old Latin manuscripts, and the Old Syriac (Head 2000, 11).

One of these recently discovered manuscripts deserves special notice. P[115] (P.Oxy. 4499) consists of twenty-six fragments from Revelation, the most poorly attested book in the New Testament canon (Hoskier 1929; Schmid 1955–1956). As we saw in chapter 2, the only manuscript of Revelation available to Erasmus lacked the last six verses, so he in essence made up a Greek translation from the Latin text. Today there are 306 known Greek manuscripts of Revelation, but only fourteen of them from prior to the ninth century. Only three of these are majuscules (Sinaiticus [ℵ], Alexandrinus [A], and Ephraemi [C]). The oldest papyrus fragment, P[98] (second century), contains only part of seven verses; the oldest extensive papyrus witness, P[47] (third century), contains ten leaves, with the text of Rev 9:10–17:2. The new Oxyrhynchus find, P[115] (third/fourth century), contains nine fragmentary leaves, with portions of chs. 2, 3, 5, 6, and 8–15. P[115] famously provides the earliest manuscript support for the "number of the beast" in Rev 13:18 as 616 rather than 666.

In addition to papyrus fragments that continue to be identified, David Parker points out that other manuscripts, particularly minuscules, are added to the Gregory-Aland list with some regularity by scholars who visit monasteries, churches, and libraries around the world (Parker 2008, 45–46). Although the nineteenth and twentieth centuries appear to have been the age of discovery for New Testament manuscripts, we should never discount the possibility of new and important finds.

Movers and Motives

In chapter 8 we traced the heightened interest in textual variation as a window into the social world of early Christianity, especially as the text was affected by theological debates and developments in liturgy and leadership. Studies devoted to such textual variation routinely attribute these changes to scribes. For centuries, "scribes" and "scribal alterations" have been referred to as casually and uncritically as "original text," but can we really be certain who bears responsibility for the introduction of those 180 christological variants Ehrman deals with in his groundbreaking book profiled in the last chapter? How much do we really know about ancient scribal education, authority, responsibility, and practice? How much freedom did scribes have to alter the text? The late postmodern era has marked an "empirical turn" (Schmid 2008, 9) in the study of scribes, readers, and other tradents[6] who had roles in the production of manuscripts and in the transmission of the text of the New Testament. We turn now to some examples of these newer developments.

Scribes and Variants[7]

Ascribing all textual changes to copyists is an ancient convention, as we will remember from Origen's comments in chapter 2. But this assumes that scribes not only made mechanical errors—accidents in transcription—but also deliberately introduced changes from the parent text into their copies. Ehrman frequently accounts for "orthodox corruptions" of the text by such phrases as "some scribes modified," "orthodox scribes interpolated," "some scribes assimilated," and the like.[8] The casual reader gets the impression that the individual scribe of each manuscript being referenced made a deliberate decision to substitute different wording from that of his or her exemplar. Such a picture runs counter to the old dictum "identity of reading implies identity of origin," that is, manuscripts attesting the same variant reading likely have a common ancestor; their scribes

---

6. Parker 2008, 133–58, borrows this term to refer to the New Testament manuscripts themselves but includes also the editors, scribes, and users of the manuscripts and their texts.

7. I take the title of this section from Ulrich Schmid's provocative and important essay (2008, 1–23).

8. See Schmid 2008, 5 and n. 18. Similar loose references can be found broadly in the literature; Parker 1997 routinely attributes harmonizations, theological corrections, and other conscious alterations to copyists.

did not independently decide to make the same alteration.⁹ The default reference to all textual changes as "scribal" also treats scribes not only as copyists but as editors and authors (Schmid 2008, 2–3).

One of the most promising recent developments in New Testament textual criticism is the attention being given to the production of manuscripts and the transmission of their texts within the social contexts of early Christianity. There was no book-length study of the social world of early Christian scribes available until Kim Haines-Eitzen's doctoral dissertation appeared in print in 2000 under the title *Guardians of Letters: Literacy, Power, and the Transmitters of Early Christian Literature*. She confirms previous findings that a great many professional scribes during the Roman era were slaves or freedpersons working at the behest of social elites or governmental officials or making copies for the book trade (see Gamble 1995, 87–95). Nevertheless, there is evidence that other literate persons, not professional scribes, sometimes made copies for their own use, and Haines-Eitzen takes this to be the predominant reality in early Christianity.¹⁰ With a few exceptions, early Christian papyri do not betray the hand of professional scribes accustomed to copying literary texts (Epp 1997, 66). Haines-Eitzen envisions, rather, a series of "private scribal networks" engaged in the reproduction and transmission of Christian literature during the second and third centuries (2000, 16, 78–104), but it is not altogether clear from her account how the role of scribes was distinguished from that of readers and hearers of the texts.¹¹ Like her mentor Ehrman, she routinely attributes the deliberate modification of texts for theological reasons to scribes.¹² Thus, she sees scribes as participants in the "contests over readings" during the church's debates about self-definition, theology, and Christology (107).

---

9. There are exceptions, of course, such as independent correction of a grammatical or spelling error.

10. Haines-Eitzen (2000, 40) cites the Shepherd of Hermas as the only example of a literary Christian source illustrating the copying practices and transmission of texts. Although we do not know the occupation of Hermas, nothing in the text suggests he was a professional scribe.

11. From a colophon at the conclusion of the Martyrdom of Polycarp that traces the copying of these writings through a scribe named Gaius to another named Socrates and finally to one Pionius, she posits a "web" of relationships between these scribes (Haines-Eitzen 2000, 80–83).

12. One of her theses is that "scribes, as readers, were also simultaneously, interpreters" (ibid., 111).

The Fifth Birmingham Colloquium on the Textual Criticism of the New Testament (2007) was devoted to studies relating to the various stages in the production and transmission of Christian texts, with special concern for theological textual variation (Houghton and Parker 2008). Several essays in the published proceedings argue against the notion that scribes acted also as editors and authors of the works they were copying. Ulrich Schmid asks the question, "Who contributed what and when to a manuscript?" He draws up a "typology of literary production/reproduction" that includes the tasks of authoring a text, editing it (adding titles and prefaces, dividing the work into books or chapters, suiting the text to its intended readers), manufacturing the copy (preparing the writing materials, the pen and ink, ruling the lines, copying the text), and using the books (reading, displaying, lending, and annotating them; Schmid 2008, 9–10). Rather than imagining an all-purpose scribe or even a scribal network as responsible for all these stages of book production and transmission, Schmid attributes the impetus for the production and transmission of Christian books to individuals, some of them wealthy, who saw the need for multiplying books rapidly enough to keep up with the spread of the Christian movement (12).[13] As a model he suggests Marcion, who sponsored an edited version of the New Testament that must have been disseminated widely from the beginning in identical copies (except for unconscious errors), since the text remained stable for a period of more than 150 years (13).[14]

As an example of editorial variation that transcends the work of scribes, Schmid points to the difficult problem of the conclusion of Paul's letter to the Romans. Forms of the text exist showing the letter (1) ending at Rom 14:23, (2) extending to 16:23 or (3) to 16:24 or (4) with a doxology added at 16:25–27.[15] Each of these variant forms requires a series of thoughtful decisions about the proper way to end the letter, decisions that cannot reasonably be attributed to scribes working "on the fly" (Schmid 2008, 15–16). They are the work of editors, their decisions then perpetuated by copyists who were not themselves responsible for the redactional changes. Schmid also points to the probable effect of readers' marginal

---

13. Metzger (1981, 21) refers to the "rapid expansion and consequent increased demand by individuals and by congregations for copies of scripture" as requiring "the speedy multiplication of copies."
14. He refers to his study of Marcion's text, Schmid 1995.
15. This is a simplified account; altogether, there are fourteen different versions.

notes on the subsequent history of the text, illustrating by means of a photographic image from P.Bod. XIV (P^{75}) at the place where Jesus cleanses the ten leprous men. At Luke 17:14, where Jesus tells them, "Go, show yourselves to the priests," an interlinear mark and a marginal sign direct the reader to a note in the bottom margin, clearly written in a different hand, saying "I will. Be clean. And immediately they were cleansed." Schmid infers that the comment was added by a reader who was familiar with one or more of the accounts of the healing of a leprous man in Mark 1:41–42, Matt 8:3, or Luke 5:13, all of which contain these words. We cannot know whether the author of the marginal note intended the words to be added to the text or simply placed the note there as a connection to the other account(s). Although the note was not added to any of the manuscripts examined for the IGNTP text of Luke, other, similar additions to the story are found in some manuscripts, perhaps having arisen as readers' notes, not scribal alterations (Schmid 2008, 16–21).

I have cited extensively from Schmid's essay because it reflects concerns that were addressed also by others in the volume and it offers a challenge to the casual reference to all textual variations as "scribal alterations." Parker also engages the question "did scribes revise the text they were copying?" (Parker 2008, 151). He points out that a scribe in the middle of the copying process is unlikely to have made the theological changes Ehrman cites. Such changes are more likely to have occurred while the exemplar was being examined prior to copying, when its errors were checked and corrected (154).

The ultimate source of many of the conscious alterations of New Testament manuscripts is probably amateur readers, as James Zetzel has found to be the case with many classical Latin manuscripts (Zetzel 1981, 232–39).[16] These book-lovers "wrote comments in the margins, made corrections of errors where they noticed them, and generally created a book that was of service to themselves" (ibid., 238). These comments and corrections were then taken up into the text of subsequent copies. This process need not imply that the readers and annotators were disconnected from the theological influences of their church settings. John Brogan is probably on the right track in attributing many of the theological alterations to the leaders of Christian communities who shaped the thinking of

---

16. I am grateful to Michael W. Holmes, whose references in several essays first made me aware of the importance of Zetzel's book.

those who heard their sermons and commentaries relative to the theological controversies of their day, but he is probably mistaken in imagining the scribes as "ponder[ing] over these theological and scriptural questions during times of prayer, meditation, and study" and then reading and copying the text "through the eyes of their interpretive community" (Brogan 2003, 25).

The studies surveyed above and related ones make it clear how difficult it is to reconstruct the history of Christian texts in the earliest period of their production and transmission, when so much textual variation occurred. Even the use of the terms conscious and unconscious in reference to scribal alterations entails some psychological assumptions about scribes (Parker 2008, 151–58). Although Hort referred to "the observed proclivities of average copyists" (Westcott and Hort 1881, 2:23), he was not naïve. He went on to point out that scribes were motivated by more different impulses than often imagined; that different scribes responded to different impulses; and that two readings in conflict could often each be explained by impulses operative on scribes in other cases (ibid., 25). The only way to be sure of a particular scribe's copying habits is to study the work of that scribe. Fortunately, we have several such studies now available.

Scribal Habits in New Testament Manuscripts

Paleographers have routinely analyzed scribal hands in New Testament manuscripts in order to identify how many copyists were involved and to distinguish the original hands from those of correctors (see Milne and Skeat 1938). Such paleographical studies have also enabled scholars to classify the most frequent kinds of scribal errors (omitting, duplicating, transposing, and so on). But the discovery of New Testament papyri containing substantial amounts of text has made it possible to investigate scribal practices in manuscripts a century or two older than our oldest majuscules.[17] I referred in chapter 7 to several such efforts. But by far the most detailed study appeared in 2008, James R. Royse's *Scribal Habits in Early Greek New Testament Papyri*, a revision of his 1981 ThD dissertation.

Royse gives detailed attention to "the big six" of NT papyri: P^{45}, P^{46}, P^{47}, P^{66}, P^{72}, and P^{75}. He determines that the only way to distinguish the

---

[17]. Many scholars have posited that scribes copying New Testament texts after the canon was formally established were not as free with their changes as in earlier times.

variants produced by scribes from the readings found in the scribe's exemplar is to adopt Colwell's method of concentrating on singular readings, that is, those without the support of other manuscripts. Since it is impossible to establish that a reading has no support at all in any manuscript, version, or father, the best a researcher can do is compare the reading in question to the widest possible database. Royse has used Tischendorf's eighth edition, von Soden, Nestle-Aland (25th, 26th, and 27th), UBS (3rd and 4th), Aland's *Synopsis,* the IGNTP, *Das Neue Testament auf Payprus,* and Reuben Swanson's *New Testament Greek Manuscripts* (1995–2001). To minimize the difficulties of distinguishing between accidental and intentional alterations, Royse simply uses the term "error" for any reading that was not in the scribe's exemplar (Royse 2008, 97).[18]

Royse uses such categories as nonsense readings, additions, omissions, transpositions, substitutions, conflations, and harmonizations to discuss the scribal errors of each manuscript. He also treats corrections, whether by the original hand or later hands. He gives due attention to readings that have been identified by others as motivated by theological interests. After each of the six chapters devoted to the manuscripts, he provides a summary listing the main copying habits of the scribe of that manuscript, based solely on its singular readings.

In addition to the wealth of data collected in this volume, Royse makes two findings of great importance to textual criticism: (1) the scribes of all six manuscripts omit more often than they add to the text; and (2) all six scribes tend to harmonize to the immediate context (2008, 737). So important is the first of these discoveries that Royse devotes a complete chapter to the shorter-reading canon first devised by Griesbach (705–36). Although Griesbach's canon preferring the shorter reading was subject to a number of conditions, it has often been used uncritically.[19] On the basis of his own findings, Royse formulates a new text-critical canon. In general, the longer reading is to be preferred, except where: (1) the longer reading appears, on external grounds, to be late; or (2) the longer reading may have arisen from harmonization to the immediate context, to parallels, or to general usage; or (3) the longer reading may have arisen from an attempt at grammatical improvement (Royse 2008, 735).

---

18. For reflections on the uses of accidental, intentional, conscious, unconscious, and the relation of Freudian theory to scribal errors, see Royse's comments at 97 n. 108 and supplementary n. 8 at 754–55.

19. See Metzger and Ehrman 2005, 166.

With respect to theologically motivated changes, among the total of 1,386 singular readings in the six manuscripts, Royse identifies only three variants as most likely due to theological motivation, all of them in P[72]. First, at 1 Pet 5:1, where all other witnesses refer to the sufferings "of Christ" (χριστου, *christou*), P[72] reads "of God" (θεου, *theou*). Second, at 1 Pet 1:2, where all other witnesses read "Grace and peace be multiplied to you in knowledge of God and Jesus our Lord," P[72] omits the "and" between "God and Jesus," to read "God Jesus our Lord" (θεου Ιησου του κυριου ημων, *theou Iēsou tou kuriou hēmōn*). Third, in Jude 5, where other witnesses attribute the salvation of the people from Egypt to "God," "the Lord," or "Jesus," P[72] alone reads "God Christ" (θεος χριστος, *theos Christos*). Although this last example is more complicated than the other two, all three underscore the deity of Christ (Royse 2008, 611). It is striking that Royse finds no other likely examples among the five other manuscripts, even though several scholars, including Ehrman, have identified some readings in these papyri as theologically motivated.[20]

Manuscripts as Artifacts

Many of the studies referenced above open up fruitful new trajectories for New Testament textual criticism by concentrating attention on the manuscripts themselves and not simply on the texts they contain. To be sure, several older studies attended carefully to the physical properties of manuscripts, their manufacture, and the history revealed through annotations and colophons,[21] but recent research, especially on the papyri, has

---

20. For example, the original hand of P[66] at John 10:33 has "the Jews" saying to Jesus, "you, although a human, are making yourself God" (τον θεον, *ton theon*); but the article making the word "god" definite has been corrected, so that Jesus is understood to claim to be not "God" but "a god." Ehrman (1993, 84, 114 n. 184) takes the addition of the article to be a theologically motivated change, whereas: (1) It is easily explained as an accidental doubling of the second syllable of the preceding word, "yourself" (σεαυτον, *seauton*). (2) The scribe corrected his own mistake, a fact not noticed by Ehrman (this example cited by Royse 2008, 459). It is difficult to know whether a change that affects *a reader's understanding* theologically was therefore *motivated* by a scribe's theology. Barbara Aland (2006, 122) points out how important it is to know the habits of individual scribes before attributing conscious motives to their work.

21. See, for example, the series of studies by T. C. Skeat on the codices Sinaiticus, Vaticanus, and Alexandrinus, as well as selected papyri, now gathered into section b of Skeat 2004.

sought to open still more windows into the world of early Christianity. Exemplary of this research are the efforts to solve two of the greatest puzzles about early Christian manuscripts. As I mentioned briefly in chapter 1, early Christian literature is distinguished from other writings contemporary with it by two scribal practices: a preference for the codex form of book over the roll (scroll) and the use of a system of abbreviations (the *nomina sacra*) to set apart a number of words deemed to be of special importance.

In the 1930s Frederick Kenyon had already realized that the great majority of Christian writings coming from the sands of Egypt were in codex, or leaf, form, even though the roll continued to be used almost universally for most other literature copied during the second and third centuries. Why did Christians prefer the codex to the roll? Kenyon attributed the choice of the codex to the desire of early scribes to include more texts in one book than even the largest rolls would hold (Kenyon 1937, 18). In 1940 Colin Roberts tackled the question more systematically and intentionally (Roberts 1940, 169–204). Since the codex originated in Rome in the form of parchment notebooks, Roberts hypothesized that the Gospel of Mark was originally written in Rome in a parchment notebook and that the same format was used when that Gospel traveled to Egypt and was copied on papyrus. The status of the Alexandrian church and its traditional association with Mark would have given the papyrus codex status among Christians (187–89). In the revised and enlarged edition of his small work on the codex, Roberts and T. C. Skeat offered a new hypothesis, namely, that Christians adopted the codex from the practice of the Jewish community in Rome or Antioch, where papyrus tablets were used to write down decisions in the Mishnah and rabbinic sayings. Possibly early Christians assembled papyrus tablets into a "primitive form of codex" and used this to record the materials of a "Proto-Gospel" (Roberts and Skeat 1983, 58–59). The common element in these hypotheses is that there must have been some powerful event or promulgation from a major Christian center before 100 c.e. to account for such a massive migration from roll to codex.

Subsequent studies on the codex have benefited from the huge databank assembled by Eric G. Turner in his *Typology of the Early Codex*. Turner's purpose is not to address the issue of the origins of the codex but to "map the territory" (1977, 2) of the codex by comparing the formats, construction, page sizes, and other codicological details, so as to arrive at a typology similar to that which archaeologists create from a comparative study of clay pots. His primary subjects are Greek and Latin papyri (both biblical and secular) from the second through the sixth centuries. In addition to observations about and illustrations of the manufacture of codices, scribal preparation for laying out the work, and issues of dating, the book contains tables listing papyrus and (separately) parchment codices grouped by page size, makeup (number of gatherings), date, and other variables. Although Turner's work is indispensable to those seeking to account for the Christian preference for the codex, the data are open to varying interpretations.[22]

Some theories focus on pragmatic reasons: comparative cost advantage over the roll, ease of consultation of texts, portability, familiarity with the codex from its use in elementary education or daily business. Others invoke the concept of a deliberate decision from an influential church center. Although each of these rationales may sound initially plausible, none of them is more than an educated guess.

Consider three examples. Having recognized fatal weaknesses in his first two hypotheses, T. C. Skeat offered yet another suggestion in a 1994 article (Skeat 1994, 263–68). Observing that every single papyrus fragment of the Gospels is from a codex, he suggested that the four-Gospel canon, which is already taken for granted by Irenaeus (about 185), is inseparable from the four-Gospel codex, since only a codex could contain all four (ibid.; cf. Skeat 1992, 194–99). Once the church had decided to adopt this Roman innovation, the codex became the standard for manuscripts of the Gospels, so that even a copy of one or two Gospels would have been made in a codex (Roberts and Skeat 1983, 83–85). Harry Gamble offers a second example. He agrees with Roberts and Skeat that some decisive event in the publication of Christian literature must have occurred to elevate the codex to preeminence, but he posits collections of Pauline letters, rather than Gospels, as the catalyst (Gamble 1995, 58–65). Roger Bagnall argues that there is no necessary connection between the choice of book format and the volume of material included in it. He asks, "Would the Christians have used the book roll for the gospels if there had been only three of them? Or for Paul's letters if there had been only half as many of them?" (Bagnall 2009, 81). Similarly, Eldon Epp puts no empha-

---

22. E. Turner 1977, 63–69. The most important studies on the origin and development of the codex include Roberts and Skeat 1983; Blanchard 1989; Gamble 1995, 49–66; Epp 2005, 522–36; Stanton 2004, 165–91.

sis on the volume of material as a rationale for the Christian adoption of the codex but focuses instead on the need of itinerant Christian preachers for books of modest enough size to be easily carried, citing Turner's list of early papyrus codices that tended toward just such modest size. Epp's thesis does not depend on the *contents* of the books (whether Gospels, Epistles, or just lists of scriptural texts), only on their portability and visibility. Having once seen respected traveling evangelists using such "props," Christian scribes would have been encouraged to adopt the codex as the standard for copying Christian literature in general (Epp 1998, 21).

The scribal practice involving the *nomina sacra* has proved equally resistant to a consensus. As I indicated briefly in chapter 1, beginning with the earliest identifiably Christian manuscripts, scribes routinely abbreviated certain words, most notably the words "God," "Lord," "Jesus," and "Christ."[23] The usual practice was to write the first and last letters (case endings were taken into account), although variations occurred: (Θεος [*Theos*] as $\overline{Θς}$, Κυριος [*Kyrios*] as $\overline{Κς}$, Χριστος [*Christos*] as $\overline{Χς}$ or $\overline{Χρς}$, Ιησους [*Iēsous*] as $\overline{Ις}$ or $\overline{Ιης}$). By the late second century some scribes extended the practice to additional words, including "spirit" (πνευμα, *pneuma*), "human being" or "man" (ανθρωπος, *anthropos*), and "cross" (σταυρος, *stauros*). By the fifth century eight more words were frequently or routinely abbreviated, namely, the words for "father" (πατηρ, *patēr*), "son" (υιος, *huios*), "savior" (σωτηρ, *sōtēr*), "mother" (μητηρ, *mētēr*), "heaven" (ουρανος, *ouranos*), "Israel" (Ισραελ, *Israēl*), "David" (Δαυειδ, *Daueid*), and "Jerusalem" (Ιερουσαλημ, *Ierousalēm*). For all the longer words, not only the first and last (or first and second) but also medial consonants and vowels could become parts of the compendium. Almost always, a horizontal stroke was added above the abbreviation to show it was not a complete word.[24] The manuscripts exhibit the difficulty scribes faced in deciding when certain of the words ("son," "mother," "father") were used sacrally or commonly.

The designation *nomina sacra* was given by Ludwig Traube in his 1907 study of the phenomenon, well before "the age of the papyri"

---

23. *Nomina sacra* occur not only in biblical texts but also in other Christian writings, including apocryphal literature, and even on artifacts such as amulets, mosaics, and icons. They are routinely found in texts written in Greek, Latin, and Coptic but often also those in Armenian and Slavonic.

24. Since the Greek alphabet was also used for numerals, scribes used a supralinear stroke in these cases as well.

brought earlier examples to light.[25] Traube and many subsequent scholars attributed the innovation to Jewish scribes preparing a Greek translation of the Hebrew Bible. It is well-known that by the first century C.E., if not before, scribes and readers gave the Hebrew divine name special care both orally and in writing. Since the name consists of four Hebrew letters (*yod, hē, waw, hē*), scholars refer to this name as the Tetragrammaton (usually transliterated as YHWH and spelled out as Yahweh). This name, regarded as so sacred as to be unpronounceable, was often set apart for special treatment by scribes. In some Hebrew manuscripts, scribes inserted the Tetragrammaton in an archaic form of Hebrew, as in several of the manuscripts from Qumran (Tov 2004, 218–19). Similarly, Jewish scribes copying Greek biblical manuscripts used a variety of means for indicating the special significance of the Tetragrammaton, including the insertion of Hebrew characters into the Greek text (303–15). Thus, many scholars have assumed or asserted that Christian scribes borrowed this practice from Jewish copyists, extending the treatment to the word "Lord," then "Christ" and "Jesus," and gradually the additional terms.[26]

Other scholars looked to the imitation of Greek scribal conventions for abbreviating words, as illustrated from ostraca or pre-Christian Greek inscriptions (Rudberg 1910, 71–100; 1913, 156–61; Nachmanson 1910, 100–144).

Colin H. Roberts devoted major attention to this puzzling phenomenon in his Schweich Lectures for 1977. Roberts advanced the discussion in three particulars. First, he suggested that the *nomina sacra* were strictly a Christian innovation, originating in the abbreviation for the name Jesus (Ιησους, *Iēsous*) in a curious passage in Barn. 9:8. Here the author, commenting on the Greek text of Gen 14:14, notes that the number 318 is there expressed as eighteen (*iota-eta*, IH) and 300 (*tau*, T): "so he reveals Jesus in two letters, and in the remaining one the cross." Since the writer does not offer his interpretation as a novelty, Roberts holds that the abbreviation for the name Jesus was probably well-known and may have been a fixture in Christian manuscripts prior to the date of

---

25. Traube's work was expanded in light of the papyri by Paap 1959 and O'Callaghan 1970.

26. Traube supposed that all of the fifteen words except "Jesus," "Christ," "son," "savior," "mother," and "cross" originated among Jewish scribes.

Barnabas, that is, before 100 C.E. (Roberts 1979, 35–36).[27] Second, Roberts locates the motive for giving special attention to the name of Jesus and related words and titles in a "theology of the Name" found in the New Testament (41–44). Thus, the primary four words "Jesus," "God," "Lord," and "Christ" are used in the church's earliest confessional statements about Jesus; the other terms come to express the core beliefs of the Christian community (46). Third, Roberts accounts for the rapid adoption of the convention by tracing it back to directions given by leaders in the Jerusalem church.[28]

In 1998 Larry Hurtado published a programmatic essay surveying all the relevant literature on the *nomina sacra* and offering a new proposal (Hurtado 1998). He agrees with Roberts that the *nomen sacrum* for "Jesus" was already in place by the late first century, prior to its usage in Barnabas. He speculates that it may have derived from the numerical value of the Hebrew word for "life" (*heth-yod*, חי = 18). Christians acquainted with Jewish gematria (number symbolism) and familiar with texts and traditions connecting Jesus with life may well have transferred the Hebrew gematria to a Greek equivalent (Hurtado 1998, 665–69). One advantage of Hurtado's theory is that it accounts for the supralinear stroke over all the *nomina sacra*, namely, that the very first of these compendia was both a number and the first two letters of the name of Jesus.

More recently David Martinez has carried forward Roberts's suggestion that the *nomina sacra* have a creedal core. Martinez notes "the possibility that one or more authoritative texts, which had a creedal flavor, set (or at least helped to set) the roster" (Martinez 2009, 593). He calls attention to the last sentence of Peter's speech in Acts 2:14–36, which contains the creedlike statement, "Let all the house of Israel know with certainty that God has made Lord and Christ this Jesus whom you crucified." Not only are the "big four" *nomina sacra* found here, but two others (Ισραηλ [*Israēl*] and σταυρος [*stauros*] in the verbal form εσταυρωσατε [*estaurōsate*]). Moreover, many other of the fifteen standard terms appear somewhere in the Pentecost speech (611–12). I myself had noted in 1993 in a contribution to a Festschrift that Acts 2:14–36 contains eleven of the fifteen *nomina sacra*

---

27. Clement of Alexandria (*Strom.* 6.278–280) also knows this numerological interpretation of Gen 14:14.

28. Roberts 1979, 46. Roberts's last suggestion seems particularly speculative, since we have no reason for attributing to the Jerusalem church the authority to set standards for scribal treatment of the name of Jesus.

and that "the importance of many of these words in the explication of the faith in a Jewish-Christian environment could well account for their special treatment in the church's literary tradition" (Hull 1993, 37–38).

In his 2006 book *The Earliest Christian Artifacts: Manuscripts and Christian Origins*, Hurtado summarized and critiqued the most substantial studies on early Christian manuscripts in their historical and social contexts, extending the research in fruitful directions. Hurtado points out that the earliest Christian manuscripts may, in fact, also be the earliest examples of Christian material culture in existence, a possibility overlooked by most historians of Christianity. Therefore, the texts contained in the manuscripts, but also the physical makeup, scribal practices, and intended use of the manuscripts, are critically important concerns for those who study early Christianity (Hurtado 2006a, 1–13). One of the most instructive features of the book is a table of "Christian Literary Texts in Manuscripts of the Second and Third Centuries" (209–29). We find laid out in six columns descriptions of 246 manuscripts, giving textual content, current location and inventory numbers, date, writing material (papyrus or parchment), form (codex or roll), and comments (characteristics of the handwriting, presence of *nomina sacra*, readers' helps). After detailed comparative studies of the various proposals as to the relative Christian preference for the codex, Hurtado does not offer a new solution, although he leans toward Gamble's hypothesis that an early collection of the Paulines may have set the pattern (73, 80). But he does offer one observation by way of stimulating further research: early Christians were quite willing to continue to use the bookroll for many Christian texts (including, for example, the Gospel of Mary and Gospel of Thomas), but there is not a single example of any document that became part of the New Testament canon found on the recto (front side) of a roll; all are in codex form except for three fragments written on the verso (back) of a reused roll. Therefore, "it is reasonable to judge that the use of a roll to copy a text signals that the copyist and/or user for whom the copy was made did not regard that text (or at least that copy of that text) as having scriptural status" (81).

Hurtado gives equally thorough attention to the history of research on the *nomina sacra*, including responding to criticisms of his 1998 proposals. His major point is that although there is no consensus regarding the origin and significance of this scribal practice, the *nomina sacra* embody "an interesting and significant visual expression of early Christian piety" that should be of interest to students of early Christianity (Hurtado 2006a, 133). Still under debate is the question whether there are any certain examples of Jewish scribes using a *nomen sacrum* (see Tuckett 2003, 433–35; Kraft 2003, 51–72). Hurtado admits the possibility, but contends that there are no *pre-Christian* examples of such usage. Recently a single example of the *nomen sacrum* for "God" in the genitive case (Θ̅Υ̅) in a Greek inscription (dated 360–370 C.E.) from the synagogue at Sardis has been reported (Edwards 2009, 813–21), but this example does not suffice to answer the question of where the practice originated.

WHENCE THE *STAUROGRAM*?

Hurtado also gives attention to a peculiar way of abbreviating the words for "cross" (σταυρος, *stauros*) and "crucify" (σταυροω, *stauroō*) in three early Christian manuscripts: P⁷⁵, P⁶⁶, and P⁴⁵ (in order of date). In a handful of instances, these manuscripts combine the *tau* and *rho* such that the *rho* is superimposed on the *tau* in a compendium that has come to be called a *staurogram*: (Hurtado 2006a, 135–54).²⁹

Although the *chi-rho* (☧) and other Christograms appear to be adaptations of pre-Christian symbols found in secular inscriptions and literature (McNamee 1981), the *tau-rho* is uniquely Christian; moreover, in its earliest attested usages, it appears only within abbreviated forms for words, never as a freestanding device (as it later became). Since we find the staurogram in three early manuscripts with no scribal connections among them, Hurtado suggests the *tau-rho* must have been developed independently of any of these manuscripts (Hurtado 2006a, 142). This would make the *tau-rho* the earliest Jesus monogram, as Aland noted. Following up suggestions of Kurt Aland (1967a) and Erich Dinkler (1967, 134–78) and incorporating the results of his own earlier study (Hurtado 2000, 271–88), Hurtado underscores the possibility that the *tau-rho* functioned as "a stylized reference to (and visual representation of) Jesus on the cross" (Hurtado 2006a, 151). That is, the rounded top of the *rho*, which projects just above the crossbar of the *tau*, might well

---

29. For an example see ibid., 237, plate 5, which shows a close-up of Luke 14:27 in P.Bod. XIV (P⁷⁵). This term takes its origin from such words as "monogram" and "Christogram." Kurt Aland first called attention to this feature (1967a, 173–79). For an image of the staurogram (without overstroke), go to http://gospel-thomas.net/pictures/cross.jpg.

suggest the head of the crucified Jesus.[30] If so, the *tau-rho* was the most ancient of all visual representations of Jesus on the cross, indeed, perhaps the oldest example of Christian iconography extant, belying the conventional views of art historians that Christian art is not attested prior to the age of Constantine.[31]

Models

The above examples of the "empirical turn" in textual studies suggest the rich possibilities that lie ahead for younger students wishing to make their mark in New Testament textual criticism. Several of the books and articles I have referenced serve as good models for future research, but I will focus on one book not mentioned there and one text-critical issue as specific examples of the fruits that may be gathered from close attention to the physical properties of the manuscripts.

What Do We Know about Codex Bezae?

Of all the studies of specific New Testament manuscripts, none can match for thoroughness of detail David C. Parker's *Codex Bezae: An Early Christian Manuscript and Its Text* (1992). Divided into five parts, the book devotes nearly fifty pages to the paleography of the original hand and the numerous correctors and annotators. Parker has instructive comments on the codicology not only of Codex Bezae but of dozens of other Greek-Latin bilingual codices. His close reading and shrewd detective work enable him to describe the format of the scribe's exemplar and to demonstrate how the scribe changed that format, most notably by altering the sense-lines in the Gospels. He is able to show even that the Greek and the Latin columns represent different customs in reference to the *nomina sacra* (Parker 1992, 106). He suggests a date of around 400 for the manuscript, locates its original provenance in Berytus (Beirut), and identifies the scribe as probably a copyist of Latin legal texts working in the scriptorium of a law school (279–86). He argues that the kind of *text* contained

---

30. See the patristic references to the visual symbolism of the *tau* in Hurtado 2006a, 146–50.

31. Hurtado (2006a, 141–52) cites the commendable example of Robin Margaret Jenson, who, alone among art historians, references the staurogram in the three papyri as "a kind of pictogram" of a crucified man (2000, 138).

in the manuscript "is as old as the beginnings of the Gospel traditions" (280) and that it developed in the second half of the second century, after the four Gospels had become a recognized quantity in some churches and had begun to be harmonized and expanded through the addition of oral traditions about Jesus and the early church. I cite Parker's study as a model not because all of his conclusions will necessarily hold up to future scrutiny, but to show what is possible by means of a study that pays minute attention not only to former studies of the Codex but to every aspect and characteristic of the manuscript itself.[32]

Now, in keeping with earlier chapters, I cite a model treatment of an important New Testament textual variant.

Is 1 Corinthians 14:34–35 an Interpolation?

For more than a century some scholars have insisted that this passage, bidding the wives at Corinth to be silent during "the assembly," is a non-Pauline interpolation into the text, perhaps originally a gloss modeled on 1 Tim 2:11–12.[33] The arguments have been based largely on internal considerations (linguistic peculiarities, interruption of its context, contradiction of other Pauline texts). A few interpreters have defended the view that the words in question are not Paul's but are his quotation of a Corinthian slogan he rejects (Odell-Scott 2000, 68–74). With the rise of social analysis of biblical texts, literature on the passage has burgeoned, and it remains a hotly debated text. The external evidence, however, appears mostly straightforward: not a single New Testament witness omits the passage; in a number of manuscripts, however, the passage follows verse 40.[34] All but two of the witnesses for the displaced text are Western (the other two are Byzantine). The majuscule manuscripts are all Greek-Latin bilingual texts, and F and G probably derive from a common archetype closely related to Codex Bezae, which would reduce the testimony of the three witnesses to one.

---

32. For an insightful demonstration by Parker of the information that can be gleaned from close study of a double page of Codex Bezae, see Parker 2003b, 43–50.

33. As long ago as 1863 the Dutch pastor J. W. Straatman conjectured that the verses were interpolated, a view that earned him a place in the apparatus of Nestle-Aland. For the history of scholarship and response to it, see Thiselton 2000, 1146–62.

34. The witnesses are Greek manuscripts D (06) F (010) G (012) 88 915, Sy^P, Latin a (61) b (89), Ambrosiaster, Sedulius Scotus.

In a series of articles, Philip B. Payne has demonstrated that the external evidence is not, in fact, as straightforward as it appears, and I cite his studies to illustrate the value of close study of the manuscripts themselves, rather than simply the texts the manuscripts contain. In a careful analysis of the sixth-century Latin Codex Fuldensis, Payne shows that the manuscript contains the text of 1 Cor 14:34–40 following verse 33, but at the end of verse 33 there is a scribal mark (similar to "hd") keyed to a note in the bottom margin, where verses 36–40 are repeated. Payne judges that the marginal note is by the original scribe, who was directed by Victor of Capua, reviser of the Codex, to indicate variant readings in a number of places in the manuscript using the "hd" mark. Payne interprets the marginal note as showing that Bishop Victor knew of one or more witnesses lacking verses 34–35 and that he preferred such a reading (Payne 1995).

Payne bolstered this theory by an analysis of extratextual scribal marks in the left-hand margin of Codex Vaticanus: sometimes a double dot, which Payne dubs an umlaut, after the German vowel marker, and sometimes the umlaut accompanied by a short line projecting into the margin (similar to a *paragraphus*), a compendium Payne calls a bar-umlaut. Payne discovered these scribal markers at numerous places in Vaticanus, in a high percentage of the occurrences placed on a line just preceding one of the textual variants recorded in the apparatus of Nestle-Aland. (The markers appear just opposite the last line of v. 33 in 1 Cor 14; see Payne 1995, 24–62.) Payne responded to his critics and refined his argument in three respects in subsequent studies. (1) By studying the original codex in the Vatican under magnification with the aid of Paul Canart, senior paleographer at the Vatican, he was able to detect the original apricot color of the ink showing at the edges of these dots in fifty-one places in the manuscript (Payne and Canart 2000, 105–13). (2) He deemphasizes the significance of the bar, since its function is not always clear and there are many examples where the umlaut appears alone at a place where other textual witnesses attest a textual variant (Payne 2004, 105–12). (3) After consultation with experts, he agrees that the umlaut should be called a *distigme* (pl. *distigmai*) and the bar an *obelos*, which is the usual designation for this scribal feature when it is used to mark a textual variant. He labels the combination a *distigme-obelos* (Payne and Canart 2000, 199–225). Payne urges that these textual phenomena strongly support the thesis that there were manuscripts prior to Codex Vaticanus that did not contain 1 Cor 14:34–35. The presence of these verses in two different places in the textual tradition shows that the context made it difficult to know where to insert the gloss, since it does not really fit in either place. He argues that the strong internal evidence combined with the recently noticed scribal phenomena mark 14:34–35 as a non-Pauline interpolation. My point here is not to validate Payne's conclusions[35] but to hold up his work with the realia, the actual manuscripts in their physicality, as a model well illustrating the "empirical turn" characteristic of textual research in the twenty-first century.

Future Tasks

It is my hope that this chapter has captured some of the excitement and vigor of New Testament textual criticism in its current practice. There is no shortage of opportunities for younger scholars entering the field or thinking about it. Following are ten suggestions for research culled from recent studies (Hurtado 1999, 33–48, and Metzger 2003, 348–49) and from my own reflections.

1. Other manuscripts need to be studied with the meticulous care exhibited by Parker in his work with Codex Bezae.

2. There is a need for sophisticated analyses of patristic quotations, following the models of the volumes in the SBL series The New Testament in the Greek Fathers.

3. A study of the history of the Greek lectionary text has still not been undertaken.

4. Much work needs to be done on the textual witnesses to the book of Revelation. Especially intriguing is the phenomenon that copies of Revelation are frequently found in manuscripts containing other, nonbiblical texts; conversely, Revelation is very often lacking in manuscripts that contain the rest of the New Testament.[36] What do these phenomena suggest

---

35. Parker 2008, 276, calls attention to a paper read by J. Kloha in the 2006 New Testament Textual Criticism Section of the SBL Annual Meeting, in which Kloha references a "large number" of other dislocations of text in bilingual manuscripts of Paul, so that the dislocation Payne refers to in Fuldensis may contribute little or nothing to the discussion about the original text.

36. The data are striking: there are fifty-nine Greek manuscripts containing the entire New Testament, but there are 150 manuscripts that contain the whole New Testament *except for* Rev; see Parker 2008, 283.

about the canonical status of the book and its reception in the Christian community?[37]

5. What can we learn from the analysis of New Testament quotations and allusions in noncontinuous sources (inscriptions, amulets, private letters, unidentified papyrus texts)? (See S. Pickering 1999, 121–40; S. Porter 2003, 167–86.)

6. More research is needed on the education and responsibilities of scribes and their relation to editors, readers, and other users of texts.

7. We must continue our efforts to explain the Christian "addiction"[38] to the codex and the origin and function of the *nomina sacra*.

8. The field is wide open for those who would pioneer new techniques in electronic editing of texts and electronic management of data.

9. The interface between orality (or "orality/scribality") studies and textual criticism is only beginning to be explored. The old idea from form criticism that there was a long period of exclusively oral tradition in early Christianity has been largely abandoned (see Gamble 1995, 28–32), but the phenomenon that ancient literature was mostly consumed (and even produced) orally/aurally has not been sufficiently explored in biblical studies (see Kelber 2007, 1–24).[39] Parker's *Living Text of the Gospels* may point the way to further exploration of the influence of oral tradition on the transmission of literary texts.

10. Bible translators and translation committees have generally done a very poor job in communicating text-critical decisions to their readers.[40] There is room for a handbook with guidelines sufficiently comprehensive to serve translators working across the whole spectrum of target audiences.

The opening paragraph of this chapter referenced a paper delivered by Eldon Jay Epp in the Textual Criticism Section at the 1977 Society of

---

37. See Metzger 2003, 205–6, for the statistics.

38. Graham Stanton (2004, 71, 166) draws attention to F. G. Kenyon's statement that the Chester Beatty papyri "confirm the belief that the Christian community was *addicted to the codex* rather than to the roll" (Kenyon 1933–1937, 1:12); emphasis Stanton's.

39. Paul J. Achtemeier placed the issue front and center in his presidential address to the SBL in 1989 (Achtemeier 1990, 3–27). James D. G. Dunn sharpened the focus in his presidential address at the Studiorum Novi Testamenti Societas in 2002 (Dunn 2003, 139–75, esp 154 n. 47); but see the cautions of Gamble (1995, 28–32) about setting up an oral/literary dichotomy in early Christianity.

40. See the valuable survey by Holger Szesnat (2007, 1–18). This electronic resource can be accessed at http://purl.org/TC.

9. REASSESSING THE DISCIPLINE

Biblical Literature Annual Meeting. Frustrated at the small number of participants in the section over several years and the lack of progress in major projects, Epp entitled his paper "New Testament Textual Criticism in America: Requiem for a Discipline" (Epp 1979). His major criticisms had to do with the perceived decline of interest in the discipline in the United States. Happily, this final chapter points not to a requiem but to a rebirth of interest in New Testament textual criticism, both in the United States and in many other countries. The *new* textual criticism (as some have labeled it) is not simply the "lower criticism" of generations ago—reconstruction of the text as a preliminary task before the exegetical, theological, and practical disciplines take over. Textual criticism today is a holistic enterprise, incorporating paleography, church history, social-world studies, and even psychology in its toolkit. My aim has been to sketch the history of this vital enterprise, in the hopes of awakening further interest and appreciation in the readers. My hope, as I wrote in the introduction, is that some of you will help to write the next chapter in the development of New Testament textual criticism.

Bibliography

Achtemeier, Paul. 1990. *Omne Verbum Sonat*: The New Testament and the Oral Environment of Late Western Antiquity. *JBL* 109:3–27.

Aland, Barbara. 2006. Sind Schreiber Früher neutestamentlicher Handschriften Interpreten des Textes? Pages 114–22 in Childers and Parker 2006.

———, ed. 1986. *Die grossen katholischen Briefe*. Vol. 1 of *Das Neue Testament in syrischer Überlieferung*. ANTF 7. Berlin: de Gruyter.

———, ed. 1997. *Katholische Briefe*. Vol. 4 of *Novum Testamentum graecum: Editio critica maior*. Stuttgart: Deutsche Bibelgesellschaft.

Aland, Barbara, and Joël Delobel, eds. 1994. *New Testament Textual Criticism, Exegesis and Church History: A Discussion of Methods*. CBET 7. Kampen: Kok Pharos.

Aland, Barbara, and A. Juckel, eds. 1991–2002. *Die paulinischen Briefe*. Vol. 2 of *Das Neue Testament in syrischer Überlieferung*. ANTF 14. Berlin: de Gruyter.

Aland, Barbara, et al., eds. 1993a. *The Greek New Testament*. 4th rev. ed. Stuttgart: Deutsche Bibelgesellschaft.

Aland, Barbara, et al., eds. 1993b. *Novum Testamentum Graece, post Eberhard et Erwin Nestle*. 27th ed. Stuttgart: Deutsche Bibelgesellschaft.

Aland, Kurt. 1965. The Significance of the Papyri for Progress in New Testament Research. Pages 325–46 in *The Bible in Modern Scholarship*. Edited by J. Philip Hyatt. Nashville: Abingdon.

———. 1967a. Bemerkungen zum Alter und Entstehung des Christogramms anhand von Beobachtungen bei P66 und P75. Pages 173–79 in idem, *Studien zur Überlieferung des Neuen Testaments und seines Textes*. ANTF 2. Berlin: de Gruyter.

———. 1967b. Die Bedeutung des P75 für den Text des Neuen Testaments: Ein Beitrag zur Frage des "Western Non-Interpolations." Pages

155–72 in idem, *Studien zur Überlieferung des Neuen Testaments und seines Textes*. ANTF 2. Berlin: de Gruyter.

Aland, Kurt, and Barbara Aland. 1989. *The Text of the New Testament*. 2nd ed. Translated by Erroll B. Rhodes. Grand Rapids: Eerdmans.

The American and British Committees of the International Greek New Testament Project, eds. 1984, 1987. *The Gospel according to St. Luke*. 2 vols. The New Testament in Greek 3. Oxford: Clarendon.

Baarda, Tjitze. 1995. The Syriac Versions of the New Testament. Pages 97–112 in Ehrman and Holmes 1995.

Bagnall, Roger S. 2009. *Early Christian Books in Egypt*. Princeton: Princeton University Press.

Bauckham, Richard. 1998. For Whom Were the Gospels Written? Pages 9–48 in *The Gospels for All Christians: Rethinking the Gospel Audiences*. Edited by Richard Bauckham. Grand Rapids: Eerdmans.

Bentley, James. 1986. *Secrets of Mount Sinai: The Story of the World's Oldest Bible*. Garden City, N.J.: Doubleday.

Birdsall, J. Neville. 1970. The New Testament Text. Pages 308–77 in vol. 1 of *The Cambridge History of the Bible*. Edited by Peter R. Ackroyd and Christopher F. Evans. 3 vols. Cambridge: Cambridge University Press.

———. 1992. The Recent History of New Testament Textual Criticism (from Westcott and Hort, 1881, to the Present). *ANRW* 26.1:99–197.

———. 2002. Irenaeus and the Number of the Beast: Revelation 13, 18. Pages 349–59 in *New Testament Textual Criticism and Exegesis*. Edited by A. Denoux. Leuven: Peeters.

Birdsall, J. Neville, and Robert W. Thomson, eds. 1963. *Biblical and Patristic Studies in Memory of Robert Pierce Casey*. Freiburg: Herder.

Black, David Alan, ed. 2002. *Rethinking New Testament Textual Criticism*. Grand Rapids: Baker Academic.

Blanchard, Alain, ed. 1989. *Les débuts du codex: Actes de la journée d'étude organisée à Paris les 3 et 4 juillet 1985 par l'Institut de papyrologie de la Sorbonne et l'Institut de recherché et d'histoire des textes*. Turnhout: Brepols.

Brock, Sebastian P. 1995. The Use of the Syriac Fathers for New Testament Textual Criticism. Pages 224–36 in Ehrman and Holmes 1995.

Brogan, John J. 2003. Another Look at Codex Sinaiticus. Pages 17–32 in McKendrick and O'Sullivan 2003.

Brown, Schuyler. 1970. Concerning the Origin of the *Nomina Sacra*. *SPap* 9:7–19.

Burgon, John W. 1883. *The Revision Revised*. London: John Murray.

Burkitt, Frederic C. 1904. *Evangelion da-Mepharreshe: The Curetonian Syriac Gospels*. 2 vols. Cambridge: Cambridge University Press.
Callahan, Allen D. 1996. Again: The Origin of Codex Bezae. Pages 56–64 in Parker and Amphoux 1996.
Caragounis, Chrys C. 2006. *The Development of Greek and the New Testament*. Grand Rapids: Baker Academic.
Childers, J. W., and D. C. Parker, eds. 2006. *Transmission and Reception: New Testament Text-Critical and Exegetical Studies*. TS 3/4. Piscataway, N.J.: Gorgias.
Clark, Kenneth W. 1956. The Effect of Recent Textual Criticism upon New Testament Studies. Pages 26–50 in *The Background of the New Testament and Its Eschatology*. Edited by W. D. Davies and D. Daube. Cambridge: Cambridge University Press. Repr. as pages 65–89 in *The Gentile Bias and Other Essays*. Selected by John L. Sharpe III. NovTSup 54. Leiden: Brill, 1980.
———. 1966. The Theological Relevance of Textual Variation in Current Criticism of the Greek NT. *JBL* 85:1–16.
Colwell, Ernest C. 1947. Genealogical Method: Its Achievements and Its Limitations. *JBL* 66:109–33. Repr. as pages 63–83 in Colwell 1969.
———. 1958. The Significance of Grouping of New Testament Manuscripts. *NTS* 4:73–92. Repr. as Method in Grouping New Testament Manuscripts. Pages 1–25 in Colwell 1969.
———. 1959. Method in Locating a Newly-Discovered Manuscript within the Manuscript Tradition of the Greek New Testament. Pages 757–77 in *Studia evangelica: Papers Presented to the International Congress on "The Four Gospels in 1957" Held at Christ Church, Oxford, 1957*. Edited by Kurt Aland et al. TUGAL 73. Berlin: Akademie-Verlag. Repr. as pages 26–44 in Colwell 1969.
———. 1961. The Origin of Texttypes of New Testament Manuscripts. Pages 128–38 in *Early Christian Origins*. Edited by Allen Wikgren. Chicago: University of Chicago Press. Repr. as Method in Establishing the Nature of Text-Types of New Testament Manuscripts. Pages 45–55 in Colwell 1969.
———. 1964. Variant Readings: Classification and Use. *JBL* 83:253–61. Repr. as Method in Classifying and Evaluating Variant Readings. Pages 96–105 in Colwell 1969.
———. 1965. Scribal Habits in Early Papyri: A Study in the Corruption of the Text. Repr. as Method in Evaluating Scribal Habits: A Study of P^{45}, P^{66}, P^{75}. Pages 106–24 in Colwell 1969.

———. 1968. Hort Redivivus: A Plea and a Program. Pages 131–56 in *Transitions in Biblical Scholarship*. Edited by J. Coert Rylaarsdam. Essays in Divinity 6. Chicago: University of Chicago Press. Repr. as pages 148–71 in Colwell 1969.

———. 1969. *Studies in Methodology in Textual Criticism of the New Testament*. NTTS 9. Grand Rapids: Eerdmans.

Colwell, Ernest C., and Donald W. Riddle, eds. 1933. *Prolegomena to the Study of the Lectionary Text of the Gospels*. Studies in the Lectionary Text of the Greek New Testament 1. Chicago: University of Chicago Press.

Colwell, Ernest C., with Ernest W. Tune. 1963. The Quantitative Relationships between MS Text-Types. Pages 25–32 in Birdsall and Thomson 1963. Repr. as Method in Establishing Quantitative Relationships between Text-Types of New Testament Manuscripts. Pages 56–62 in Colwell 1969.

Comfort, Wesley. 1990. *Early Manuscripts and Modern Translations of the New Testament*. Grand Rapids: Baker.

———. 1995. Exploring the Common Identification of Three New Testament Manuscripts: P4, P74, and P67. *TynBul* 46:43–54.

Comfort, Wesley, and David P. Barrett. 2001. *The Text of the Earliest New Testament Greek Manuscripts*. Wheaton, Ill.: Tyndale.

Conybeare, F. C. 1902. Three Early Doctrinal Modifications of the Text of the Gospels. *HibJ* 1:96–113.

Cribiore, Raffaella. 1996. *Writing, Teachers, and Students in Graeco-Roman Egypt*. Atlanta: Scholars Press.

Dain, Alphonse. 1975. *Les Manuscrits*. 3rd ed. Paris: Belles Lettres.

Deissmann, Adolf. 1910. *Light from the Ancient East: The New Testament Illustrated by Recently Discovered Texts from the Graeco-Roman World*. Translated by L. R. M. Strachan. London: Hodder & Stoughton. Repr., Grand Rapids: Baker, 1978.

Dekkers, Eliguis, ed. 1995. *Clavis patrum latinorum*. 3rd aug. and rev. ed. Brepols: Editores Pontificii.

Delling, Gerhard. 1978. Johann Jakob Griesbach: His Life, Work, and Times. Pages 5–21 in *J. J. Griesbach: Synoptic and Text-Critical Studies (1776–1976)*. Edited by Bernard Orchard and Thomas R. W. Longstaff. SNTSMS 34. Cambridge: Cambridge University Press.

Delobel, Joël. 1994. Textual Criticism and Exegesis: Siamese Twins? Pages 98–117 in Aland and Delobel 1994.

Die Griechischen christlichen Schriftsteller der ersten drei Jahrhunderte. 1897–. Leipzig: Hinrichs.

Dinkler, Erich. 1967. Älteste christliche Denkmäler: Bestand und Chronologie. Pages 134–78 in *Signum Crucis.* Edited by Erich Dinkler. Tübingen: Mohr Siebeck.

Dunn, James D. G. 2003. Altering the Default Setting: Re-envisaging the Early Transmission of the Jesus Tradition. *NTS* 49:139–75.

Edwards, James R. 2009. A *Nomen Sacrum* in the Sardis Synagogue. *JBL* 128:813–21.

Egypt Exploration Society. 1898–. *The Oxyrhynchus Papyri.* Various editors. London: Egypt Exploration Society.

Ehrman, Bart D. 1987a. Methodological Developments in the Analysis and Classification of New Testament Documentary Evidence. *NovT* 29:2–45. Repr. as pages 9–32 in Ehrman 2006.

———. 1987b. The Use of Group Profiles for the Classification of New Testament Documentary Evidence. *JBL* 106:465–86. Repr. as pages 33–56 in Ehrman 2006.

———. 1989. A Problem of Circularity: The Alands on the Classification of New Testament Manuscripts. *Bib* 70:377–88. Repr. as pages 57–70 in Ehrman 2006.

———. 1993a. *The Orthodox Corruption of Scripture: The Effects of Early Christological Controversies on the Text of the New Testament.* New York: Oxford University Press.

———. 1993b. The Theodotians as Corruptors of Scripture. Pages 46–51 in *Studia patristica: Papers Presented at the Eleventh International Conference on Patristic Studies Held in Oxford 1991.* Edited by Elizabeth A. Livingstone. Studia Patristica 25. Leuven: Peeters. Repr. as pages 300–306 in Ehrman 2006.

———. 1995. The Text as Window: New Testament Manuscripts and the Social History of Early Christianity. Pages 361–79 in Ehrman and Holmes 1995. Repr. as pages 100–119 in Ehrman 2006.

———. 2005. *Misquoting Jesus: The Story behind Who Changed the Bible and Why.* New York: Oxford University Press.

———. 2006. *Studies in the Textual Criticism of the New Testament.* NTTS 33. Leiden: Brill.

Ehrman, Bart D., Gordon Fee, and Michael W. Holmes, eds. 1992. *The Text of the Fourth Gospel in the Writings of Origen.* Atlanta: Scholars Press.

Ehrman, Bart D., and Michael W. Holmes, eds. 1995. *The Text of the New Testament in Contemporary Research. Essays on the* Status Quaestionis. SD 46. Grand Rapids: Eerdmans.
Elliott, J. Keith. 1972. Rational Criticism and the Text of the New Testament. *Theology* 75:338–43.
———, ed. 1976. *Studies in New Testament Language and Text: Essays in Honour of George D. Kilpatrick on the Occasion of His Sixty-Fifth Birthday.* NovTSup 44. Leiden: Brill.
———. 1987. *A Survey of Manuscripts Used in Editions of the Greek New Testament.* Leiden: Brill.
———. 1992. Can We Recover the Original Text of the New Testament? An Examination of the Role of Thoroughgoing Eclecticism. Pages 17–43 in idem, *Essays and Studies in New Testament Textual Criticism.* EFN 3. Cordoba: Ediciones el Elmendro.
———. 1995. Thoroughgoing Eclecticism in New Testament Textual Criticism. Pages 321–35 in Ehrman and Holmes 1995.
———. 2000. Mark 1.1–3: A Later Addition to the Gospel. *NTS* 46:584–88.
———. 2009. Manuscripts Cited by Stephanus. *NTS* 55:390–95.
Elliott, W. J., and David C. Parker, eds. 1995. *The New Testament in Greek IV: The Gospel according to St John. Vol. 1: The Papyri.* NTTS 20. Leiden: Brill.
Epp, Eldon Jay. 1966a. Coptic Manuscript G67 and the Rôle of Codex Bezae as a Western Witness in Acts. *JBL* 85:197–212. Repr. with added notes as pages 17–39 in Epp 2005.
———. 1966b. *The Theological Tendency of Codex Bezae Cantabrigiensis in Acts.* SNTSMS 3. Cambridge: Cambridge University Press.
———. 1967. The Claremont Profile Method for Grouping New Testament Minuscule Manuscripts. Pages 27–38 in *Studies in the History and Text of the New Testament in Honor of Kenneth Willis Clark, Ph.D.* Edited by Boyd L. Daniels and M. Jack Suggs. SD 29. Salt Lake City: University of Utah Press. Repr. as pages 41–57 in Epp 2005.
———. 1974. The Twentieth Century Interlude in New Testament Textual Criticism. *JBL* 93:386–414. Repr. with added notes as pages 59–100 in Epp 2005.
———. 1976a. The Eclectic Method in New Testament Textual Criticism: Solution or Symptom? *HTR* 69:211–57. Repr. with added notes as pages 125–73 in Epp 2005.
———. 1976b. Toward the Clarification of the Term "Textual Variant."

Pages 153–73 in Elliott 1976. Repr. with added notes as pages 101–24 in Epp 2005.

———. 1979. New Testament Textual Criticism in America: Requiem for a Discipline. *JBL* 98:94–98. Repr. with added notes as pages 175–84 in Epp 2005.

———. 1980. A Continuing Interlude in New Testament Textual Criticism? *HTR* 73:131–51. Repr. with added notes as pages 185–209 in Epp 2005.

———. 1989a. Decision Points in Past, Present, and Future New Testament Textual Criticism. Pages 75–126 in *The New Testament and Its Modern Interpreters*. Edited by Eldon J. Epp and George W. MacRae. Philadelphia: Fortress. Repr. with added notes as pages 228–83 in Epp 2005.

———. 1989b. The New Testament Papyrus Manuscripts in Historical Perspective. Pages 261–88 in *To Touch the Text: Studies in Honor of Joseph A. Fitzmyer, S.J.* Edited by Maurya P. Horgan and Paul J. Kobelski. New York: Crossroad. Repr. with added notes as pages 309–43 in Epp 2005.

———. 1989c. The Significance of the Papyri for Determining the Nature of the New Testament Text in the Second Century. Pages 71–103 in *Gospel Traditions in the Second Century*. Edited by William L. Petersen. Notre Dame, Ind.: University of Notre Dame Press. Repr. with added notes as pages 345–81 in Epp 2005.

———. 1991. New Testament Papyrus Manuscripts and Letter Carrying in Greco-Roman Times. Pages 35–56 in *The Future of Early Christianity*. Edited by Birger A. Pearson. Minneapolis: Fortress. Repr. with added notes as pages 383–409 in Epp 2005.

———. 1997. The New Testament Papyri at Oxyrhynchus in Their Social and Intellectual Context. Pages 47–68 in *Sayings of Jesus: Canonical and Non-canonical: Essays in Honour of Tjitze Baarda*. Edited by W. L. Petersen, J. S. Vos, and H. J. de Jonge. NovTSup 89. Leiden: Brill. Repr. with added notes as pages 497–520 in Epp 2005.

———. 1998. The Codex and Literacy in Early Christianity and at Oxyrhynchus: Issues Raised by Harry Y. Gamble's *Books and Readers in the Early Church*. *CRBR* 11:15–37. Repr. with added notes as pages 521–50 in Epp 2005.

———. 1999. The Multivalence of the Term "Original Text" in New Testament Textual Criticism. *HTR* 92:245–99. Repr. with added notes as pages 551–93 in Epp 2005.

———. 2002a. Issues in New Testament Textual Criticism: Moving from the Nineteenth Century to the Twenty-First Century. Pages 17–76 in Black 2002. Repr. as pages 641–97 in Epp 2005.

———. 2002b. Issues in the Interrelation of New Testament Textual Criticism and Canon. Pages 484–515 in McDonald and Sanders 2002. Repr. as pages 595–638 in Epp 2005.

———. 2003. Anti-Judaic Tendencies in the D-Text of Acts: Forty Years of Conversation. Pages 111–46 in Nicklas and Tilly 2003. Repr. as pages 699–739 in Epp 2005.

———. 2004. The Oxyrhynchus New Testament Papyri: "Not without Honor Except in Their Hometown"? *JBL* 123:5–55. Repr. as pages 743–801 in Epp 2005.

———. 2005. *Perspectives on New Testament Textual Criticism: Collected Essays, 1962–2004.* NovTSup 116. Leiden: Brill. Repr., Atlanta: Society of Biblical Literature, 2008.

———. 2007. Are Early New Testament Manuscripts Truly Abundant? Pages 77–106 in *Israel's God and Rebecca's Children: Christology and Community in Early Judaism and Christianity: Essays in Honor of Larry W. Hurtado and Alan F. Segal.* Edited by April D. Deconick, Helen K. Bond, and Troy A. Miller. Waco, Tex.: Baylor University Press.

Epp, Eldon Jay, and Gordon D. Fee, eds. 1993. *Studies in the Theory and Method of New Testament Textual Criticism.* SD 45. Grand Rapids, Mich: Eerdmans.

Eshbaugh, Howard. 1979. Textual Variants and Theology: A Study of the Galatians Text of Papyrus 46. *JSNT* 3:60–72.

Fascher, Erich. 1953. *Textgeschichte als hermeneutisches Problem.* Halle: Niemeyer.

Fee, Gordon D. 1968–1969. Codex Sinaiticus in the Gospel of John: A Contribution to Methodology in Establishing Textual Relationships. *NTS* 15:23–44. Repr. as pages 221–24 in Epp and Fee 1993.

———. 1974. P75, P66, and Origen: The Myth of Early Textual Recension in Alexandria. Pages 19–45 in *New Dimensions in New Testament Study.* Edited by Richard N. Longenecker and Merrill C. Tenney. Grand Rapids: Zondervan. Repr. as pages 247–73 in Epp and Fee 1993.

———. 1976. Rigorous or Reasoned Eclecticism—Which? Pages 174–96 in Elliott 1976. Repr. as pages 124–40 in Epp and Fee 1993.

———. 1978. Textual Criticism of the New Testament. Pages 127–55 in *Biblical Criticism: Historical, Literary and Textual*. Edited by R. K. Harrison et al. Grand Rapids: Zondervan. Repr. as pages 3–16 in Epp and Fee 1993.

———. 1992. Greek Patristic Citations in New Testament Textual Criticism: The State of the Question. *ANRW* 26.1:246–65.

———. 1993. On the Types, Classification, and Presentation of Textual Variation. Pages 62–79 in Epp and Fee 1993.

———. 1995. The Use of the Greek Fathers for New Testament Textual Criticism. Pages 191–207 in Ehrman and Holmes 1995.

Fischer, Bonifacius, et al, eds. 1983. *Biblia Sacra iuxta Vulgatam Versionem*. 2 vols. 3rd rev. ed. Stuttgart: Deutsche Bibelgesellschaft.

Fox, Adam. 1954. *John Mill and Richard Bentley: A Study of Textual Criticism of the New Testament, 1675–1729*. Oxford: Basil Blackwell.

Fuller, David Otis. 1975. *Which Bible?* 5th ed. Grand Rapids: Grand Rapids International.

Gamble, Harry Y. 1995. *Books and Readers in the Early Church: A History of Early Christian Texts*. New Haven: Yale University Press.

———. 2002. The New Testament Canon: Recent Research and the Status Quaestionis. Pages 267–94 in McDonald and Sanders 2002.

Geerard, Maurice, ed. 1974–. *Clavis patrum graecorum*. 5 vols. Brepols: Turnhout.

Geerlings, Jacob. 1961a. *Family 13 (The Ferrar Group): The Text according to Luke*. SD 20. Salt Lake City: University of Utah Press.

———. 1961b. *Family 13 (The Ferrar Group): The Text according to Matthew*. SD 19. Salt Lake City: University of Utah Press.

———. 1962. *Family 13 (The Ferrar Group): The Text according to John*. SD 21. Salt Lake City: University of Utah Press.

Globe, Alexander. 1980. Some Doctrinal Variants in Matthew 1 and Luke 2 and the Authority of the Neutral Text. *CBQ* 42:52–72.

Goodspeed, Edgar J. 1937. *New Chapters in New Testament Study*. New York: Macmillan.

Grant, Frederick C. 1946. The Greek Text of the New Testament. Pages 37–43 in *An Introduction to the Revised Standard Version of the New Testament*. By Members of the Revision Committee, Luther A. Weigle, Chairman. Chicago: International Council of Religious Education.

Greenlee, J. Harold. 1995. *Introduction to New Testament Textual Criticism*. Rev. ed. Peabody, Mass.: Hendrickson.

Gregory, Caspar René. 1907. *Canon and Text of the New Testament*. Edinburgh: T&T Clark.

———. 1908. *Die Griechischen Handschriften des Neuen Testaments*. Leipzig: Hinrichs.

Haines-Eitzen, Kim. 2000. *Guardians of Letters: Literacy, Power, and the Transmitters of Early Christian Literature*. Oxford: Oxford University Press.

Harris, J. Rendel. 1908. *Side-Lights on New Testament Research*. London: Kingsgate.

Harris, William. 1989. *Ancient Literacy*. Cambridge: Harvard University Press.

Hatch, William H. P. 1939. *The Principal Uncial Manuscripts of the New Testament*. Chicago: University of Chicago Press.

Head, Peter M. 1993. Christology and Textual Transmission: Reverential Alterations in the Synoptic Gospels. *NovT* 35:107–29.

———. 2000. Some Recently Published NT Papyri from Oxyrhynchus: An Overview and Preliminary Assessment. *TynBul* 51:1–16.

———. 2005. Is P4, P64 and P67 the Oldest Manuscript of the Four Gospels? A Response to T. C. Skeat. *NTS* 51:450–57.

Hengel, Martin. 2000. *The Four Gospels and the One Gospel of Jesus Christ*. Translated by John Bowden. Harrisburg, Pa.: Trinity Press International.

Hills, Edward. 1956. *The King James Version Defended!* 4th ed. Des Moines, Iowa: Christian Research.

Hodges, Zane C., and Arthur Farstad, eds. 1985. *The Greek New Testament according to the Majority Text*. 2nd ed. Nashville: Nelson.

Holmes, Michael W. 1984. Early Editorial Activity and the Text of Codex Bezae in Matthew. PhD diss., Princeton Theological Seminary.

———. 1996. Codex Bezae as a Recension of the Gospels. Pages 123–60 in Parker and Amphoux 1996.

———. 2002. The Case for Reasoned Eclecticism. Pages 71–100 in Black 2002.

———. 2003. Women and the "Western" Text of Acts. Pages 183–203 in Nicklas and Tilly 2003.

———. 2006. *The Text of the Epistles* Sixty Years After: An Assessment of Günther Zuntz's Contribution to Text-Critical Methodology and History. Pages 89–113 in Childers and Parker 2006.

Horne, T. H. 1856. *Introduction to the Critical Study and Knowledge of the Holy Scriptures*. 4 vols. 10th ed. London: Longmans, Green.

Horner, George W., ed. 1898–1905. *The Coptic Version of the New Testament in the Northern Dialect, Otherwise called Memphitic and Bohairic: With Introduction, Critical Apparatus, and Literal English Translation.* 4 vols. Oxford: Oxford University Press. Repr., Osnabrück: Zeller, 1969.

———, ed. 1911–1924. *The Coptic Version of the New Testament in the Southern Dialect, Otherwise called Sahidic and Thebaic: With Critical Apparatus, Literal English Translation, Register of Fragments, and Estimate of the Version.* 7 vols. Oxford: Oxford University Press. Repr., Osnabrück: Otto Zeller, 1969.

Hort, Arthur Fenton. 1896. *Life and Letters of Fenton John Anthony Hort.* 2 vols. London: Macmillan.

Hort, Fenton John Anthony. 1876. *Two Dissertations.* Cambridge: Cambridge University Press.

Hoskier, Herman C. 1929. *Concerning the Text of the Apocalypse.* 2 vols. London: Quaritch.

Houghton, H. A. G., and D. C. Parker, eds. 2008. *Textual Variation: Theological and Social Tendencies? Papers from the Fifth Birmingham Colloquium on the Textual Criticism of the New Testament.* TS 3/6. Piscataway, N.J.: Gorgias.

Housman, A. E. 1961. *Selected Prose.* Edited by John Carter. Cambridge: Cambridge University Press.

Howard, George. 1997. The Tetragram and the New Testament. *JBL* 96:63–68.

Howard, Wilbert F. 1941. The Influence of Doctrine upon the Text of the New Testament. *The London Quarterly and Holborn Review* 166:1–16.

Hulbert-Powell, C. L. 1938. *John James Wettstein, 1693–1754.* London: SPCK.

Hull, Robert F., Jr. 1993. Called "Christians" at Antioch: Christian Identity and the "Sacred Names" in Early Christian Manuscripts. Pages 25–50 in *Building Up the Church: A Festschrift in Honor of Henry E. Webb.* Edited by Gary E. Weedman. Milligan College, Tenn.: Milligan College.

Hulley, K. K. 1944. Principles of Textual Criticism Known to St. Jerome. *HSCP* 55:97–109.

Hurtado, Larry W. 1998. The Origin of the *Nomina Sacra*: A Proposal. *JBL* 117:655–73.

———. 1999. Beyond the Interlude? Developments and Directions in New Testament Textual Criticism. Pages 26–48 in Taylor 1999.

———. 2000. The Earliest Evidence of an Emerging Christian Material and Visual Culture: The Codex, the *Nomina Sacra*, and the Staurogram. Pages 271–88 in *Text and Artifact in the Religions of Mediterranean Antiquity: Essays in Honour of Peter Richardson*. Edited by Stephen G. Wilson and Michel Desjardins. Waterloo, Ont.: Wilfred Laurier University Press.

———. 2006a. *The Earliest Christian Artifacts: Manuscripts and Christian Origins*. Grand Rapids: Eerdmans.

———, ed. 2006b. *The Freer Biblical Manuscripts: Fresh Studies on an American Treasure Trove*. SBLTCS 6. Atlanta: Society of Biblical Literature.

Hutton, Edward Ardron. 1911. *An Atlas of Textual Criticism: Being an Attempt to Show the Mutual Relationship of the Authorities for the Text of the New Testament up to about 1000 A.D.* London: Cambridge University Press.

Jenson, Robin Margaret. 2000. *Understanding Early Christian Art*. London: Routledge.

Jeremias, Joachim. 1966. *The Eucharistic Words of Jesus*. 3rd ed. Translated by Norman Perrin. New York: Charles Scribner's Sons.

Jonge, H. J. de. 1971. *Daniel Heinsius and the Textus Receptus: A Study of His Contribution to the Editions of the Greek New Testament Printed by the Elzeviers at Leiden in 1624 and 1633*. Leiden: Brill.

Jongkind, Dirk. 2008. Singular Readings in Sinaiticus: The Possible, the Impossible, and the Nature of Copying. Pages 35–54 in Houghton and Parker 2008.

Jülicher, Adolf, Walter Matzkow, and Kurt Aland, eds. 1963–1976. *Itala: Das Neue Testament in Altlateinescher Überlieferung*. 4 vols. Berlin: de Gruyter.

Kasser, Rodolphe, ed. 1958. *Papyrus Bodmer, III: Evangile de Jean et Genèse I–IV, 2 en bohairique*. CSCO 177. Leuven: Peeters.

Keith, Chris. 2009. The Initial Location of the *Pericope Adulterae* in Fourfold Tradition. *NovT* 51:209–31.

Kelber, Werner H. 2007. Orality and Biblical Studies: A Review Essay. *RBL* 9:1–24.

Kelhoffer, James A. 2000. *Miracle and Mission: The Authentication of Missionaries and Their Message in the Longer Ending of Mark*. Tübingen: Mohr Siebeck.

Kenyon, Frederic. 1912. *Handbook to the Textual Criticism of the New Testament.* 2nd ed. London: Macmillan. Repr., Grand Rapids: Eerdmans, 1951.

———, ed. 1933–1937. *The Chester Beatty Biblical Papyri: Descriptions and Texts of Twelve Papyrus Manuscripts of the Bible.* 9 vols. London: Emery Walker.

———. 1937. *The Text of the Greek Bible.* London: Duckworth.

———. 1951. *Handbook to the Textual Criticism of the New Testament.* 2nd ed. London: Macmillan, 1912. Repr., Grand Rapids, Mich: Eerdmans.

Kilpatrick, George. D. 1943. Western Text and Original Text in the Gospels and Acts. *JTS* 44:24–36.

———. 1978. Griesbach and the Development of Textual Criticism. Pages 136–53 in *J. J. Griesbach: Synoptic and Text-Critical Studies (1776–1976).* Edited by Bernard Orchard and Thomas R. W. Longstaff. SNTSMS 34. Cambridge: Cambridge University Press.

Kiraz, George Anton. 1996. *Comparative Edition of the Syriac Gospels.* 4 vols. NTTS 21. Leiden: Brill.

Klijn, Albertus F. J. 1949. *Researches into the Western Text of the Gospels and Acts.* Utrecht: Kemink.

Kloha, Jeffrey. 2008. The Ethics of Sexuality and Textual Alterations in the Pauline Epistles. Pages 85–108 in Houghton and Parker 2008.

Knust, Jennifer Wright. 2006. Early Christian Re-writing and the History of the *Pericope Adulterae. JECS* 14:485–536.

Kraeling, Karl H., ed. 1936. *A Greek Fragment of Tatian's Diatessaron from Dura.* SD 3. London: Christophers.

Kraft, Robert A. 2003. The "Textual Mechanics" of Early Jewish LXX/OG Papyri and Fragments. Pages 51–72 in McKendrick and O'Sullivan 2003.

Krans, Jan. 2006. *Beyond What Is Written: Erasmus and Beza as Conjectural Critics of the New Testament.* NTTS 35. Leiden: Brill.

Kubo, Sakae. 1975. *P72 and the Codex Vaticanus.* SD 27. Salt Lake City: University of Utah Press.

Lagrange, Marie-Jean. 1935. *Critique textuelle.* 2 vols. 2nd ed. Paris: Gabalda.

Lake, Kirsopp. 1902. *Codex 1 of the Gospel and Its Allies.* TS 7. Cambridge: Cambridge University Press.

———. 1904. *The Influence of Textual Criticism on the Exegesis of the New Testament.* Oxford: Oxford University Press.

Lake, Kirsopp, and Silva Lake. 1941. *Family 13 (The Ferrar Group): The Text according to Mark, with a Collation of Codex 28 of the Gospels*. SD 11. London: Christophers.

Lake, Kirsopp, and Robert P. Blake. 1923. The Text of the Gospels and the Koridethi Codex. *HTR* 16:267–86.

Lakmann, M.-L. 2007. Papyrus Bodmer XIV–XV (P75) Neue Fragmente. *Museum Helveticum* 64:22–41.

Lewis, Agnes Smith. 1910. *The Old Syriac Gospels, or Evangelion da-Mephareshe*. London: Williams & Norgate.

Lyon, Robert W. 1958–1959. "A Re-examination of the Codex Ephraemi Rescriptus." *NTS* 5:266–72.

Maas, Paul. *Textual Criticism*. 1958. Oxford: Oxford University Press.

Martin, Victor, ed. 1956. *Papyrus Bodmer II*. Cologny-Geneva: Biblioteca Bodmeriana.

———, ed. 1962. *Papyrus Bodmer II, Supplement: Nouvelle edition augmentée et corrigée*. Cologny-Geneva: Biblioteca Bodmeriana.

Martin, Victor, and Rodolphe Kasser, eds. 1961. *Papyrus Bodmer XIV–XV: Evangiles de Luc et Jean*. 2 vols. Cologny-Geneva: Biblioteca Bodmeriana.

Martinez, David G. 2009. The Papyri and Early Christianity. Pages 590–622 in *The Oxford Handbook of Papyrology*. Edited by Roger S. Bagnall. New York: Oxford University Press.

Martini, Carlo M. 1977. *Il problema della recensionalità del codice B alla luce del papiro Bodmer XIV*. Rome: Biblical Institute Press.

McDonald, Lee M., and James A. Sanders, eds. 2002. *The Canon Debate: On The Origins and Formation of the Bible*. Peabody, Mass.: Hendrickson.

McKendrick, Scot, and Orlaith O'Sullivan, eds. 2003. *The Bible as Book: The Transmission of the Greek Text*. New Castle, Del.: Oak Knoll.

McLachlan, H. 1938–1939. An Almost Forgotten Pioneer in New Testament Criticism. *HibJ* 37:617–25.

McNamee, Kathleen. 1981. *Abbreviations in Greek Literary Papyri and Ostraca*. BASPSup 3. Chico, Calif.: Scholars Press.

Metzger, Bruce M. 1961–1962. Codex Bezae and the Geneva Version of the English Bible (1560). *NTS* 8:72–77. Repr. as pages 138–44 in Metzger 1968.

———. 1963a. *Chapters in the History of New Testament Textual Criticism*. NTTS 4. Grand Rapids: Eerdmans.

———. 1963b. Explicit References in the Works of Origen to Variant Readings in New Testament Manuscripts. Pages 78–95 in Birdsall and Thomson 1963. Repr. as pages 88–103 in Metzger 1968.

———. 1964. *The Text of the New Testament: Its Transmission, Corruption, and Restoration.* New York: Oxford University Press.

———. 1968. *Historical and Literary Studies: Pagan, Jewish, and Christian.* NTTS 8. Grand Rapids: Eerdmans.

———. 1975. The Practice of Textual Criticism among the Church Fathers. Pages 340–49 in *Studia patristica: Papers Presented to the Sixth International Conference on Patristic Studies Held in Oxford, 1971: Part I, Inaugural Lecture, Editiones, Critica, Philologica, Biblica, Historica.* Edited by Elizabeth A. Livingstone. Studia Patristica 12. TU 115. Berlin: Academie-Verlag. Repr. as pages 189–98 in Metzger 1980.

———. 1977. *The Early Versions of the New Testament.* Oxford: Clarendon.

———. 1979. St. Jerome's Explicit References to Variant Readings in Manuscripts of the New Testament. Pages 179–90 in *Text and Interpretation: Studies in the New Testament Presented to Matthew Black.* Edited by Ernest Best and R. McL. Wilson. Cambridge: Cambridge University Press. Repr. as pages 199–221 in Metzger 1980.

———. 1980. *New Testament Studies: Philological, Versional, and Patristic.* NTTS 10. Grand Rapids: Eerdmans.

———. 1981. *Manuscripts of the Greek Bible.* New York: Oxford University Press.

———. 1984. Bilingualism and Polylingualism in Antiquity, with a Check-List of New Testament MSS Written in More than One Language. Pages 327–34 in *The New Testament Age: Essays in Honor of Bo Reicke.* Edited by William C. Weinrich. Macon: Ga.: Mercer University Press.

———. 1994. *A Textual Commentary on the Greek New Testament.* 2nd ed. Stuttgart: Deutsche Bibelgesellschaft.

———. 1997. *Reminiscences of an Octogenarian.* Peabody, Mass.: Hendrickson.

———. 2001. *The Bible in Translation: Ancient and English Versions.* Grand Rapids: Baker Academic.

———. 2003. The Future of New Testament Textual Studies. Pages 201–8 in McKendrick and O'Sullivan 2003.

Metzger, Bruce M., and Bart D. Ehrman. 2005. *The Text of the New Testament: Its Transmission, Corruption, and Restoration.* 4th ed. New York: Oxford University Press.

Millard, A. R. 2000. *Reading and Writing in the Time of Jesus*. New York: New York University Press.

Miller, Jeffrey. 1999. (Mis)understanding Westcott and Hort. *ResQ* 41:160–62.

Milne, H. J. M., and T. C. Skeat. 1938. *Scribes and Correctors of the Codex Sinaiticus*. London: British Museum.

Muñoz, A. 1907. *Il codice purpureo di Rossano e il frammento sinopense*. Rome: Danesi.

Murphy-O'Connor, Jerome. 1995. *Paul the Letter-Writer: His World, His Options, His Skills*. Collegeville, Minn.: Liturgical Press.

Nachmanson, Ernst. 1910. Die schriftliche Kontraktion auf den griechischen Inschriften. *Eranos* 10:100–144.

Nestle, Eberhard. 1901. *Introduction to the Textual Criticism of the Greek New Testament*. London: Williams & Norgate.

Nichols, Francis Morgan. 1962. *The Epistles of Erasmus*. 3 vols. New York: Russell & Russell.

Nicklas, Tobias, and Michael Tilly, eds. 2003. *The Book of Acts as Church History: Text, Textual Traditions and Ancient Interpretations/Apostelgeschichte als Kirchengeschichte: Text, Texttraditionen und antike Auslegungen*. BZNW 120. Berlin: de Gruyter.

North, J. Lionel. 1995. The Use of the Latin Fathers for New Testament Textual Criticism. Pages 208–23 in Ehrman and Holmes 1995.

———. 1999. The Oxford Debate on the Textual Criticism of the New Testament, Held at New College on May 6, 1897: An End, Not a Beginning for the Textus Receptus. Pages 1–25 in Taylor 1999.

O'Callaghan, José. 1970. *"Nomina Sacra" in Papyris Graecis Saeculi III Neotestamentariis*. AnBib 46. Rome: Biblical Institute Press.

Odell-Scott, D. W. 2000. Editorial Dilemma: The Interpolation of 1 Cor 14:34–35 in the Western Manuscripts of D G and 88. *BTB* 30:68–74.

Osburn, Carroll D. 1995. The Greek Lectionaries of the New Testament. Pages 61–74 in Ehrman and Holmes 1995.

Paap, A. H. R. E. 1959. *Nomina Sacra in the Greek Papyri of the First Five Centuries A.D.: The Sources and Some Deductions*. Papyrologica Lugduno-Batava 8. Leiden: Brill.

Parker, David C. 1992. *Codex Bezae: An Early Christian Manuscript and Its Text*. Cambridge: Cambridge University Press.

———. 1995. The Majuscule Manuscripts of the New Testament. Pages 22–42 in Ehrman and Holmes 1995.

———. 1997. *The Living Text of the Gospels*. Cambridge: Cambridge University Press.

———. 2000. A New Oxyrhynchus Papyrus of Revelation: P115 (P.Oxy. 4499). *NTS* 46:159–74.

———. 2003a. Codex Bezae: The Manuscript as Past, Present and Future. Pages 43–50 in McKendrick and O'Sullivan 2003.

———. 2003b. The Principio Project: A Reconstruction of the Johannine Tradition. Pages 21–43 in *The New Testament Text in Early Christianity: Proceedings of the Lille Colloquium, July 2000*. Edited by Christian-Bernard Amphoux and J. Keith Elliott. Lausanne: Editions du Zebrè.

———. 2008. *An Introduction to New Testament Manuscripts and Their Texts*. Cambridge: Cambridge University Press.

Parker, David C., and J. Neville Birdsall. 2004. The Date of Codex Zacynthius (Ξ): A New Proposal. *JTS* 55:117–31.

Parker, David C., D. G. K. Taylor, and M. S. Goodacre. 1999. The Dura-Europos Gospel Harmony. Pages 192–228 in Taylor 1999.

Parker, David C., and C.-B. Amphoux, eds. 1996. *Codex Bezae: Studies from the Lunel Colloquium, June 1994*. NTTS 22. Leiden: Brill.

Parsons, Mikeal. 1986. A Christological Tendency in P75. *JBL* 105:463–79.

Parvis, Merrill M. 1952. The Nature and Tasks of New Testament Textual Criticism: An Appraisal. *JR* 32:171–73.

———. 1973. The Goals of New Testament Textual Studies. Pages 393–407 in *Studia Evangelica VI: Papers Presented to the Fourth International Congress on New Testament Studies Held at Oxford, 1969*. Edited by Elizabeth A. Livingstone. TU 112. Berlin: Akademie-Verlag.

Payne, Philip B. 1995. Fuldensis, Sigla for Variants in Vaticanus, and 1 Cor 14:34–35. *NTS* 41:24–62.

———. 2004. The Text-Critical Function of the Umlauts in Vaticanus, with Special Attention to 1 Corinthians 14:34–35: A Response to J. Edward Miller. *JSNT* 27:105–12.

Payne, Philip B., and Paul Canart. 2000. The Originality of Text-Critical Symbols in Codex Vaticanus. *NovT* 42:105–13.

Pestman, P. W. 1990. *The New Papyrological Primer*. Leiden: Brill.

Petersen, William L. 1994. *Tatian's Diatessaron: Its Creation, Dissemination, Significance, and History in Scholarship*. Leiden: Brill.

Petzer, Jacobus H. 1994. The History of the New Testament Text—Its Reconstruction, Significance and Use in New Testament Textual Criticism. Pages 11–36 in Aland and Delobel 1994.

———. 1995. The Latin Version of the New Testament. Pages 113–30 in Ehrman and Holmes 1995.

Pickering, Stuart R. 1999. The Significance of Non-continuous New Testament Textual Materials in Papyri. Pages 121–40 in Taylor 1999.

Pickering, Wilbur N. 1980. *The Identity of the New Testament Text*. Rev. ed. Nashville: Nelson.

Pierpoint, William G., and Maurice A. Robinson, eds. 1991. *The New Testament in the Original Greek according to the Byzantine/Majority Textform*. Atlanta: Original Word.

Politis, Linos. 1980. Nouveau manuscripts grecs découverts au Mont Sinaï. *Scriptorium* 34:5–17.

Porter, Calvin. 1962. Papyrus Bodmer XV (P75) and the Text of Codex Vaticanus. *JBL* 81:363–76.

Porter, Stanley E. 2003. Why So Many Holes in the Papyrological Evidence in the Greek New Testament? Pages 167–86 in McKendrick and O'Sullivan 2003.

Quecke, Hans, ed. 1972a. *Das Lukasevangelium saïdisch: Text der Handschrift PPalau Rib.-Inv.-Nr. 182 mit den Varianten der Handschrift M569*. Barcelona: Papyrologica Castroctaviana.

———, ed. 1972b. *Das Markusevangelium saïdisch: Text der Handschrift PPalau Rib. Inv.-Nr. 182 mit den Varianten der Handschrift M569*. Barcelona: Papyrologica Castroctaviana.

———, ed. 1984. *Das Johannesevangelium saïdisch: Text der Handschrift PPalau Rib. Inv.-Nr. 183 mit den Varianten der Handschriften 813 und 814 der Chester Beatty Library und der Handschrift M569*. Rome: Papyrologica Castroctaviana.

Rabil, Albert. 1972. *Erasmus and the New Testament: The Mind of a Christian Humanist*. San Antonio, Tex.: Trinity University Press.

Reicke, Bo. 1966. Erasmus und die neutestamentliche Textgeschichte. *TZ* 22:254–65.

Reuss, Eduard. 1872. *Bibliotheca Novi Testamenti Graeci*. Brunswig: C. A. Schwetschke & Sons.

Reynolds, Leighton D., and N. G. Wilson. 1974. *Scribes and Scholars: A Guide to the Transmission of Greek and Latin Literature*. 2nd ed. Oxford: Clarendon.

Rice, George E. 1974. The Alteration of Luke's Tradition by the Textual Variants in Codex Bezae. PhD diss., Case Western Reserve University.

Richards, E. Randolph. 1991. *The Secretary in the Letters of Paul*. Tübingen: Mohr Siebeck.

———. 2004. *Paul and First-Century Letter Writing: Secretaries, Composition and Collection*. Downer's Grove, Ill.: Intervarsity Press.
Richards, Larry W. 1977. *The Classification of the Greek Manuscripts of the Johannine Epistles*. SBLDS 35. Missoula, Mont.: Scholars Press.
Riddle, Donald W. 1936. Textual Criticism as a Historical Discipline. *AThR* 18:221–24.
Rius-Camps, Josep. 2007. The Pericope of the Adulteress Reconsidered: The Nomadic Misfortunes of a Bold Pericope. *NTS* 53:379–405.
Roberts, Colin H. 1935. *An Unpublished Fragment of the Fourth Gospel in the John Rylands Library*. Manchester: John Rylands Library.
———. 1940. The Codex. *Proceedings of the British Academy* 40:169–204.
———. 1968. *Greek Papyri*. Princeton: Princeton University Press.
———. 1979. *Manuscript, Society and Belief in Early Christian Egypt*. The Schweich Lectures of the British Academy, 1977. London: Oxford University Press.
Roberts, Colin H., and T. C. Skeat. 1983. *The Birth of the Codex*. London: Oxford University Press for the British Academy.
Robinson, James M. 1986. The Discovery and Marketing of Coptic Manuscripts: The Nag Hammadi Codices and the Bodmer Papyri. Pages 2–25 in *The Roots of Egyptian Christianity*. Edited by Birger A. Pearson and James E. Goehring. Philadelphia: Fortress.
Ross, J. M. 1998. Some Unnoticed Points in the Text of the New Testament. *NovT* 25:58–72.
Rotherham, J. B. 1872. *The New Testament: Newly Translated from the Greek Text of Tregelles and Critically Emphasized*. London: Bagster.
Royse, James R. 2008. *Scribal Habits in Early Greek New Testament Papyri*. NTTSD 36. Leiden: Brill.
Rudberg, Gunnar. 1910. Zur paläographischen Kontraktion. *Eranos* 10:71–100.
———. 1913. Verschleifung und Kontraktion. *Eranos* 13:156–61.
Schaff, Philip. 1883. *A Companion to the Greek Testament and English Version*. New York: Harper & Brothers.
Schenke, Hans-Martin, ed. 1981. *Das Matthaüs-Evangelium im mittelägyptischen Dialekt des Koptischen (Codex Scheide)*. TU 127. Berlin: Akademie-Verlag.
———, ed. 1991. *Apostelgeschichte 1,1–15,3 im mittelägyptischen Dialekt des Koptischen (Codex Glazier)*. TU 137. Berlin: Akademie-Verlag.
Schmid, Josef. 1955–1956. *Studien zur Geschichte des griechischen Apokalypse-Textes*. 3 vols. Munich: Karl Zink.

Schmid, Ulrich. 1995. *Marcion und sein Apostolos: Rekonstruktion und historische Einordnung der marcionitischen Paulusbriefausgabe.* ANTF 25. Berlin: de Gruyter.

———. 2008. Scribes and Variants: Sociology and Typology. Pages 1–23 in Houghton and Parker 2008.

Schmid, Ulrich, W. J. Elliott, and David C. Parker, eds. 2007. *The New Testament in Greek IV: The Gospel according to St John, Edited by the American and British Committees of the International Greek New Testament Project.* Vol. 2: *The Majuscules.* NTTSD 37. Leiden: Brill.

Schmitz, Franz-Jürgen, and Gerd Mink, eds. 1986–1991. *Liste der koptischen Handschriften des Neuen Testaments I: Die sahidischen Handschriften der Evangelien.* Parts 1 and 2. ANTF 8, 9, 13, 15. Berlin: de Gruyter.

Schürmann, Heinz. 1955. *Der Paschamahlberichte: Lk. 22, 19–20 II. Teil Einer Quellenkritischer Untersuchung des Lukanischen Abendmahlsberichtes Lk. 22, 7–38.* Münster/Westfalia: Ashendorffsche.

Scrivener, Francis H. A. 1894. *A Plain Introduction to the Criticism of the New Testament.* 2 vols. 4th ed. Edited by Edward Miller. London: Bell & Sons.

Silva, Moisés. 1995. Modern Critical Editions and Apparatuses of the Greek New Testament. Pages 283–96 in Ehrman and Holmes 1995.

———. 2002. Response. Pages 141–50 in Black 2002.

Skeat, Theodore C. 1956. The Use of Dictation in Ancient Book Production. *Proceedings of the British Academy* 42:179–208. Repr. as pages 3–32 in Skeat 2004.

———. 1992. Irenaeus and the Four-Gospel Canon. *NovT* 34:194–99. Repr. as pages 73–78 in Skeat 2004.

———. 1994. The Origin of the Christian Codex. *ZPE* 102:263–68. Repr. as pages 79–87 in Skeat 2004.

———. 1997. The Oldest Manuscript of the Four Gospels? *NTS* 43:1–24. Repr. as pages 158–92 in Skeat 2004.

———. 2004. *The Collected Biblical Writings of T. C. Skeat.* Introduced and edited by J. K. Elliott. NovTSup 113. Boston: Brill, 2004.

Smalley, Beryl. 1952. *The Study of the Bible in the Middle Ages.* 2nd ed. Oxford: Basil Blackwell.

Soden, Hermann Freiherr von, ed. 1902–1913. *Die Schriften des Neuen Testaments in ihrer ältesten erreichbaren Testgestalt hergestellt auf Grund ihrer Textgeschichte.* 4 vols. Göttingen: Vandenhoeck & Ruprecht.

Stanton, Graham. 2004. *Jesus and Gospel*. Cambridge: Cambridge University Press.
Stenger, Werner. 1975. Textkritik als Schicksal. *BZ* 19:240–47.
Steudel, J. C. F., ed. 1858. *Gnomon of the New Testament by John Albert Bengel*. Vol. 1. Translated by James Bandinel. Repr., Edinburgh: T&T Clark.
———, ed. 1863. *Gnomon of the New Testament by John Albert Bengel*. Vol. 5. Translated by William Fletcher. 5th repr. ed. Edinburgh: T&T Clark.
Streeter, Burnett Hillman. 1924. *The Four Gospels: A Study of Origins*. London: Macmillan.
Sturz, Harry A. 1984. *The Byzantine Text-Type and New Testament Textual Criticism*. Nashville: Nelson.
Swanson, Reuben, ed. 1995–2001. *New Testament Greek Manuscripts: Variant Readings Arranged in Horizontal Lines against Codex Vaticanus*. 7 vols. Pasadena, Calif.: William Carey International University Press; Wheaton, Ill.: Tyndale House.
Szesnat, Holger. 2007. "Some Witnesses Have…": The Representation of the New Testament Text in English Bible Versions. *TC: A Journal of Biblical Textual Criticism* 12:1–18. Online: http://purl.org/TC.
Tarelli, C. C. 1943. Erasmus's Manuscripts of the Gospels. *JTS* 44:155–62.
Tasker, Randolph V. G., ed. 1964. *The Greek New Testament, Being the Text Translated in the New English Bible*. Oxford: Oxford University Press; Cambridge: Cambridge University Press.
Taylor, D. G. K., ed. 1999. *Studies in the Early Text of the Gospels and Acts: The Papers of the First Birmingham Colloquium on the Textual Criticism of the New Testament*. SBLTCS 1. Atlanta: Society of Biblical Literature.
Testuz, Michel. 1959. *Papyrus Bodmer VII–IX*. Cologny-Geneva: Biblioteca Bodmeriana.
Text und Textwert der griechischen Handscriften des Neuen Testaments. 1987– . ANTF. Berlin: de Gruyter.
Thiselton, Anthony C. 2000. *First Epistle to the Corinthians: A Commentary on the Greek Text*. Grand Rapids: Eerdmans.
Thomas, Cecil K. 1958. *Alexander Campbell and His New Version*. St. Louis: Bethany.
Thompson, Herbert, ed. 1932. *The Coptic Version of the Acts of the Apostles and the Pauline Epistles in the Sahidic Dialect*. Cambridge: Cambridge University Press.
———, ed. and trans. 1924. *The Gospel of St John according to the Earliest Coptic Manuscript*. London: British School of Archaeology in Egypt.

Tischendorf, Constantin von. 1869–1894. *Novum Testamentum Graece*. 3 vols. 8th major ed. Leipzig: Giesecke & Devrient; Hinrichs.

———. 1934. *Codex Sinaiticus*. 8th ed. London: Lutterworth.

Tov, Emmanuel. 2004. *Scribal Practices and Approaches Reflected in the Texts Found in the Judean Desert*. STDJ 54. Leiden: Brill.

Traube, Ludwig. 1907. *Nomina Sacra: Versuch einer Geschichte der christlichen Kürzung*. Munich: Beck. Repr., Darmstadt: Wissenschaftliche Buchgesellschaft, 1967.

Tregelles, Samuel Prideaux. 1854. *An Account of the Printed Text of the Greek New Testament*. London: Bagster.

———, ed. 1857–1879. *The Greek New Testament*. Appendix edited by F. J. A. Hort and A. W. Streane. London: Bagster.

Tuckett, Christopher M. 2003. "Nomina Sacra": Yes and No? Pages 431–58 in *The Biblical Canons*. Edited by J.-M. Auwers and H. J. de Jonge. BETL 98. Leuven: Peeters.

Turner, C. H. 1923–1927. Marcan Usage: Notes, Critical and Exegetical, on the Second Gospel. *JTS* 25:377–86; 26:12–20, 145–56, 225–40, 337–46; 27:58–62; 28:9–30, 349–62.

Turner, Eric G. 1968. *Greek Papyri: An Introduction*. Princeton: Princeton University Press.

———. 1971. *Greek Manuscripts of the Ancient World*. Princeton: Princeton University Press.

———. 1977. *The Typology of the Early Codex*. Philadelphia: University of Pennsylvania Press.

Ulrich, Eugene. 1999. *The Dead Sea Scrolls and the Origins of the Bible*. Grand Rapids: Eerdmans; Leiden: Brill.

Vetus Latina: Die Reste der altlateinischen Bibel nach Petrus Sabatier neu Gesammelt von der Erzabtei Beuron. 1949–. Freiburg: Herder.

Vogels, Heinrich J. 1929. *Codicum Novi Testamenti Specimina*. Bonn: Hanstein.

Wachtel, Klaus, and Klaus Witte, eds. 1986–. *Das Neue Testament auf Papyrus*. Berlin: de Gruyter.

Walker, William O. 1987. The Burden of Proof in Identifying Interpolations in the Pauline Letters. *NTS* 33:610–18.

Wallace, Daniel B. 1995. The Majority Text Theory: History, Methods, and Critique. Pages 297–320 in Ehrman and Holmes 1995.

West, Martin L. 1971. *Textual Criticism and Editorial Technique*. Stuttgart: Teubner.

Westcott, Arthur. 1903. *Life and Letters of Brooke Foss Westcott*. 2 vols. London: Macmillan.
Westcott, Brooke F., and Fenton J. A. Hort. 1881. *The New Testament in the Original Greek*. 2 vols. London: Macmillan. 2nd ed., 1896.
Wikgren, Allen. 1963. Chicago Studies in the Greek Lectionary of the New Testament. Pages 96–121 in Birdsall and Thomson 1963.
Williams, Charles. S. C. 1951. *Alterations to the Text of the Synoptic Gospels and Acts*. Oxford: Oxford University Press.
Willis, William H. 1990. The Letter of Peter (1 Peter). Pages 135–216 in *The Crosby-Schøyen Collection*. Edited by J. E. Goehring. CSCO 521. Leuven: Peeters.
Wisse, Frederik. 1982. *The Profile Method for the Classification and Evaluation of Manuscript Evidence as Applied to the Continuous Greek Text of the Gospel of Luke*. SD 44. Grand Rapids: Eerdmans.
———. 1990. Textual Limits to Redactional Theory in the Pauline Corpus. Pages 172–78 in *Gospel Origins and Christian Beginnings in Honor of James M. Robinson*. Edited by James E. Goehring et al. Sonoma, Calif.: Polebridge.
———. 1995. The Coptic Versions of the New Testament. Pages 131–41 in Ehrman and Holmes 1995.
Witherington, Ben, III. 1984. The Anti-feminist Tendencies of the "Western" Text in Acts. *JBL* 103:82–84.
Wright, John. 1988. Origen in the Scholar's Den: A Rationale for the Hexapla. Pages 48–92 in *Origen of Alexandria: His World and His Legacy*. Edited by Charles Kannengiesser and William L. Petersen. Notre Dame, Ind.: University of Notre Dame Press.
Zetzel, James E. G. 1981. *Latin Textual Criticism in Antiquity*. New York: Arno.
Zuntz, Günther. 1953. *The Text of the Epistles: A Disquisition upon the Corpus Paulinum*. The Schweich Lectures of the British Academy, 1946. London: Oxford University Press.

Index of Biblical Citations

Old Testament

Genesis
14:14	182

Leviticus
7:13	101

Isaiah
53	165

New Testament

Matthew
3:9	112
3:15	112
5:20–22	112
5:22	35
5:25–28	112
5:27–32	158
6:9–13	158
6:13	68
8:3	175
8:28	20
16:2–3	106
19:3–9	158
20:28	119
25:6	52
27:16–17	34, 121, 136
27:49	20, 104

Mark
1:1–3	157
1:1–5:30	120
1:2	20
1:41	20
1:41–42	175
5:1	20
5:31–16:20	120
6:33	101n27
8:26	101n27
9:2–12	158
9:38	101n27
9:49	101
10:45	165
12:12	156n8
14:24	165
15:13–38	120
16:8	91, 106
16:9–20	33, 91, 105, 106, 107
16:14	120

Luke
1:1–4	13
1:1–8:12	120
1:1–11:33	91
5:13	175
6:4	55
6:5	55
6:10	55
6:50–8:52	52
8:13–24:53	120
8:26	20
9:10	101n27
9:54	101n27
11:2	122
11:2–5	158
12:18	101n27

Luke (cont.)

14:8–10	119
14:27	185n29
16:18	158
16:19	118
17:14	175
20:19	156n8
22:17–18	162–163
22:19b–20	3, 104, 162–167
22:43–44	106
23:34	106
24:3	105
24:6	105
24:12	105
24:36	105
24:40	105
24:51	105
24:52	105
24:53	101n27, 105

John

1:1–14:26	116
1:34	171
3:6	62
6:11–35	116
5:12–21:25	120
7:53–8:11	3, 68, 92, 105, 106, 116
10:7	118
11:30–31	116n17
14:25–16:7	120
14:29–21:9	116
18:31–33	115
18:37–38	115
19:33	178n20
19:34	20
21:22	55

Acts

1:1–15:3	128
1:14	43
2:14–26	183
2:22–36	165
2:30–37	170
2:46–47	170
3:1–2	170
3:12–16	165
5:8–12	165
7:51–56	165
8:32–33	165
13:26–41	165
17:4	155n6
17:12	155n6
18:27–19:6	113
19:12	113
19:16	113
23:11–17	113
23:25–29	113

Romans

1:1–5:16	114
1:7	14
1:15	14
5:1	19
5:17	114n12
12:8	18
14:23	174
15:33	115
16:1	19
16:1–2	11
16:3–15	11
16:22	7, 9
16:23	7, 174
16:24	174
16:25–27	174

1 Corinthians

1:27	125n33
4:17	11
11:23–25	163
11:24–25	166
14:33	155n7, 188
14:34–35	155, 187–89
14:24–40	188
14:40	155n7
15:49	19
16:10	11

INDEX OF BIBLICAL CITATIONS

1 Corinthians (cont.)
16:21 — 9

2 Corinthians
4:13–12:6 — 52
7:15–16 — 11

Galatians
2:5 — 35
4:25 — 46
6:11 — 9

Ephesians
1:1 — 156
6:21 — 11

Philippians
2:25 — 11
2:25–30 — 11
4:6 — 18
4:14–18 — 11

Colossians
4:7 — 11
4:17 — 11
4:18 — 9

1 Thessalonians
5:27 — 12

2 Thessalonians
3:17 — 9

1 Timothy
2:11–12 — 187
3:16 — 63

2 Timothy
4:13 — 8

Titus
3:2 — 11

Philemon
19 — 9

Hebrews
5:7 — 125n33
9:14 — 121
9:15 — 53

1 Peter
1:2 — 178
5:1 — 178

1 John
5:7 — 37, 68, 69
5::8 — 69

Jude
5 — 178

Revelation
9:10–17:2 — 115, 118, 171
13:18 — 32, 34, 171

Index of Persons

Alcuin, 28, 31
Achtemeier, Paul J., 190n39, 193
Ackroyd, Peter R., 194
Aland, Barbara, 1, 3, 26, 30, 43, 94n15, 122n25, 125n30, 126n35, 128, 132n3, 134n6, 139n12, 140–42, 152, 160–61, 177, 178, 187n3, 188, 193, 194, 196, 197
Aland, Kurt, 1, 3, 26, 30, 43, 94n15, 122n25, 125n30, 126n35, 128, 129, 132n3, 134n6, 139n12, 140–42, 152, 155, 160, 164, 177, 185, 187n3, 188, 193, 194, 195, 197, 204, 209
Alexander II, Tsar of Russia, 88
Ambrose of Milan, 62
Amphoux, Christian-Bernard, 195, 202, 209
Aphrahat, 125
Augustine, 28, 93
Augustus, Frederick, 88
Auwers, J. M., 214
Baarda, Tjitze, 125n33, 194, 199
Bagnall, Roger S., 15, 180, 194, 206
Bandinel, James, 213
Barrett, David P., 112n6, 196
Bauckham, Richard, 14n7, 194
Beatty, Chester, 113–15, 205
Bengel, Johann Albrecht, 39, 47–53, 58, 62, 64–67, 69–74, 83, 98–100, 133, 141, 213
Benoit, Pierre, 164
Bentley, James, 87n1, 194
Bentley, Richard, 45–61, 68, 75–77, 83, 201

Beza, Theodore, 40–42, 51, 54–58, 62
Birdsall, J. Neville, 1, 91, 132, 147n21, 154, 196, 207, 209, 215
Black, David Alan, 170n3, 194, 200, 202, 212
Black, Matthew, 160, 207
Blake, Robert P., 121, 136, 206
Blanchard, Alain, 180n22, 194
Bodmer, Martin, 116
Bond, Helen K., 200
Bowden, John, 202
Bowyer, William, 50n17, 67n47, 68
Brock, Sebastian P., 125n33, 129, 194
Brogan, John J., 90, 175–76, 194
Brown, Schuyler, 194
Bude, William, 36
Burgon, John W., 3, 84, 149, 152, 194
Burkitt, Frederick C., 92n11, 110, 125, 195
Callahan, Allen D., 54, 195
Campbell, Alexander, 97n20, 213
Canart, Paul, 188, 209
Caragounis, Chrys C., 18, 195
Casey, Robert Pierce, 194
Chabot, I. B., xi
Charlemagne, 61
Charles I, King of England, 43, 52
Childers, J. W., 193, 195, 202
Chrysostom, John, 102
Cicero, 60
Clark, Kenneth W., 146, 152, 156, 195, 198
Clement of Alexandria, 13, 20, 30, 103, 123, 183

INDEX OF PERSONS

Clericus, 48
Colinus, Simon de, 68
Courcelles, Etienne de, 68
Collins, Anthony, 67
Colwell, Ernest C., 101n26, 116, 123, 131, 132n1, 137–39, 142, 146–47, 153–55, 165n18, 177, 195, 196
Comfort, Wesley, 112n6, 161n12, 196
Constantine, Emperor, 26, 186
Conybeare, F. C., 152, 196
Creed, J. M., 163
Cribiore, Raffaella, 8, 15, 196
Cureton, William, 92, 110
Cyprian of Carthage, 76, 93
Dain, Alphonse, 18, 196
Damasus, Pope, 28
Daniels, Boyd L., 198
Daube, D., 195
Davies, W. D., 105
de Jonge, H. J., 41n3, 199 204, 214
Deconick, April D., 200
Deissmann, Adolf, 111n3, 196
Dekkers, Eligius, 196
Delling, Gerhard, 72, 74–75, 196
Delobel, Joël, 107n33, 193 196, 209
Denoux, A., 194
Desjardins, Michel, 204
Dinkler, Erich, 185, 197
Diocletian, Emperor, 26, 30, 114, 149
Dunn, James D. G., 190n39, 197
Easton, B. S., 163
Edwards, James R., 185, 197
Ehrman, Bart, 5, 18–20, 27, 30–31, 36–38, 39, 41, 42n4, 44, 46, 51n20, 52n21, 58, 62n39, 67nn47, 48, 72n1, 73, 77, 93, 112n6, 114, 117, 118n21, 119n22, 120, 122, 123, 125n34, 129n44, 134, 137n10 139n13, 140n14, 144n17, 149, 153–55, 158, 160n11, 162–67, 172–78, 194, 197, 198, 201, 207, 208, 210, 212, 214, 215
Elliott, J. Keith, 40, 122n24, 144–45, 157, 198, 209

Elliott, W. J., 161, 198, 199, 212
Elzevir, Abraham, 41–42, 44, 50, 51, 74
Elzevir, Bonaventure, 41–42, 44, 50, 51, 74
Ephraem of Syria, 54, 125
Epp, Eldon Jay, ix, 8n1, 11, 15, 24, 43, 48n14, 50, 64n43, 65n45, 66, 73–74, 77, 79n8, 81–82, 85, 98n23, 110–11, 114, 117, 128, 132n1, 125, 142–43, 145n19, 146, 150, 153, 156–57, 159, 161, 165n19, 169, 173, 180–81, 190, 191, 198, 199, 200, 201
Erasmus, 24, 27–28, 31–33, 36–42, 52–4, 57, 59, 61–62, 68–69, 97, 171, 205, 208, 210, 213
Eshbaugh, Howard, 54, 200
Eugenius, Bishop of Carthage, 69
Eusebius, 13, 26, 30, 34, 62, 80, 107, 134
Evans, Christopher F., 194
Farstad, Arthur, 149, 202
Fascher, Erich, 152, 200
Fee, Gordon, 29, 43, 90, 94n18, 118n20, 129 30, 139, 145, 150, 197, 200, 201
Fell, John, 44, 126n38
Ferrar, W. H., 91
Fischer, Bonifacius, 129, 201
Fitzmyer, Joseph A., 199
Fletcher, William, 213
Fox, Adam, 45–47, 54, 67–68, 201
Froben, John, 36
Fuller, David Otis, 149, 201
Gamble, Harry, 7–8, 12, 14–16, 173, 180, 184, 190, 199, 201
Geerard, Maurice, 201
Geerlings, Jacob, 123, 201
Globe, Alexander, 153, 201
Goehring, James E., 211, 215
Goltz, E. von der, 123, 124
Goodacre, Mark S., 125, 209
Goodspeed, Edgar J., 97, 201
Grant, Frederick C., 145, 201
Greenlee, J. Harold, 43, 201
Gregory, Pope, 94

Gregory of Nyssa, 122
Gregory, Caspar René, 49, 75, 79, 89–91, 132, 202
Grenfell, Bernard, 111
Griesbach, Johann Jacob, 71–75, 80–85, 95, 97–98, 105, 108, 124, 177, 196, 205
Gutenberg, Johannes, 31
Haase, Wolfgang, xi
Haines-Eitzen, Kim, 10, 15, 117, 173, 202
Hanson, R. P. C., 1
Harding, Stephen, 28, 31
Harris, J. Rendel, 152, 202
Harris, William, 8
Harrison, R. K., 201
Harwood, Edward, 67
Hatch, William H. P., 54n29, 164, 202
Head, Peter M., 113, 153, 170–71, 202
Headlam, A. C., 93n13
Heinsius, Daniel, 41n3, 204
Hengel, Martin, 13, 202
Henry II, King of France, 40
Hermas, 15, 173n10
Hesychius, 34, 134
Hilary, 76
Hills, Edward, 149, 202
Hippolytus of Rome, 30, 62n39, 153
Hodges, Zane C., 149, 202
Holmes, Michael W., 32, 130n44, 146n20, 147n21, 148, 153n2, 155n6, 175n16, 194, 197, 198, 201, 208, 210, 212, 214, 215
Homer, 32, 60
Horgan, Maurya P., 199
Horne, T. H., 80n9, 202
Horner, George W., 93n13, 126–27, 203
Hort, Arthur Fenton, 203
Hort, Fenton John Anthony, 5, 41n2, 71, 80, 82–85, 87, 90, 92–94, 96–111, 113, 115, 116, 118, 122–26, 129–40, 143–52, 154, 159–60, 162–66, 176, 194, 196, 203, 208, 214

Hoskier, Herman C., 171, 203
Houghton, H. A. G., 174, 203, 204, 205
Housman, A. E., 17, 151, 203
Howard, George, 203
Howard, Wilbert F., 152, 203
Hug, J. L., 124
Hulbert-Powell, C. L., 49n15, 50n18, 63, 69, 203
Hull, Robert F., Jr., 203
Hulley, K. K., 33, 203
Hunt, Arthur, 111
Hurtado, Larry, 113, 120, 169n2, 170n3, 171, 183–85, 186n31, 189, 200, 203
Hutton, Edward A., 138n11, 204
Hyatt, J. Philip, 193
Irenaeus, 20, 23, 30, 32–34, 55, 76, 83, 103, 123, 153, 180, 194, 212
James I, King of England, 37
Jenson, Robin Margaret, 186n31, 204
Jeremias, Joachim, 164, 204
Jerome, 19, 28, 30–35, 58, 61n38, 107, 120, 134, 203, 207, 208
De Jonge, H., 41n3, 199, 204, 214
Jongkind, Dirk, 204
Juckel, A., 126, 193
Jülicher, Adolf, 129, 204
Justin Martyr, 30, 33, 93, 103, 153
Kannengiesser, Charles, 215
Karavidopoulos, Johannes, 160
Kasser, Rodolphe, 117n18, 128, 204, 206
Keith, Chris, 105n32, 156n8, 204
Kelber, Werner H., 190, 204
Kelhoffer, James A., 34, 204
Kenyon, Frederic, 78, 113–14, 135n7, 139n12, 142, 152, 164, 179, 190, 205
Kilpatrick, George D., 72, 144–45, 198, 205
Kiraz, George Anton, 126, 205
Klijn, Albertus F. J., 114n9, 205
Kloha, Jeffrey, 155, 189n35, 205
Klostermann, E., 163
Knust, Jennifer Wright, 205

INDEX OF PERSONS

Kobelski, Paul J., 199
König, Elise, 134
Kraeling, Karl H., 125n34, 205
Kraft, Robert A., 185, 205
Krans, Jan, 36, 38n4, 41, 205
Kubo, Sakae, 117, 205
Küster, Ludolph, 54
Lachmann, Karl, 58, 71, 75–78, 80–82, 85, 94–96, 105
Lagrange, Marie-Jean, 144n16, 205
Lake, Kirsopp, 90n5, 121, 123, 135, 136, 152, 205, 206
Lake, Silva, 123, 206
Lakmann, M.-L., 117n19, 206
Legg. S. C. E., 164
Lewis, Agnes Smith, 124, 125n31, 206
Lightfoot, J. B., 93n13
Livingstone, Elizabeth A., 197, 207, 209
Longenecker, Richard N., 200
Longstaff, Thomas R. W., 196, 205
Lucar, Cyril, 43,
Lucifer of Cagliari, 76, 93
Luther, Martin, 69, 97
Lyon, Robert W., 54n29, 206
Maas, Paul, 132, 206
Mace, Daniel, 46–47, 67n47, 68
Macedonius II, 63n42
MacRae, George W., 199
Marcion, 83, 122, 151, 166, 174, 212
Martial, 9n3, 15
Martin, Victor, 116n16, 117nn18–19, 206
Martinez, David G., 183, 206
Martini, Carlo M., 118, 160n20, 206
Mastricht, Gerhard von, 64–65
Matzkow, Walter, 129, 204
McDonald, Lee M., 200, 201, 206
McKendrick, Scot, 194, 205, 206, 207, 209, 210
McLachlan, H., 46, 206
McNamee, Kathleen, 185, 206
McReynolds, Paul, 139–40

Melito of Sardis, 113, 117, 127
Metzger, Bruce, v, 1, 3n1, 17, 18, 19, 26, 27, 28, 30–42, 44, 46, 50n–54n, 56n32, 58, 61n38, 62, 67nn47–48, 68, 72n1, 73, 77, 90n5, 92n10, 93, 99n24, 104n30, 108n34, 112n6, 114, 115n13, 116, 117, 118n21, 119–23, 125–28, 124, 137, 144n17, 145, 149, 155, 160, 162n16, 169n2, 170, 174n13, 177n19, 189, 190n37, 206, 207
Mill, John, 44n7
Millard, A. R., 8n1, 208
Miller, Edward, 212
Miller, J. Edward, 209
Miller, Jeffrey, ix, 151, 208
Miller, Troy A., 200
Milne, H. J. M., 90n5, 176, 208
Mink, Gerd, 127n39, 212
Mommsen, Theodor, 110n1
Muñoz, A., 119n22, 208
Murphy-O'Conner, Jerome, 7, 9n4, 208
Nachmanson, Ernst, 182, 208
Nestle, Eberhard, 160, 208
Nestle, Erwin, 1, 30, 43, 152, 161n12, 164, 187n32, 188, 193
Nichols, Francis Morgan, 36, 208
Nicklas, Tobias, 200, 202, 208
North, J. Lionel, 125n32, 129, 208
O'Callaghan, José, 182n25, 208
O'Sullivan, Orlaith, 194, 205, 206, 207, 209, 210
Odell-Scott, D. W., 187, 208
Orchard, Bernard, 196, 205
Origen, 17, 20, 23, 24, 30, 32–35, 45, 51, 60, 62, 72, 76, 103, 121, 123, 134, 126, 127, 148, 158, 172, 197, 200, 207, 215
Osburn, Carroll D., 27, 45n8, 57, 123, 208
Ovid, 60n37
Paap, A. H. R. E., 182, 208
Palmer, Edwin, 84n14

Papias, 13
Parker, David C., 17–18, 24, 26, 27, 31, 43, 50n18, 53n25, 54, 56n31, 91, 117n19, 125, 132, 157n9, 158–59, 160n11, 161, 162, 171, 172n6,8, 174, 175, 176, 186, 187, 189, 190, 193, 195, 198, 202, 203, 204, 205, 208
Parsons, Mikeal, 153, 209
Parvis, Merrill M., 128, 209
Payne, Philip B., 188–89, 209
Pearson, Birger A., 199, 211
Pelt, M. R., 153
Perrin, Norman, 204
Pestman, P. W., 8n2, 113n8, 209
Petersen, William L., 126, 199, 209, 215
Petzer, Jacobus H., 128, 140, 209
Pickering, Stuart R., 190, 210
Pickering, Wilbur N., 149, 210
Pierpoint, William G., 149, 210
Pionius, 173
Pliny, 15
Plummer, A., 163
Politis, Linos, 170, 210
Porter, Calvin, 118n20, 210
Porter, Stanley E., 190, 210
Priscillian, 69
Quecke, Hans, 127, 210
Quintilian, 15
Rabil, Albert, 36, 210
Reicke, Bo, 36, 207, 210
Reuchlin, John, 36
Reuss, Eduard, 47, 74n2, 210
Reynolds, Leighton D., 32, 60, 210
Rhodes, Erroll B., 194
Rice, George E., 153n2, 210
Richards, E. Randolph, 7–10, 12, 210
Richards, Larry, 139, 211
Richardson, Peter, 204
Riddle, Donald W., 123n29, 151, 152, 196, 211
Rius-Camps, Josep, 156n8, 211
Roberts, Colin H., 8, 16, 26n1, 109, 113, 115, 179, 180, 182, 183, 211

Robinson, James M., 116, 211, 215
Robinson, Maurice, 149, 210
Ross, J. M., 145n18, 211
Rotherham, J. B., 97, 211
Royse, James R., 15, 116n17, 117, 118n21, 176–78, 211
Rudberg, Gunnar, 182, 211
Rylaarsdam, J. Coert, 196
Sabatier, Pierre, 58, 59, 128, 214
Schaff, Philip, 41, 98n22, 211
Schenke, Hans-Martin, 128, 211
Schmid, Josef, 171, 211
Schmid, Ulrich, 161, 172–75, 212
Schmitz, Franz-Jürgen, 127n39, 212
Scholz, J. M. A., 71, 80
Schürmann, Heinz, 164, 212
Scrivener, Francis H. A., 36, 44, 46, 52n21, 53n25, 56, 57n34, 58, 59n36, 74, 76, 78, 84, 85, 90n6, 92, 95, 97, 98n22, 106, 126, 212
Scrivener, Frederick, 84
Segal, Alan F., 200
Semler, Johann Salomo, 50–52, 72, 83
Sharpe, John L., III, 195
Silva, Moisés, 157, 158, 160n11, 161n13, 206, 212
Simon, Richard, 107
Skeat, Theodore C., 8, 10, 16, 90n5, 113, 176, 178n21, 179, 189, 202, 208, 211, 212
Smalley, Beryl, 31, 212
Socinus, Laelius, 63n41
Soden, Hermann von, 134–35, 139, 177, 212
Stanton, Graham, 113, 180n22, 190n28, 213
Stenger, Werner, 63n42, 213
Stephanus, Robert, 40–44, 47–48, 51, 54–56, 62, 67, 84n14, 198
Steudel, J. C. F., 47n12, 48n13, 53, 65, 69, 213
Straatman, J. W., 187n32
Strachan, L. R. M., 196

INDEX OF PERSONS

Streane, A. W., 80, 214
Streeter, Burnett Hillman, 136, 141, 213
Stunica, D. L. de, 37
Sturz, Harry A., 149n24, 150n27, 213
Suggs, M. Jack, 198
Swanson, Reuben, 177, 213
Szesnat, Holger, 190n40, 213
Tarelli, C. C., 36, 213
Tasker, Randolph V. G., 145, 163n17, 213
Tatian, 83, 94, 103, 125, 205, 209
Taylor, D. G. K., 125, 204, 208, 209, 210, 213
Temporini, Hildegard, xi
Tenney, Merrill C., 200
Testuz, Michel, 116, 117, 213
Theodulf, 28
Thatcher, Tom, ix
Thiselton, Anthony C., 187, 213
Thomas, Cecil K., 97n20, 213
Thompson, Herbert, 127, 213
Thomson, Robert W., 194, 196, 207, 215
Tilly, Michael, 200, 202, 208
Tischendorf, L. F. Constantin von, 2, 54n29, 71, 78-82, 85, 87-91, 93-97, 105, 106, 110, 130, 132, 160, 177, 214
Tov, Emmanuel, 182, 214
Traube, Ludwig, 26, 181, 182, 214
Tregelles, Samuel Prideaux, 71, 75n4, 79-82, 85, 91, 95-97, 98n21, 105-6, 130, 211, 214
Tuckett, Christopher M., 185, 214
Tune, Ernest W., 138, 196
Turner, C. H., 144, 214
Turner, Eric G., 8n2, 9, 12, 111, 179-81, 214
Tyndale, William, 97
Ulrich, Eugene, 157n9, 214
Usher, Archbishop, 58
Valla, Lorenzo, 61
Victor of Antioch, 34
Victor of Capua, 94, 188
Vogels, Heinrich J., 58n35, 126n35, 214
Vos, J. S., 199
Wachtel, Klaus, 112n6, 214
Walker, William O., 157n10, 205, 214
Wallace, David B., 149, 150, 214
Walton, Brian, 42-44, 49n16, 50n19, 51, 53, 55-58
Webb, Henry E., 203
Weedman, Gary E., 203
Weigle, Luther, 3, 201
Weiss, B., 160
Wells, Edward, 45, 46, 67n47
West, Martin L., 48, 60n37, 214
Westcott, Arthur, 215
Westcott, Brooke Foss, 5, 41n2, 71, 82-85, 87, 90, 92-94, 96-108, 109-11, 113n7, 116, 122, 124-26, 129-39, 143, 149-52, 159-60, 162, 163, 166, 176, 194, 208, 215
Wettstein, Johann Jakob, 49-50, 52, 54, 56-59, 62-64, 66-74, 95, 98, 123, 132, 203
Weymouth, R. F., 160
Whitby, Daniel, 46n9, 67
Wikgren, Allen, 123, 160, 195, 213
Williams, C. S. C., 152, 164, 215
Willis, William H., 127, 215
Wilson, N. G., 32, 60, 210
Wilson, R. McL., 207
Wilson, Stephen G., 204
Winer, G. B., 78
Wisse, Frederik, 127, 139, 140, 157, 215
Witherington, Ben, III, 155, 215
Witte, Klaus, 112, 214
Wright, John, 33, 215
Ximenes de Cisneros, F., 36
Zahn, T. H., 163
Zetzel, James E., 175, 215
Zuntz, Günther, 45, 72, 75n3, 77, 115, 147-48, 150n26, 152, 153, 202, 215

Index of Subjects
(excludes manuscripts mentioned only in lists)

Alexandrian scholarship, 31–32, 34–35, 60, 84, 92
Alexandrian text, 72, 83, 84, 90, 91, 102, 103, 104, 109, 111, 113n7, 114, 117, 120, 122, 123, 124, 126n36, 134, 136, 141, 142
Asiatic text, 83; *see also* Byzantine text
Authorized Version, *see* King James Version
Arabic version, 41, 69
archetype, 91n9, 134, 144, 147, 189
Armenian version, 29, 57, 69, 125, 181n23
Biblia patristica, 129
bilingual manuscripts, 30–31, 40, 55, 61, 103, 187, 189n35
Bodmer papyri, 2, 116–19, 211
Bohairic version, 44, 51, 72, 103, 126, 128, 134
books, materials and manufacture of, 8–10, 12, 15–17
Byzantine text, 27, 71, 83, 90, 91, 94, 101–2, 109, 110, 111, 120, 121, 122, 123, 136, 141, 149, 150, 213
Caesarean text, 92n10, 114, 119, 120, 121, 124, 136–37, 142, 147
canons of textual criticism, 47, 48, 49–50, 64–67, 73–74, 78–79, 80–81, 100, 159, 177
Chester Beatty Biblical Papyri, 109, 113–15, 205
Chester Beatty Manuscripts A and B, 127

Claremont Profile Method, 140, 198
classification of manuscripts, 40, 42, 43, 44, 48, 49, 57, 58, 64, 71, 138–42
Clavis patrum graecorum, 129, 201
Clavis patrum latinorum, 129, 201
codex, development of, 8–9, 179–80; use of for Christian texts, 8–9, 16, 25, 179–181; *see also* glossary
Codex Alexandrinus, 43–44, 48, 49n16, 50, 51, 52–53, 63, 72, 83, 87, 117, 121, 142
Codex Amiatinus, 94
Codex Athous Laurae, 91
Codex Augiensis, 92
Codex Beratinus, 119
Codex Bezae, 40, 41, 43, 54–56, 58–59, 72, 87, 103, 113, 121, 122, 134, 141, 142, 153, 155, 163, 186–87, 189, 196, 198, 202, 206, 208, 209, 210
Codex Bobiensis, 93
Codex Claromontanus, 41, 56, 78, 87, 103
Codex Ephraemi, 49, 54, 72, 78, 171, 206
Codex Freerianus, 119–20; *see also* Codex Washingtonianus
Codex Fuldensis, 94, 155, 188, 189, 209
Codex Gigas, 93
Codex Koridethi, 120, 134, 136, 186, 206
Codex Lindisfarnensis (Lindisfarne Gospels), 94
Codex Palatinus, 93

INDEX OF SUBJECTS

Codex Purpureus Petropolitanus (N), 90–91, 119
Codex Rossanensis, 119
Codex Sinaiticus, 2, 78, 80, 82n11, 84, 87–90, 97, 104, 106, 107, 109, 110, 115, 118, 121, 133, 134, 139, 171, 178, 194, 200, 204, 208
Codex Sinopensis, 119
Codex Vaticanus, 44n6, 45, 53–54, 56, 57, 80, 82n11, 84, 87, 90, 91, 97, 104, 105, 107, 109, 110, 113, 117, 118, 121, 134, 137, 142, 143, 165, 178, 205, 209, 210, 213
Codex Washingtonianus, 120, 121, 142
Codex Zacynthius, 79, 91, 209
Comma Johanneum, see Johannine Comma
Complutensian Polyglot, 35–36, 37, 40, 59
Comprehensive Profile Method, 140
conflation of readings, 20, 101–2, 109
conjectural emendation, 46–47, 48, 66, 96, 157
Constantinopolitan text, 72, 83; *see also* Byzantine text
Coptic versions, 28–29, 57–58, 69, 103, 118, 126–27, 160
critical apparatus, 1, 40, 45, 47, 50, 51, 52, 64, 67, 68, 83, 161, 162
Crosby Codex, 127
Curetonian Syriac version, 92, 103, 109, 124–25, 195
Diatessaron, 94, 125–26, 205, 209
dictation, 8–10, 16, 19, 30, 210
Distigme-obelos, 188
Eastern text, 51, 83; *see also* Byzantine text
eclectic method, 5, 144–46, 148, 198, 200, 202
Editio critica maior, 159, 161–62, 193
error in manuscripts, 17–19, 151, 172, 176, 177
Ethiopic version, 29, 42, 51, 69

Eusebian canons, 26, 106
external evidence, 49, 66, 69–70, 77, 78, 80, 96, 102, 143–44, 163n17, 164, 187–88
family, definition of, 91, 134
Family 1, 121, 135, 136, 137
Family 13, 91, 121, 123, 134, 135, 136, 137, 201, 206
Fayyumic version, 126
Fleury Palimpsest, 93
Ferrar Group, 92, 123, 135, 201, 206
Freer Logion, 120n23
Geneva Bible, 40
genealogical method, 98, 100–101, 135, 137, 195
Georgian version, 29
Glazier Codex, 128
Gothic version, 29, 44, 150
group, definition of, 138–40, 142
harmonization, 158, 177
Harklean version, 126
helps for readers, 26, 27, 32
Hesychian recension, 134
Hexapla, 32, 60, 215
Homoeoteleuton, 74; *see also* glossary
I-H-K text, 134
initial text, 159
Institut für neutestamentliche Textforschung (Institute for New Testament Textual Research, INTF), 24, 128, 133, 140, 161
internal evidence, 34, 35, 44, 77, 78, 81, 97, 98–100, 101, 102, 104, 107, 143–46, 149, 150, 189
International Greek New Testament Project (IGNTP), 123n28, 139, 140, 161, 162, 169n1, 175, 177, 212
intrinsic probability, 98–100, 143, 145n18, 146, 147165
Johannine Comma, 37, 68–70
King James Version, 3, 37, 41, 82, 97, 107, 108, 149, 202
Koine text, 134; *see also* Byzantine text

Latin versions, 27–28, 51, 93, 128; Old Latin versions, 28, 35, 48, 58, 62, 69, 76, 93, 103, 128–29, 135, 136, 163, 171; Vulgate, 28, 31, 35, 37, 38, 42, 45, 58, 61, 69, 76, 93, 94, 128–29

lectionaries, 24, 25, 27, 30, 49, 57, 73, 123–24, 132n2, 133, 170, 208

letter-carriers, 11–12

literacy, 7–8, 15, 173, 199, 202

local texts, 26, 136, 140, 141

Lord's Prayer, 158

Majority text, 142, 148–50, 202, 214

majuscule script, 25, 91

Manuscript 33, 57, 72, 96, 124

Manuscript 565, 121, 122, 136

Manuscript 579, 122

Manuscript 614, 122, 124

Manuscript 700, 121, 122, 136

Manuscript 1241, 123

Manuscript 1739, 30, 123, 124, 148n23, 150n26

Manuscript 2053, 124

Manuscript PPalau. Rib. Inv.-Nr. 181, 182, 183, 127

Manuscript Q, 127

Middle Egyptian version, 126, 128

minuscule script, 25, 30

mixture, 101, 120, 121, 133, 135, 137, 139, 140, 147

neutral text, 84, 98, 103–5, 109, 111, 115, 118, 134, 136, 140, 164, 201

Nestle-Aland text, 1, 30, 43, 128, 152, 160, 161, 164, 177, 187n33, 188

New English Bible, 145, 163, 213

nomina sacra, 25–26, 179, 181–85, 186, 190, 194, 203, 204, 208, 214

ostraca, 182, 206

Oxyrhynchus papyri, 2, 111, 113, 170, 171, 197, 199, 200, 202, 209

Papyrus Bodmer III, 128, 204

P^4, P^{64}, P^{67}, 112–13

P^{38}, 113, 142

P^{45}, 25, 114, 118, 137, 142, 176, 185, 195

P^{46}, 18, 19, 25, 114–15, 118, 147–48, 176

P^{47}, 114, 115, 118, 171, 176

P^{52}, 115–16

P^{66}, 2, 116, 117, 118, 147, 176, 178n20, 185, 193, 195, 200

P^{72}, 116–17, 176, 178, 205

P^{75}, 2, 25, 116, 117–19, 137, 142, 147, 164, 165n18, 175, 176, 185, 193, 200, 206, 209, 210

P^{91}, 170n4

P^{106}, 171

P^{115}, 32n3, 171, 209

papyri, 109, 110–18, 131, 161, 165; important, 2, 112–18; writing on, 10, 25

patristic quotations, 29–30, 32, 33, 34, 42, 44, 59, 60, 61, 69, 72, 76, 94, 102, 105, 128, 129, 158, 189

Peshitta version, 27, 73, 92, 102, 110, 125, 126

plenary verbal inspiration, 62, 75, 149

publication in antiquity, 7, 12, 14, 15, 16, 60, 180

punctuation, 27, 32, 160

quantitative method, 137–40, 196

Received Text, *see* Textus Receptus

recensions, 51, 74, 118, 137, 142, 200, 202, 206

Revised Standard Version, 3–4, 5, 46, 145, 163, 164

Revised Version, 3, 82, 84, 97–98, 107, 152, 163, 201

Sahidic version, 103, 126, 127, 134

Scheide Codex, 128

secretary, 8–11, 14, 16, 118, 210, 211; *see also* scribes

scribes, 10, 15, 16, 18, 19–21, 25, 98–99, 117, 146–47, 151, 153–56, 159, 164, 167n21, 172–77, 181–185, 188–89; *see also* secretary

scrolls, 2, 8, 9, 14, 16, 179, 184, 214

shorthand, 10

Sinaitic Syriac, 110, 124–25

INDEX OF SUBJECTS

singular readings, 116, 138, 147, 177, 178, 204

Slavonic version, 69, 181

social world of early Christianity, 3, 152–55, 158–59, 171–73, 187, 191

Syriac versions, 27, 41, 42, 51, 57–58, 62, 69, 73, 92, 192, 103, 109, 110, 124–25, 126, 135, 136, 171, 194, 195, 205, 206

Syrian text, 83, 84, 85, 101–2, 103, 104, 109, 110; *see also* Byzantine text

Teststellen, 141

textual criticism, definition of, 17, 151; motivation for, 17, 23, 32, 33, 59, 95–97

Textus Receptus, 3, 41, 42, 45, 50, 51, 56, 60, 62, 63, 64, 67, 68, 70, 71, 74, 75, 77, 78, 80, 81, 82, 95, 96, 97, 98, 102, 105, 109, 110, 113, 122, 125, 135, 137, 138, 139, 140, 149, 150, 161, 204, 208

transcriptional probability, 98–100, 143, 146, 147, 165–66

United Bible Societies *Greek New Testament*, 2–3, 43, 48, 55, 145, 160–61, 164, 177

variant readings, collection of, 40, 43, 44, 51, 58; causes of, 17–19, 62, 151–55, 166, 177; criteria for evaluating, 33, 34, 38n4

Vetus Latina, 128, 214

Western noninterpolations, 103n29, 104, 106, 163, 193

Western order, 55, 58, 93, 120

Western text, 72, 83, 84, 90, 102–3, 104, 109, 111, 113, 114, 119, 120, 121, 128, 136–37, 142, 153, 163, 164, 202, 205, 215

writing equipment, 8–9, 10, 174

www.ingramcontent.com/pod-product-compliance
Lightning Source LLC
Chambersburg PA
CBHW021808220426
43662CB00006B/222